CROSS ROADS

Illustrations by Margie Greve

CROSS ROADS

HOW THE BLUES SHAPED ROCK 'N' ROLL (AND ROCK SAVED THE BLUES)

John Milward

Northeastern University Press | Boston

Northeastern University Press
An imprint of University Press
of New England
www.upne.com
© 2013 John Milward
All rights reserved
Manufactured in the United States of America
Designed by Mindy Basinger Hill
Typeset in Minion Pro

Illustrations courtesy of Margie Greve, 2013

University Press of New England is a
member of the Green Press Initiative.
The paper used in this book meets their
minimum requirement for recycled paper.

For permission to reproduce any of the material
in this book, contact Permissions, University
Press of New England, One Court Street, Suite
250, Lebanon NH 03766; or visit www.upne.com

Library of Congress Cataloging-in-
Publication Data

Milward, John.
Crossroads : how the blues shaped rock 'n' roll
(and rock saved the blues) / John Milward ;
illustrations by Margie Greve.
        pages   cm
Includes bibliographical references and index.
ISBN 978-1-55553-744-9 (cloth : alk. paper) —
ISBN 978-1-55553-823-1 (ebook)
1. Blues (Music)—History and criticism.
2. Blues (Music)—Influence.
3. Rock music—History and criticism. I. Title.
ML3521.M56 2013
781.66'1643—dc23   2012047684
5 4 3 2

Denim texture © Ccat82 | Dreamstime.com
Paper texture © Tuja66 | Dreamstime.com

CONTENTS

PREFACE

In a suburban living room in 1967, two teenage rock 'n' roll fans, happy to have the house to themselves on a Saturday night, slipped an LP onto the turntable and cranked up the volume. The record was not a predictable favorite by the Beatles or the Rolling Stones, but one by an American artist that they'd seen mentioned in articles about Britain's most heralded electric guitarist, Eric Clapton. It was a live recording of a concert, and as the needle hit the grooves, the murmur of the audience seemed to fill the room. "Ladies and gentleman," said the announcer, "how about a nice warm round of applause to welcome the world's greatest blues singer, the king of the blues, B.B. King!"

B.B. King's *Live at the Regal* was recorded in November of 1964 in front of an enthusiastic black audience in Chicago, and for a couple of white suburban kids, it made for thrilling, even exotic listening. King's music was certainly different from the blues-rock Clapton was making with Cream. The choice of that record with my friend Paul reflects the way that many in the 1960s got introduced to the blues, the soulful bedrock of American music.

Crossroads explores a history of connections between blues musicians, folk singers, and rockers, and how that influenced both their lives and the music they played. It's neither an encyclopedic history of the blues, nor a full accounting of the blues-rock universe (apologies to, among many others, Albert Collins and Rory Gallagher). Rather, *Crossroads* chronicles the evolution of a musical tradition through the careers and personal interactions of a crew of extraordinary musicians who built a bridge between black and white, as well as rock and the blues.

Blues fans are forever worrying about the health of the genre, but in fact, the music and the context in which it has been heard has been in constant flux for the past one hundred years. The pre-Depression country blues of Blind Lemon Jefferson and Charley Patton was rarely heard outside a community of poor Southern blacks. The more urbane styles of players like

Lonnie Johnson and pianist LeRoy Carr found a broader national audience alongside the big bands of the 1930s. In the '50s, the electric blues of such Chicago titans as Muddy Waters and Howlin' Wolf appealed to both urban and rural blacks. The gradual integration of white fans into the audience for blues in the 1950s and '60s was the last big change in the demographic drawn to the blues, but it was far more radical in its implications.

Consider the Newport Folk Festival, which in the mid-1960s, presented such rediscovered Depression-era blues legends as Son House, Skip James, and Mississippi John Hurt. It was as if these musicians had walked right out of the Delta past onto the contemporary stage. "They were not ghosts up there," said Eric Von Schmidt. "It was a minor miracle." In 1962, John Lee Hooker, who'd been rocking ghetto clubs with his electric guitar since he hit it big with 1949's "Boogie Chillen," played his acoustic guitar in a Greenwich Village coffee house with an unknown folk singer named Bob Dylan as an opening act. Off-stage, they bonded over drinks and guitars. In San Francisco, B.B. King pulled up to the Fillmore Ballroom and was confused to see not his usual black audience, but a crowd of longhaired hippies. After promoter Bill Graham introduced King to a standing ovation, his life was forever changed. In Chicago, Muddy Waters disappeared backstage thinking that the white guy who'd entered the crowded club just had to be from the I.R.S. Instead, Paul Butterfield had come to learn about the blues from a primary source. A few years later, the Butterfield Blues Band featuring guitarist Mike Bloomfield would cause a stir of its own at the Newport Folk Festival.

Muddy Waters also had a small but devoted following in England, where a scruffy band of blues lovers named itself the Rolling Stones after one of his classic songs. For bluesmen like Waters and King, the interest of famous rock musicians and exposure to their fans during the 1960s gave them commercial life even as they lost much of their traditional black audience to the more contemporary sounds of soul and rhythm and blues. And for the rockers, the blues offered a more mature musical vocabulary than what was typically found at the top of the pop charts.

Sixty years ago, the few who cared had to work hard to learn about and listen to the blues, which was largely the domain of a clique of opinionated purists known as the "blues mafia." Record collectors drawn to the blues would go door knocking in a quest to buy rare 78 rpm records, while folklorists became song catchers, traveling the countryside to document players who never got near a recording studio. The blues revival of the 1960s prompted record labels to reissue the cream (and much more) of their catalogs. These days, the whole history of the blues is available on disc or to be downloaded; for instant gratification, you can listen to virtually any artist mentioned in *Crossroads* on such on-line outlets as YouTube and Spotify.

Blues has traveled a long way from its birth in the Mississippi Delta and other Southern black communities. In 2012, Barack Obama, the country's first black president, hosted a public television concert called "Blues at the White House." Both sides of the *Crossroads* were on the guest list, including B.B. King, Buddy Guy, Jeff Beck, and Mick Jagger. "If you come from the cotton fields like I did," said Buddy Guy, "and now you're up there in the White House playing for the Commander in Chief and the First Lady, how high can you go?" At the end of the show, Guy cajoled Obama into singing a few lines from *the* classic blues about his adult hometown, "Sweet Home Chicago." Robert Johnson, who wrote the song in the mid-1930s, and who came to embody the intersection of blues and rock, composed "Sweet Home Chicago" when he was a "walking musician" in the Mississippi Delta. And as he rambled, Johnson couldn't help but find himself at the crossroads.

CROSS
ROAD
BLUES

Robert Johnson was just shy of unknown when his short life ended in 1938. Today, following the centennial of his 1911 birth, he's considered one of the most significant artists in the history of the blues. Johnson is said to have started his journey at a crossroads. The story goes that to obtain his virtuosic skills, the aspiring musician had to sell his soul to the Devil. The deal was struck at an intersection near Clarksdale in the Mississippi Delta. Johnson arrived a little before midnight, and quietly picked the strings of his guitar. At the top of the hour, an outsized, fearsome black man approached the bluesman, took his instrument, twisted its tuning pegs, and played a sweet, scary song. He handed the guitar back to Johnson, and for the promise of an extraordinary musical gift, pocketed the pledge of the young man's soul.

Son House went to bat for this tall tale. House said that Johnson would come to see him perform with his partner Willie Brown and pester them to let him play the guitar during their breaks. But Johnson made such an unholy racket that House had to make him stop. The next time Johnson saw House, less than a year had passed; he now had a guitar slung over his shoulder, and once more asked for a chance to play. With a re-

Robert Johnson 1911–1938

luctant shrug, and a roll of his eyes, House offered Johnson his seat. "When he finished, all our mouths were standing open," said House. "I said, 'Well, ain't that fast! He's gone now!'"

Truth be told, Robert Johnson stood at a number of crossroads. Johnson's collected works offer a persuasive argument that he was at the pivot point between down-home rural blues and the style of electric blues that was born in Chicago in the years after his death. More than most early bluesmen, who'd typically draw lyrics from a pool of commonly used verses, Johnson's best tunes revealed him to be a much more artful, and creative songwriter. In that regard, he was the most modern of the rural bluesman, and ended up influencing not just the music that Muddy Waters created in the 1940s and '50s, but the entire blues-rock aesthetic of the 1960s. Time has served his legend well. The most famous among many rock-era interpretations of Johnson's songs was "Crossroads," Cream's high-octane update of "Cross Road Blues" that was cut live at San Francisco's Fillmore Auditorium in 1968. That now forty-five-year-old track was recorded just thirty-one years after Johnson's original.

Johnson spent the 1930s as a "walking musician," traveling the country-side in search of music gigs while fashioning songs from his fingers, his imagination, and everything he heard on the radio and the jukebox. He was of the first generation of blues musicians that learned songs not just from other players, but also from records. Entertaining on a street corner or for a party hosted by the local bootlegger, it was important for a musician to be able to play the latest hits, and Johnson was a famously quick study. According to bluesman Johnny Shines, an occasional traveling companion, Johnson was just as likely to sing a song by pop crooner Bing Crosby or country star Jimmie Rodgers as a blues by Blind Blake or Lonnie Johnson.

Johnson didn't make his first recordings until the mid-1930s, a somewhat unlikely occurrence given that the market for down-home blues had largely passed. Fortuitously, the improved studio technology endowed Johnson's records with much better sound quality than discs cut early in the decade. Between surface noise and the quick deterioration of the cheap shellac used to produce so-called "race records," those discs offered less than high fidelity; by contrast, Johnson's recordings let the listener accurately hear the sweet, silvery sound of his slide guitar and the dramatic range of his savvy vocals.

Johnson's first recordings for ARC Records were made over three days in November of 1936 in San Antonio, Texas. That week, the company also cut records by two Mexican groups and a country swing band called the

Chuck Wagon Gang. Johnson famously positioned himself facing the corner of the room, prompting suggestions that he was either hiding his guitar technique from the other musicians, creating a reverb-like effect by bouncing the sound off the hard plaster walls, or was simply shy on the occasion of cutting his first record. In any event, he did two takes apiece of sixteen different songs, including songs that would become latter-day blues standards ("Sweet Home Chicago" and "I Believe I'll Dust My Broom") and performances that would define his singular artistry ("Cross Road Blues" and "Come On in My Kitchen").

Johnson, like many other blues musicians, used elements of existing songs to create new ones. "Sweet Home Chicago" owed a musical debt to a 1934 tune by Kokomo Arnold, "Old Original Kokomo Blues," which in turn looked back to Scrapper Blackwell's "Kokomo Blues." In hindsight, it's easy to see why an ode to Chicago as opposed to a small city in Indiana would become an evergreen for blues bands all over the world (Junior Parker turned it into an R&B hit in 1959).

"I Believe I'll Dust My Broom" drew from songs by Arnold and Leroy Carr but didn't become a blues classic until Elmore James outfitted his 1951 version with an electrifying slide guitar lick. Johnson's original employed a walking bass line derived from ragtime and boogie-woogie piano. "In the early thirties, boogie was rare on the guitar," said Johnny Shines. "Because of Robert, people learned to complement [themselves], carrying their own bass as well as their own lead with this one instrument." Guitarist Eddie Taylor, who in the 1950s helped Jimmy Reed create his influential shuffle rhythm, said "I got the style from Charley Patton and Robert Johnson."

"Come On in My Kitchen" was a song of sexual seduction that shared a lyric line with a ghostly tune recorded in 1931 by Skip James, "Devil Got My Woman." But it's the sensual swing of Johnson's slide guitar that made it a masterpiece. Johnson had a sophisticated ear for arrangement, and his guitar parts mixed passages picked with his fingers alongside melodies carved with his slide. "Cross Road Blues" featured Johnson's virtuosic slide and lyrics about trying to hitch a ride that led some listeners to wonder what else he might have been looking for where one road crossed another.

Johnson's first session, for which he was paid around $100, included the song that would be his biggest hit, "Terraplane Blues," a hard-driving car song that was thick with the kind of sexual double entendres that is a familiar lyrical technique in the blues. "Terraplane Blues," released in March of 1937, and backed with "Kind Hearted Woman Blues," was estimated to have sold four or five thousand copies. The record's success prompted ARC to summon Johnson for a second round of recording sessions in June 1937. He arrived at the Dallas studio with thirteen more songs, including tunes that would in later decades be covered by the Rolling Stones ("Love in Vain," "Stop Breaking Down Blues"), Cream ("From Four Until Late"), and Led Zeppelin ("Traveling Riverside Blues"). He also recorded more songs that alluded to his relationship with the fiery underworld, including "Me and the Devil Blues" and "Hell Hound on My Trail."

In 1961, Columbia Records released a compilation of the blues musician's work entitled *Robert Johnson: King of the Delta Blues Singers*. Over the next decade, it sold around twelve thousand copies. A second volume of Johnson songs was released in 1970. Interest continued to quietly percolate over the decades—in 1987, he was inducted into the Rock and Roll Hall of Fame—until 1990, when *Robert Johnson: The Complete Recordings* was released on compact disc and sold over a million copies. The collection received a Grammy Award for "Best Historical Recording." Fifty-three years after he died, Johnson had become a platinum-selling, Grammy-winning star.

This remarkable posthumous career was due to more than just the finely wrought songs that appealed to generations of blues-rock musicians. There was also the allure of the crossroads myth and a dramatic death involving two staples of the blues life, whiskey and women. Johnson was such a hard-drinking ladies man that even the liquor-loving Son House was moved to give him some advice. "When you playing for these balls," said House, "and these girls get full of corn whiskey and snuff mixed together, and you be playing a good piece and they like it and call you. 'Daddy, play it again, daddy,' well, don't let it run you crazy. You liable to get killed."

In August of 1938, Johnson was playing a Saturday night gig with Dave "Honeyboy" Edwards in Three Forks, Mississippi. They'd played there before, and according to Edwards, the promoter had become convinced that Johnson was fooling around with his wife and conspired to have a pint of poisoned whiskey passed along to the philandering musician. After a good long drink, Johnson continued to perform until he finally collapsed and was taken to his lodgings in nearby Greenwood. Accounts vary as to the precise circumstances of his death. Aleck "Sonny Boy Williamson" Miller claimed to have seen Johnson crawling on the floor and barking like a dog. Others have said that he succumbed not to the effects of poison, but to pneumonia or syphilis. The only thing that's fairly certain is the date of his death: August 16, 1938. Numerologists take note: Elvis Presley died exactly thirty-nine years later.

John Hammond was hoping to book Johnson for a concert at New York's

Carnegie Hall called "From Spirituals to Swing" that was designed to celebrate the breadth of African American music, from blues and gospel to jazz. Hammond had written about Johnson's ARC recordings, calling him "the greatest Negro blues singer who has cropped up in recent years," and adding, "Johnson makes Lead Belly sound like an accomplished poseur." Hammond was sorely disappointed when he found out that Johnson would be unavailable to play the big show, and enlisted Big Bill Broonzy, a sophisticated Chicago musician, to represent down-home blues. But Johnson was still part of the program, as Hammond played two of his songs , "Walking Blues" and "Preachin' Blues (Up Jumped the Devil)," over the hall's public address system.

Great songs, superb performances, sex, booze, jealous husbands, endless travel, a command performance at Carnegie Hall, still-to-come hit records, litigation, and paternity suits—no wonder Johnson became a vital link from the Delta to not only the Chicago blues stars of the 1950s, but to the blues-rock musicians of the 1960s. His visit to the crossroads had transformed Robert Johnson into both the last of the great Delta bluesman and America's first rock star.

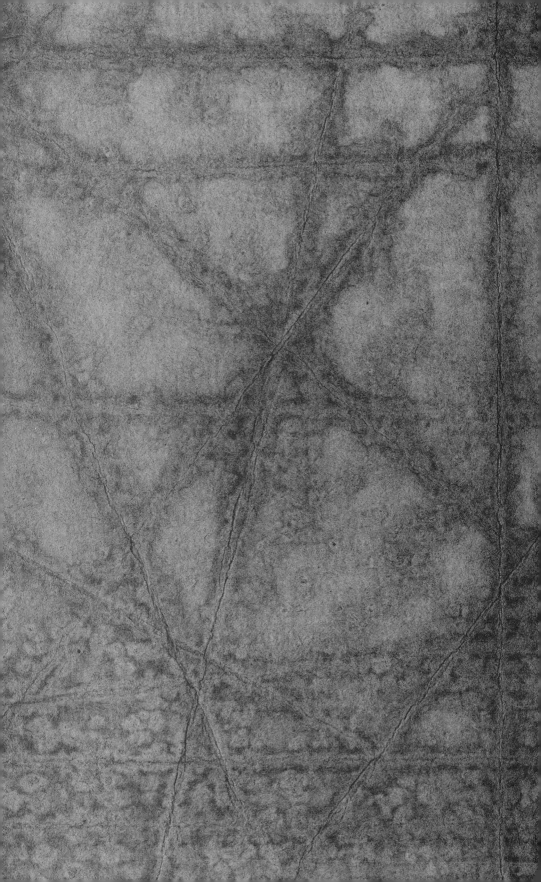

ONE RARE RECORDS AND WORKING MUSICIANS

There was a smudge of crayon on the black-and-yellow label of the 78 rpm Paramount disc with its signature logo of an eagle astride the earth. Otherwise, the thick, hefty record was remarkably clean considering the journey that it had taken from its 1931 pressing in a Wisconsin chair factory to a used-record store in Washington, D.C., in 1952. Because discs were actively recycled for their shellac during World War II, some prewar recordings were now quite rare if not all but extinct.

The record was "Hard Time Killin' Floor Blues" by Skip James. Dick Spottswood had never heard of Skip James, but at age fifteen he already had a record collector's taste for the odd, the obscure, and the valuable. The store let you sample records before you bought them, and the song's minor-key guitar lines and the singer's eerie falsetto voice intrigued Spottswood. The "killin' floor" referred to the violent heart of a slaughterhouse, but at the dawn of the Depression, James saw danger wherever he looked. While the blues typically traded in the downbeat, Skip James was downright dire.

At that moment, however, James had reason to be hope-ful. He'd won the chance to re-

Son House 1902–1988

cord after auditioning for H. C. Speir, the Jackson, Mississippi talent scout who'd already found Charley Patton and Tommy Johnson, and would later discover Robert Johnson. Speir tried out performers in a room above his store, and James won his approval by singing a haunting song called "Devil Got My Woman." Speir gave James a $65 guitar and put him on an Illinois Central train to Grafton, Wisconsin. James recorded eighteen tunes (and possibly a couple more) on both guitar and piano, and declined a flat fee for his efforts, opting instead for future royalties. James figured he was going to be a star like Patton or Blind Lemon Jefferson. But by the end of 1931, he had slipped back into obscurity with $40 in royalties.

Spottswood bought two Skip James records in 1952: "Hard Time Killin' Floor Blues" backed with "Cherry Ball Blues" cost him a dollar, and a worn "22-20 Blues" backed with "If You Haven't Any Hay Get On Down the Road" went for sixty cents. "Hard Time Killin' Floor Blues" was not made with a white teenager in mind. Recorded on the cheap to sell to poor southern blacks, it was a so-called "race record." A thumbnail history of the blues would start with the early-1920s popularity of female singers like Bessie Smith, and later in the decade, with male singers accompanying themselves on guitar. Charley Patton and Blind Lemon Jefferson fit that bill, and the South was thick with other "walking musicians" who'd wander the countryside playing for tips on the street or for the local bootlegger. Good Christians considered the blues singers to be no-good sinners playing the Devil's music. But for people wearied by a long week in the fields, dancing and partying was an earthly taste of Heaven. And the guilty could always make amends on Sunday morning.

The young Spottswood was savvy enough about the vintage record market to know a clean King Oliver jazz record was worth more than an obscure blues by a virtual unknown. At the same time, collectors also knew that a rare disc could draw unexpected attention among the small fraternity of fanatics who perused the classified ads in a magazine like *Record Changer*. In this case, James McKune, a New York blues fan, telephoned Spottswood about his Skip James records.

"I guess he [McKune] knew I had the records because I had come to know [collector] Pete Whelan by that time," said Spottswood. "They had apparently been offered at auction in the *Record Changer* in 1948, but nobody had bid on them, and they wound up in the used record store where I found them." After Spottswood told McKune that the records weren't for sale, McKune made arrangements to travel to Washington to simply listen to the rare 78s. "He took a Greyhound bus," said Spottswood, "and since

I wasn't old enough to drive, he somehow found his way to my house in Bethesda. He listened to those Skip James records once, maybe twice, and then turned around and went back home to Brooklyn."

McKune lived in a single room at a Brooklyn YMCA where he kept his collection of 78s stored in boxes beneath the bed. Through the 1940s and '50s, he was at the center of a group of blues aficionados who'd swap shoptalk at the Jazz Record Center (also known as "Indian Joe's") on West Forty-Seventh Street and argue the merits of various blues musicians. McKune had initially preferred traditional jazz, but in 1944, after buying a crackly copy of Charley Patton's "Some These Days I'll Be Gone," he became obsessed by the raw, lonesome power of a solitary guitar player singing a down-home blues. He soon trolled stores with a wish list of thirteen hundred records.

McKune's pilgrimage to hear the Skip James records was perhaps motivated by the memory of the two boxes of mint-condition Paramount 78s that he let get away. McKune had discovered the cache on a 1942 visit to the Central General Store on Long Island, but because he'd yet to discover his passion for blues, he passed on the deal and alerted a West Coast record collector with whom he corresponded. Harry Smith promptly bought them all. Ten years later, some of those discs would be included on the *Anthology of American Folk Music*, a highly influential collection of vintage recordings that Smith compiled for Folkways Records

Harry Everett Smith was a world-class bohemian who became known not just for the *Anthology*, but also for his experimental films, his study of Native American rituals, and his expertise with string figures. "If he was in a good mood," said Patti Smith, who met him when they both lived in the Chelsea Hotel in the late 1960s, "he would pull a loop of string several feet long from his pocket and weave a star, a female spirit, or a one-man cat's cradle. We all sat at his feet in the lobby like amazed children watching as his deft fingers produced evocative patterns by twisting and knotting the loop."

Harry Smith grew up around Seattle, Washington, where as a schoolboy, he studied the customs, music, and languages of the Lummi, Nootka, and Kwakiutl Indian tribes. Beginning in 1942, he studied anthropology at the University of Washington and worked nights at a Boeing plant manufacturing bombers. The job gave him money to buy old 78s, for while the government was destroying discs for their shellac, the effort had also brought a bounty of records out of dusty attics. During those years, said Smith, "there were big piles of 78s. Enormous groaning masses of them . . . I rapidly amassed many thousands of records. It became like a problem. . . . It was an obsessive, investigative hobby."

Smith had eclectic tastes, and was drawn to the early country music of the Carter Family and Jimmie Rodgers as much as to the blues of Charley Patton and Sleepy John Estes. "I was looking for exotic records," said Smith, who quit school after a couple of years and relocated to Berkeley, California. "Exotic in relation to what was considered to be the world culture of high-class music." A "race record" certainly fit that criterion. After Smith won a Guggenheim grant to pursue his work in film, he moved his massive collection to New York City in the early 1950s. When money got tight, he offered to sell the records to Moses Asch, president of Folkways Records, who instead challenged him to pick the cream of the crop for a compilation.

The *Anthology* package, which Smith artfully designed and fully annotated, was essentially a bootleg recording, with none of the artists or original recording companies compensated for the eighty-four individual songs. Like later compilers of old 78s, Asch reasoned that the record labels had relinquished their rights by letting the recordings go out of print. Because of the relative obscurity of the material, few noticed the legal sleight-of-hand, but history certainly took note of the profound effect the recordings (initially released as three, two-record sets) had on the folk revival of the 1950s and the blues revival that would follow.

"In 1952 fiddler Eck Dunford, blues guitarist Furry Lewis, the Eck Robertson and Family string band, bluesman Blind Lemon Jefferson, and Cannon's Jug Stompers were only twenty or twenty-five years out of their time," said Greil Marcus, who wrote about the profound influence the *Anthology* had on Bob Dylan. "Cut off by the cataclysms of the Great Depression and the Second World War by a national narrative that had never included their kind, they appeared now like visitors from another world, like passengers on a ship that had drifted into the sea of the unwritten."

Musicians had a more pragmatic view of the *Anthology*. "The set became our Bible," said Dave Van Ronk, who would become a central player in the Greenwich Village folk-blues scene. "It is how most of us first heard Blind Willie Johnson, Mississippi John Hurt, and even Blind Lemon Jefferson. And it was not just blues people. . . . It was an incredible compendium of American traditional musics, all performed in the traditional styles. . . . Without the Harry Smith anthology we could not have existed, because there was no other way for us to get hold of that material."

John Fahey, who went on record collecting trips with Dick Spottswood and would become an influential acoustic guitarist, was also smitten by the collection. "I'd match the *Anthology* up against any other single compendium of important information ever assembled," said Fahey. "Dead Sea

Scrolls? Nah. I'll take the *Anthology*. Make no mistake: there was no 'folk' canon before Smith's work. That he had compiled such a definitive document only became apparent much later, of course. We record-collecting types, sifting through many more records than he did, eventually reached the same conclusions: these were the true goods."

"Hard Time Killin' Floor Blues" by Skip James did not appear on the *Anthology*, and chances are it wasn't among the records purchased by Smith after being alerted to the cache of Paramounts by Jim McKune. That's because according to *78 Quarterly*, a collector magazine started in 1967 by McKune's friend Pete Whelan, only two copies of the record were known to exist. These days, you can download the song from iTunes, or purchase a CD of the complete Paramount recordings of Skip James. But in 1952, you had to work to hear music that had nearly been lost to history. Twelve years later, in the thick of the 1960s blues revival, a living, breathing Skip James would himself enter the lives of John Fahey and Dick Spottswood.

Record collectors constitute a community of connoisseurs who typically celebrate music that isn't heard on the radio or listed on the pop charts. In this case, they helped to nurture an interest in Depression-era blues that had rarely been heard outside the black community. Folklorists go even further, seeking out music that's not just obscure, but that was rarely recorded, or heard outside of earshot. The aim of the folklorist is to document the music before it disappears. In 1933, John Lomax, an author and musicologist, struck a deal with the Library of Congress to collect field recordings using the Library's state-of-the-art recording machine. Lomax and his eighteen-year-old son Alan tore out the back seat of the family Ford to transport a 315-pound disk recorder, along with playback equipment, a microphone, and a large stash of blank aluminum discs. It was on this trip that the pair discovered a singer named Huddie Ledbetter at the Louisiana State Prison at Angola. The world would come to know the seminal folk singer as Lead Belly.

By 1937, Alan Lomax had established his own curatorial relationship with the Library of Congress. In 1941, he traveled through the Mississippi Delta with John Work, an African American musicologist from Fisk University. The men were looking for musicians in general, and information about Robert Johnson in particular. At Stovall Plantation, they recorded McKinley Morganfield, a musician who'd once seen Johnson perform. "It was in Friar's Point," said Morganfield, already known as Muddy Waters, "and this guy had a lot of people standin' around him. He coulda been Robert, they *said* it was Robert. I stopped and peeked over, and then I left. Because he was a dangerous man."

Singing into Lomax's microphone, Waters performed "Country Blues," which was his version of Robert Johnson's "Walkin' Blues," which was in turn Johnson's re-write of Son House's "My Black Mama." That's the way songs were passed between Delta musicians, with variations of guitar licks and lyrics transforming one song into another. When Lomax replayed the disc for the singer, it was the first time Waters had heard himself on record. "Man, you don't know how I felt that Saturday afternoon when I heard that voice and it was my own voice," said Waters. "Later on he sent me two copies of the pressing and a check for twenty bucks, and I carried that record up to the corner and put it on the jukebox. Just played it and played it and said, 'I can do it, I can do it.'"

When Lomax asked what other musicians he should record, Waters directed him to one of the most powerful musicians in the Delta, Son House. "I used to say to Son House, 'Would you play so and so?' because I was trying to get that touch on that [bottleneck slide] thing he did," said Waters. "Once he played a month in a row every Sunday night. I was there every night, close to him. . . . I loved Son House because he used the bottleneck so beautiful."

House had traveled to Wisconsin to record for Paramount in 1931, and appreciated the fact that a waitress from the hotel next to the studio would bring the musicians drinks. "Anytime that you end a piece," said House, "she's right there with . . . your whiskey—that old, real good dark whiskey smells good, taste good, and make you so high you rock like a rockin' chair. Ten years later, Lomax recorded House at Klack's country store in Tunica County, Mississippi. Lomax subsequently wrote that "with [House] the sorrow of the blues was not tentative, or retiring, or ironic. Son's whole body wept, as with eyes closed, the tendons in his powerful neck standing out with the violence of his feeling and his brown face flashing." But at this session, there was no brown whiskey. "He [Lomax] came down and recorded me and [guitarist] Willie Brown and he didn't give us but one Coca-Cola," said House. "Willie grabbed up the Coca-Cola first and I didn't get nothing."

Folklorists and record collectors are more interested in history than the hits of the day, which during the late 1940s and early '50s, included seminal blues recordings by Lightnin' Hopkins, John Lee Hooker, B.B. King, Howlin' Wolf, and Muddy Waters. These artists drew from the past, but were also professional musicians creating songs for the here and now. All five, with the exception of Hopkins, moved north from Mississippi, an artistic subset of the Great Migration that saw hundreds of thousands of blacks flee sharecropper lives on rural plantations for jobs in urban factories. For these transplants, the blues was like a letter from home. But these five bluesmen would do more than just score a couple of hit records; over subsequent decades, they would also bring their down-home blues into the broader American culture, and across the ocean to Britain. Through these and other gifted musicians, the blues would come to have a profound influence on popular culture in general, and rock 'n' roll in particular.

The late 1940s were a time in which major changes were occurring in black popular music. Early in that decade, big jazz bands led by Duke Ellington and Earl Hines shared chart success with singers like Ella Fitzgerald and Billie Holiday. But as the years passed, smaller combos led by Louis Jordon and Nat King Cole came into fashion, with others like Roy Brown and Joe Liggins and his Honeydrippers anticipating the hard-driving sound of rhythm and blues. Reflective of both a change in taste and sensibility, in the summer of 1949, the trade magazine *Billboard* changed the name of its African American bestseller list from "Race Records" to "Rhythm and Blues Records."

A bluesman now had the chance to go nationwide. Sam "Lightnin'" Hopkins was born in Centerville, Texas, in 1912, and spent his adult life in Houston. At the age of eight, he saw country blues singer Blind Lemon Jefferson playing at a gathering of the General Baptist Association of Churches. Hopkins is said to have traded a few guitar licks with the popular musician, and to later serve as a guide for the bluesman. He also spent time rambling and playing music with his cousin, Texas Alexander.

Hopkins got his big break in 1946 when a talent scout saw him playing in Houston's Third Ward and arranged a deal with Aladdin Records in Los Angeles. Because he was paired with a pianist named Wilson "Thunder" Smith, Hopkins was dubbed "Lightnin'." He immediately scored a regional hit with "Katie May," and then reached the national rhythm and blues charts with tunes like "Shotgun Blues" and "Short Haired Woman." Hopkins came to define Texas country blues with a guitar style that decorated a steady-thumping bass with melodic lines played on the treble strings. His lyrics seemed to come off the top of his head (and often did).

Rayfield Jackson played gigs with Hopkins in the early '50s when he was still in high school. "We was playing in little old joints," Jackson said, "with about three or four tables in them, and when you had five or six people in there, you had a crowd. . . . Wouldn't have no drummer, just two guitars—and Lightnin' stomping his feet. That's it. He'd have them big old shoes on and a big old wide hat with a feather stuck up in it—looked like a peacock."

Hopkins didn't like to travel, which is why he'd play the local bars. He also didn't put much faith in recording contracts or the promise of royalties, which is why he cut discs (earning flat fees) for a dizzying number of labels. Working without a manager, Hopkins knew that he was selling his songs outright, but figured he'd just as soon leave the studio with $100 to $150 a side instead of royalties that might never materialize. When his pockets were empty, Hopkins would simply make up some more songs for another record label.

The music of John Lee Hooker could make the blues of Lightnin' Hopkins seem almost ornamental; his propulsive guitar typically revolved around one chord while his big voice wailed to the persistent thump of his foot. He broke out of Detroit in 1948 playing big-city, big-beat blues that bore the stylistic stamp of the Mississippi Delta. Hooker was born in 1917, one of eleven children in a family of sharecroppers in Clarksdale, Mississippi. He learned guitar from his stepfather, Will Moore, a popular local musician who was a friend and host to such famous pickers as Charley Patton, Blind Lemon Jefferson, and Blind Blake, a master of ragtime guitar. Hooker took off for Memphis as a teenager, and relocated to Cincinnati before finally settling in Detroit in 1943. He worked the auto plants by day and the noisy clubs along Hastings Street by night, playing an electric guitar to cut through the cacophony.

In 1948, Hooker entered a Detroit recording studio. After laboring over the presumed A-side, "Sally Mae," he tossed off "Boogie Chillen,'" a mesmerizing performance that nailed the gritty ruminative style that would become his musical signature. With Hooker's voice drenched in echo, and the tone of his guitar perched on the edge of distortion, the insistent beat conjured a kind of urbane Delta trance. When the track was picked up by Modern Records for national distribution, it became an R&B smash. Bernard Besman, the local record distributor who'd financed the session, was listed as the cowriter of "Boogie Chillen."

Like Hopkins, Hooker created a crazy quilt of a recorded library that was spread over a couple dozen labels. His driving license might have read John Lee Hooker, but his records bore names like Texas Slim, Delta John, Birmingham Sam, John Lee Booker, and Boogie Man. But nobody was fooled, for by the time he scored another national hit with a seductive blues ballad, 1951's "In the Mood," Hooker's sound was one of a kind.

Muddy Waters, born in April 1915 in Rolling Fork, Mississippi, was different, a stay-at-home bluesman; where walking musicians wandered the countryside to find gigs, Waters ran his own Saturday night juke so that instead of just picking up change for playing music, he could also sell moonshine and fried fish sandwiches. The craps games were strictly between the customers.

Waters traveled north in 1943, not long after being recorded by Alan Lomax. "I came to Chicago on a train," he said. "Alone. With a suitcase, one suit of clothes, and a guitar. Got here Saturday morning, got a job Saturday evening. Boy, luck was with me." Music opportunities weren't far behind, first as a sideman with piano players like Eddie Boyd and Memphis Slim. Two solo sides for Columbia went unreleased, but in 1947, when an Aristocrat session for Sunnyland Slim ended early, Waters again stepped up to the microphone. He performed two songs ("Little Anna Mae" and "Gypsy Woman") that were good enough to earn him his own session, which produced his breakthrough 1948 hit, "I Feel Like Going Home." That tune was a variation of "Country Blues," the Lomax cut from 1941.

"All of a sudden I became Muddy Waters," said the man born McKinley Morganfield about the effect of having "I Feel Like Going Home" climb the R&B charts. "Just over night. People started to hollerin' across the streets at me. When they used to hardly say 'good morning,' you know?" But this early hit, cut with just his guitar and a stand-up bass, was low-key compared to the music Waters was making with his musician friends.

"We come in, plug up the amp, get us one of these half-pint or pint bottles and get some ideas," said guitarist Jimmy Rogers of his early rehearsals with Waters. "We'd run through a few verses and finally, after maybe three or four days fooling around, you'd done built a number." They were soon joined by Marion Walter Jacobs—Little Walter—whom Rogers had spotted playing for tips at the outdoor market on Maxwell Street, and who revolutionized the sound of the harmonica through his innovative use of amplification. "When I run up on Little Walter," said Waters, "he just fitted me." The band played on. "Muddy would cook some rice and chicken gizzards," said Rogers. "We have a pot on the kitchen and we'd get us a bowl, get us some water and get a little drink. Then we'd sit back down and do it some more."

Muddy's live band, which also included Otis Spann on piano, was nicknamed "The Headhunters" because they'd drop into clubs, play when the featured attraction took a break, and show up the headliner with their superior musicianship. In 1950, Leonard Chess, who'd bought out his partners in the Aristocrat label and renamed it Chess Records, let Waters record with the band. The result was powerful group performances of songs like "Baby

Please Don't Go" and "Blow Wind Blow" that gave Waters's rural blues a potent urban sound, and also established the instrumental format (bass-drums-guitar plus keyboards and/or harmonica) of the rock and roll band.

"Muddy was playing when I was plowing," said B.B. King. "Mules that is." King, born in 1925, met bluesman David "Honeyboy" Edwards as a child. "Christmas of 1937 I was playing the streets in Inverness and I made fifteen dollars in dimes and quarters," said Edwards. "I noticed a young boy, standing there listening at me play. The next day I was going down the road walking and this boy was out in a field plowing. He came over and talked to me, said, 'I saw you playin' on the streets. My name is Riley King and I play the guitar, too.' That was B.B. . . . . The next time I saw him was in Memphis, and he was the Beale Street Blues Boy."

King hit Memphis in 1946 and stayed with his cousin Bukka White, who played a steel-bodied guitar and knew a thing or two about the blues. "He'd [Bukka] been a boxer and a baseball pitcher and served a long time in the famous Parchman Farm Prison for murdering two men," said King. "Said he killed in self-defense. And was quick to warn me to stay out of trouble."

He got his first break singing Ivory Joe Hunter's "Blues at Sunrise" on the West Memphis radio show of Sonny Boy Williamson; later that night, King subbed for Williamson at a gig he couldn't make at the 16th Street Grill. "That night I couldn't sleep for the pictures running through my head," said King of his first live performance. "I saw them [women] dressed and undressed, bending over and stretching, grinding and grinning and showing me stuff I ain't ever seen before."

King, who was billed as the Beale Street Blues Boy (the moniker was quickly shortened to B.B.), soon got his own show on WDIA in Memphis, the first radio station specifically programmed for a black audience. During his show, King would hawk an alcohol-based elixir called Peptikon. The radio helped to generate demand for live appearances, which brought King to Clarksdale, Mississippi, where he ran into Ike Turner, who offered to sit in with King's band. "He played piano and made us sound a whole lot better," said King. "Whatever little money I got, I gave some to Ike, who seemed to appreciate it."

King encouraged Turner, who'd gotten his first childhood piano lesson from Pinetop Perkins, to see Sam Phillips in Memphis about recording. Turner's group, the Kings of Rhythm, worked up a song called "Rocket 88" on the drive from Clarksdale to Memphis. Turner arranged the tune, which was recorded in 1951 by Phillips at his Memphis Recording Service. Before Phillips launched Sun Records, he'd lease recordings made in his studio to various labels. "Rocket 88," credited to singer Jackie Brensten and his Delta Cats, became the first number 1 hit in the history of Chess Records, with its piano-pumping four-four beat prompting some historians to declare it the very first rock 'n' roll record. The band earned $20 each for the session.

Turner also attended a 1951 B.B. King recording session and ended up playing piano on King's breakthrough hit, "Three O'Clock Blues," which hit number 1 on the R&B charts and lingered for three months. King represented a different side of the blues than a player like Lightnin' Hopkins. King wasn't a solitary singer-guitarist but a bandleader with a great voice and a killer touch on the electric guitar. Indeed, King would let his guitar speak up where his voice left off. He played melodic, emotional guitar solos, evocative of T-Bone Walker (who wrote the definitive slow blues tune, "Call It Stormy Monday"), but was also influenced by jazz musicians like Charlie Christian and Django Reinhardt. B.B. King became not just the most important electric guitarist in the blues, but also an essential role model for future blues-rock guitar heroes.

It was at the "Three O'Clock Blues" session that Ike Turner met producer Joe Bihari, the co-owner of Modern/RPM Records. Bihari hired Turner for $100 a week plus expenses to be his talent scout. "The top job for anybody was something like $45 a week," said Turner. "I had more money than anybody." Turner would hit a town, inquire about local musicians at the local bar or barber shop, then hold auditions and take note of what he found. Bihari would periodically drive from California with a four-input Magnecord tape recorder and make demonstration recordings of Turner's discoveries. All things considered, this scenario was not unlike the endeavor of a folklorist like Alan Lomax, except in this case, the motive was not preserving history, but finding hit records.

Some of Turner's finds weren't exactly exclusive. Chester "Howlin' Wolf" Burnett was a blues singer who was born in June of 1910 and who had a squawking harmonica style reminiscent of Sonny Boy Williamson. When he was eighteen Wolf met Charley Patton, who inspired him to become a musician as well as a farmer. By 1948, he had a radio show in West Memphis and was the leader of a band that would soon drive around in a twelve-passenger, black-and-yellow DeSoto with "Howlin' Wolf" painted on the side. Between Muddy Waters in Chicago and Howlin' Wolf in West Memphis, the Delta blues was going electric.

"Muddy, Jimmy Rogers, and Little Walter were shaping their definitive ensemble sound during these years, and, as another amplified group playing updated versions of traditional Delta Blues, Wolf's band, one would think, would have been comparable," said critic Robert Palmer about the ground-breaking music created between 1948 and 1950. "In fact, it was both more primitive and more modern than Muddy's group, for while Wolf was moaning and screaming like Charley Patton and Son House and blowing unreconstructed country blues harmonica, his band featured heavily amplified single-string lead guitar by Willie Johnson and Destruction's rippling, jazz-influenced piano."

Sam Phillips first heard Wolf sing on the radio. "When I heard Howlin' Wolf," said Phillips, "I said, 'This is for me. This is where the soul of man never dies.'" Phillips invited Wolf to check out his recording facility. "He would sit there with these feet planted wide apart," said Phillips, "playing nothing but the French harp, and I tell you, the greatest thing you could see to this day would be Chester Burnett doing one of those sessions in my studio." Nobody who's heard Howlin' Wolf's "Moanin' at Midnight" or "How Many More Years" would question the word of Sam Phillips, who leased his Wolf tracks to Chess Records. Ike Turner, meanwhile, took Wolf to a studio in West Memphis to recut some of the same songs for Bihari's Modern Records. A settlement was eventually reached whereby Wolf would record for Chess in exchange for that label giving Modern the recording rights to Roscoe Gordon, who'd just enjoyed a number 1 hit called "Booted."

"Leonard Chess kept worryin' me to come to Chicago," said Howlin' Wolf. "They talked me into the notion to give up my business and come. I turned my farming business over to my brother-in-law, my grandfather's farm that he left me. I moved to Chicago in 1952 or 1953. I had a $4,000 car and $3,900 in my pocket. I'm the onliest one drove out of the South like a gentleman."

But Wolf was not alone. He and his blues were on a trip alongside Waters and Hooker and Hopkins and King. Their music was rooted in its southern past, but having traveled to the city, would now be heard in a broader environment where it would mix it up with folk music and rock 'n' roll. Waters and Wolf would record songs that, a decade later, would become essential material for British rock bands. Hooker would pick up an acoustic guitar and beguile the coffee house crowd, while King would ultimately become a worldwide celebrity. Just as surprising, these bluesmen were also heading to a time when they would once more make music alongside long-forgotten figures of the Delta blues: Skip James, Son House, Mississippi John Hurt, and Robert Johnson, who was still dead, but not yet a legend.

TWO CHICAGO BLUES AND THE BIRTH OF FOLK-BLUES

Club Zanzibar on the West Side of Chicago was like a second home to Muddy Waters and his band from 1948 until the mid-1950s. If they weren't on tour, you'd find them there most every week. Fourteen-year-old Otis Rush saw Waters at the Zanzibar when he was visiting his sister in Chicago and knew right away that he wanted to be a guitar player. Texas-born Freddie King lived next door to the club as a teenager, and soaked up the sounds. A few years later, King and Earl Hooker (John Lee's cousin) would barnstorm the city's bars with their guitars. "They'd be shaking when we walked in," said King. "They'd say, 'Here they come again, man. Watch all your scotch. Watch your women.'"

Clubs like the Zanzibar were the laboratories where Muddy sculpted his sound. "The beat is almost like somebody falling off a bar stool," said Paul Oscher, who played harmonica in one of Waters's later bands. "It's not a straight, steady thing. . . . Muddy worked the audience, and he used time to do that. He'd sing, 'You say you love me baby . . .' and he'd wait, drag that shit out. There was no time there, you'd just wait on him. 'Please

Muddy Waters 1913–1983

call me on the phone sometime.' He'd wait till he thought it was right to tell the story."

Willie Dixon spent many nights at the Zanzibar, but when he first came to Chicago from Mississippi, he wanted to be a boxer. The stocky, six-foot-two Dixon won the novice division of the Illinois Golden Gloves Heavyweight Championship in 1937; he went professional, but after four fights had a falling out with his manager over money, and turned to music, not yet aware that it had the same business ethics as boxing. Dixon went to prison for ten months during World War II after declaring himself a "conscientious objector." "Why should I fight to save somebody that's killing me and my people?" he said. He performed songs like "Violent Love" with the Big Three Trio when he got out, wrapping his enormous frame around a stand-up bass. After playing a 1948 session for Robert Nighthawk, he became an integral part of the Chess Records family as house bassist, arranger, talent scout, and songwriter.

One night, Dixon was in the bathroom at the Zanzibar teaching a song to Muddy Waters. He told him to get a little rhythm pattern going, and since Waters couldn't read, Dixon coached him through the lyrics. "The gypsy woman told my momma," da-da-da-da-da! "before I was born," da-da-da-da-da! During the next set, Waters gave the song a shot. The crowd got louder at each blast of the band—"You got a boy child coming," da-da-da-da-da! "He's going to be a son of a gun"—until Muddy seemed to float above the stage like the sexiest man in Chicago, if not the world. A big hit (and a blues standard) had been born: "(I'm Your) Hoochie Coochie Man."

Dixon had by then become the preeminent composer of the modern blues song. The components were still drawn from a reservoir of overlapping lyrics and melodies that constitute the musical aquifer of Delta blues, but Dixon spiced his songs with hints of big-city panache and was careful to compose stylish intros and instrumental hooks. Not insignificantly, Dixon was also a tireless self-promoter, and working at Chess, he was blessed to have the inside track on selling songs to two of the best voices in blues, Waters and Howlin' Wolf.

When Wolf arrived in Chicago, Leonard Chess asked Waters to make him feel at home. Waters let Wolf stay at his house, and introduced him around town. "He took me in and I respect him for it today," said Wolf. "But while I was there, I paid for every mouthful of food I ate and every night I slept there. He didn't do it for nothing.'"

Wolf had no trouble finding work in Chicago clubs, as his records had preceded him, and a rivalry inevitably developed between the two Chess stars. Their live performances were quite different, with Muddy centered and commanding but relatively sedate compared to Wolf, who might choreograph a lyric by crawling across the stage (if not the bar). One night, when Wolf was exciting the women in the audience, a jealous girlfriend stabbed him in the thigh with a butcher knife. Wolf kept singing as he headed out the door (and to the hospital). Both Wolf and Muddy were known to do the bottle trick, in which the singer would shake up a bottle of Coca-Cola and slip it into his slacks. Then, looming over the crowd from the lip of the stage, the singer would slowly unzip his fly, pop the cap, and spray soda over the first few rows.

Waters and Wolf both worried that Dixon was giving his best songs to the other guy, prompting him to play the angles. "It got to the place where they thought I was writing better songs for the other," said Dixon. "Wolf would say, 'You giving Muddy the best songs,' and Muddy would say the same thing. So if I wanted Wolf to do the song, I'd say this is a song I wanted Muddy to do, and vice versa. Then everybody would be satisfied." Waters recorded such Dixon songs as "I'm Ready," "I Just Want to Make Love to You," and "You Shook Me" while Wolf cut "Evil," "Spoonful," and "Little Red Rooster."

At the Zanzibar, Muddy would often let the band start the show, and sit ringside with his brandy and lady friends before taking the microphone at mid-stream. Wolf would be on the stage for the first downbeat. They both worked hard to keep a steady line-up of musicians, but after Little Walter left Waters's live band after scoring a major 1952 hit instrumental called "Juke," Muddy's group was more often in flux.

Junior Wells was the first replacement for Little Walter. When Wells dropped out during a southern tour, Muddy sought out James Cotton, who'd recently recorded a single for Sun Records. Cotton had just finished a day of hauling gravel when a sharply dressed man introduced himself as Muddy Waters. "That's nice," said Cotton. "I'm Jesus Christ." Identities were soon confirmed. "We worked the Hippodrome on Beale Street [in Memphis] Saturday night," said Cotton. "That Sunday we played the state line of Arkansas and Missouri, and that Monday we was in Chicago. I moved in on the second floor." Cotton's rent was $12.50 a week.

"Muddy had a plantation mentality when it came to Chess Records," said Jimmy Rogers, who besides playing guitar with Waters, cut his own sides for Chess. "Leonard was the boss and Muddy did as the bossman said. Smart but unlettered, Muddy knew he could get what he wanted out of Leonard, and he flaunted it in the new cars he rode and the flashy clothes he wore. But Wolf was a rebel who'd left the plantation behind. All his life, he strove to be his own man." Wolf bought his own cars—Waters paid for his via uncollected record royalties—and considered Chess Records merely his place of employment.

Wolf was barely literate when he arrived in Chicago, and he took adult education classes to get basic skills in reading, writing, and math. He also took guitar lessons from Reggie Boyd, who played on Chess sessions, and taught Wolf how to read music and the rudiments of theory. During intermission at a gig, Wolf was apt to put on his glasses and do his homework. He also looked at his band as a business, and took deductions for Social Security and unemployment insurance out of the musician's salary. Wolf's accountant taught his wife Lillie how to do his books. "Wolf had to match whatever he took out for those boys," said Lillie, adding, "He wanted to shoot straight with them."

Wolf's right-hand man was guitarist Hubert Sumlin, who first saw Wolf when he was playing a juke in Seypel, Arkansas. Sumlin, who was a curious kid, climbed up on a stack of Coca-Cola crates to peek into the club. "Well, these Coke cases started to come unbalanced," said Sumlin, "and I fell through the window into the club, in the middle of a song. Over on the old Wolf's head I landed—right on the dude's head." Wolf shrugged him off and planted him in a proper seat. When the show was over, Wolf drove his youngest fan home. "When he got there," said Sumlin, "he made me wait in the car while he went in to see Momma. And he told her, 'Don't punish him, Mother, he just wanted to hear the music.' That's the first time I saw Wolf and I followed him ever since."

Waters and Wolf ruled Chicago, but throughout the '50s, a second generation of blues musicians arrived from the South. Buddy Guy, born in Lettsworth, Louisiana, in 1936, got to Chicago in September of 1957 with $100 in his pocket. "I was as green as a pool table and twice as square," said Guy, who aimed to play like B.B. King but with the flamboyant showmanship of Eddie "Guitar Slim" Jones. Guy carried an extra-long electric guitar cord so that he could recreate Slim's shtick of stepping out onto the street while playing a gnarly solo. He also chose Slim's hit "The Things That I Used to Do" when Otis Rush challenged the newcomer to take the stage at Chicago's 708 Club. His playing won over the discerning crowd, and a couple days later, Waters came by to meet the new kid in town.

"I'm in there trying to get a glimpse of Muddy Waters," said Guy, "and somebody grabbed me from behind and say, 'I'm Muddy Waters. I hear you're hungry.'" Waters figured a newly arrived country boy just had to be starving, so he brought Guy out to his Chevy and made him a salami sandwich. Guy was soon playing the 708 Club three nights a week (at $25 per) and getting the occasional all-night recording session at Chess (for $40). He also shared the stage with B.B. King, who invited him to come by his hotel. "It was like a father-and-son talk," said Guy of his visit with King, "and it got rid of a lot of shyness in me. . . . B.B. is the only person who ever shown me anything on the guitar. Other than what he taught me, I'm completely self-taught." On that day, following King's advice, Guy started playing with a flat pick.

B.B. King had learned many lessons since his early days in Memphis. Where Waters and Wolf were in Chicago for weeks at a time between periodic, mostly Southern tours, King was on the road constantly. In 1956, he played 342 shows, and subsequently averaged 330 dates a year. During his travels, he ran into a wide variety of musicians. Dizzy Gillespie introduced him to Charlie Parker. "I'm a blues player, B.," said Parker. "We're all blues players." King went to see Miles Davis and John Coltrane play at Birdland. Standing at a urinal, he heard the trumpeter's unmistakable rasp: "Motherfucking blues-singing B.B. King. Yeah, that's one cat who plays his ass off." King was also stirred by a recital by classical guitarist Andrés Segovia, and wore out Frank Sinatra's *In the Wee Small Hours*.

Nights off, however, were rare, and keeping a band on the road was a constant struggle. On the weekend his insurance lapsed, his tour bus ("Big Red") crashed and killed two men in another vehicle. King had to pay out $250,000 and finance another bus, and then ran into trouble with the IRS, which kept him fiscally underwater for a decade. Record sales didn't help. King claims that RPM Records paid him a penny or less per disc, but that wasn't the worst of it. "They would take a song I'd write and add another name to it and copyright the new one," says King, who said he never met such "cowriters" as Joe Josea and Jules Taub.

"They never had a lawyer look at their contracts," said Scott Cameron who would in later years handle the business affairs of Waters, Wolf, and Dixon. "It [Chess Records] was like a family affair. Somebody would put something in front of them with a pen, say sign it, and zip, they'd sign it, take the money and run." As always, the devil was in the details; Arc's publishing contracts were often "work-for-hire" arrangement wherein a songwriter would collect a salary but not own the publishing rights to their songs. "That generation [of record executives] was terribly paternal," said veteran record executive Bob Krasnow. "James Brown would come off the road, and Syd Nathan at King Records would buy him a bunch of clothes, a Cadillac, a case of wine, and send him home to take a couple of weeks off. Then charge it to his royalties." The record company kept the books, of course, and the artists rarely got a look inside.

Leonard Chess and his brother Phil got into the record business after running a Chicago liquor store and then a popular black nightclub, the Macomba Lounge. He knew nothing about song publishing until 1953 when Gene and Harry Goodman (clarinetist Benny's brothers) proposed a partnership called Arc Music. Arc would specifically handle international rights and Chess-owned songs covered by non-Chess acts. Covers turned into a goldmine when pop singers like Bill Haley, Pat Boone, and the McGuire Sisters had hits with Chess songs. The songwriters didn't profit, however, as Arc's early publishing contracts said that royalties were not to be paid on such recordings.

Record executives know that musicians often have a blind spot when it comes to business. Chuck Berry was encouraged by Muddy Waters to approach Leonard Chess about the chance to make a record. (Berry had sought out his favorite blues singer during a visit to Chicago, and later showed Waters around his hometown of St. Louis.) Chess liked a country-ish Berry tune called "Ida May," but pressed for a catchier title. It became "Maybellene," and was cut at Berry's first recording session in May of 1955 along with "Wee Wee Hours," "Thirty Days," and "You Can't Catch Me." During those few hours, with Willie Dixon on string bass, Berry helped to create rock 'n' roll by building a bridge between the blues and country music, a combination that was also exploited by Elvis Presley. Berry's musical signature became rocking double-stop guitar licks and teen-friendly lyrics; his secret weapon was pianist Johnnie Johnson. After the session, hamburgers and soda pop were brought into the studio for the hungry musicians. Around ten o'clock at night, Chess took Berry into his office to sign a few papers.

Berry read every word of the two contracts. "Some of the statements were beyond my knowledge of the record business," said Berry, "such as the 'residuals from mechanical rights,' the 'writer and producer's percentages,' and the 'performance royalties and publishers fees,' but I intentionally would frown at various sections to give the impression that a particular term (I actually knew nothing of) was rather unfavorable." Berry said he also knew "full well that I'd sign that darn thing anyway."

When "Maybellene" became a huge hit—number 1 R&B, and number 5 pop—Berry noticed that there were two other writers listed on the record label. One was Alan Freed, the influential New York (via Cleveland) deejay who'd famously coined the term "rock 'n' roll." Payola ruled the airwaves in the 1950s, and Marshall Chess did his part to grease the wheels of commerce. He even declared his pay-for-play payouts as a business expense on Chess's corporate tax returns, which is why he wasn't dragged into the payola scandal that ruined Freed's career. Offering the disc jockey a piece of the song's publishing was simply another (extremely generous) way to insure airplay. Berry didn't obtain full ownership of his first hit until the copyright held by Arc Music expired.

Chuck Berry became the most successful artist on Chess, which also recorded rock 'n' roll records by Bo Diddley (including some songs written by Dixon). Meanwhile, in Memphis, B.B. King met Elvis Presley, who was fast becoming the biggest star in popular music. "The roots of rock 'n' roll went back to my roots, the Mississippi Delta," King said, adding, "I understood it, but couldn't embrace it. I lacked the flash of other black entertainers like Little Richard, Chuck Berry, or Bo Diddley. I missed the boat."

The audience for the blues was aging, but while the genre's popularity would begin to wane in the late 1950s, the influence of the bluesmen would linger. "When I was a little kid," said James Hendrix of Seattle, Washington, "I heard a record playing at a neighbor's house turned way up. That song called to me, and now I don't even remember which one it was. I left my yard, went down the street, and when the song was over, I knocked on the door and said, 'What was that playing?' 'Muddy Waters,' the guy said. I didn't quite understand. He repeated it and spelled it out—'M-U-D-D-Y.'"

"Sometime around 1954 or 1955," said Dave Van Ronk, "I happened to be walking across Washington Square Park on a Sunday afternoon, and I noticed this guy playing an old New Yorker Martin, a very small, very sweet guitar, and he was doing something that sounded an awful lot like 'Stackalee.' It immediately grabbed my attention, because he was doing the whole thing by himself. His thumb was picking out the bass notes while he was playing the melody with his fingers." When the music stopped, Van Ronk asked the guitarist (Tom Paley, who later played with the New Lost City Ramblers) to show him what he was doing.

Van Ronk hurried home for the first of many practice sessions devoted to learning how to fingerpick. He considered himself a jazz guitarist, and would typically use a flat pick to either play rhythm chords or single-note melodies. The integration of bass, rhythm, and melody in this different style of guitar playing encouraged Van Ronk to experiment with a wide variety of music, including ragtime tunes typically played on the piano. The burgeoning interest in folk and blues also prompted him to ditch his jazz band and perform as a solo singer-guitarist.

Van Ronk, who made his living as a merchant seaman, played the opening night of a Greenwich Village club called the Café Bizarre in August of 1957. Odetta, the evening's headliner, offered to pass along a tape of Van Ronk to the man who ran the Gate of Horn in Chicago, a show-business newcomer named Albert Grossman. Smelling the potential for a big break, he quickly made a recording, but unbeknownst to him, the tape never made it to Odetta, let alone Grossman. Frustrated, Van Ronk impulsively hitchhiked to Chicago. Grossman, seated at the bar of his empty club, told Van Ronk to take the stage for an impromptu audition. "When I got off," said Van Ronk, "Albert still had not batted an eyelash. 'Do you know who works here?' he asked. 'Big Bill Broonzy works here. Josh White works here. Brownie McGhee and Sonny Terry play here a lot. Now tell me, why should I hire you?'" Van Ronk was back at Washington Square the following Sunday.

"The musicians were in different groups scattered around the fountain and near the arch," said guitarist Happy Traum describing a typical Sunday in the Greenwich Village park. "There were Pete Seeger-type folk singers, there were old-timey musicians, there were a couple of different bluegrass bands, there were people singing the blues. At first I went to the folk group, but I also started liking blues, and met Dave Van Ronk for the first time there, playing 'St. James Infirmary' and songs like that. He was definitely one of the first people I have an image of meeting there, because he was singing real loud and you could hear him from across the other side of the park."

When Traum studied at the Bronx campus of New York University, he met a charismatic student who rode a motorcycle and played the guitar. "His name was Ian Buchanan," said Traum, "and he pulled out this guitar and started finger picking all this obscure old blues material. He was very eclectic in his taste in music, but when he played guitar, it was blues finger picking. Here was a guy who'd play 'Canned Heat Blues' by Tommy Johnson, which was not an everyday occurrence." (Johnson, who recorded from 1928 to 1930, had a snappy guitar style and an insatiable appetite for women and liquor. "Canned Heat Blues" was about Sterno, his drink of choice when actual spirits weren't available.)

Buchanan transferred to Antioch College in Ohio, where his playing would inspire Jorma Kaukonen, who would later play in Jefferson Airplane, and John Hammond Jr., the son of the famous talent scout. "Some of the first things he taught me," said Kaukonen, "were 'Hesitation Blues,' 'Death Don't Have No Mercy,' and 'Keep Your Lamps Trimmed and Burning.' Those were my departure points, and then I went off to learn from the recordings." The three songs were all by the Reverend Gary Davis, and they became perennials in Kaukonen's post-Airplane blues ensemble, Hot Tuna.

Traum, meanwhile, found a new guitar hero when he heard a Folkways ten-inch called *Brownie McGhee Blues*. Traum telephoned McGhee, who lived in Harlem, to ask about taking lessons. "Brownie had two or three white guys like me who'd go to his apartment to take lessons," said Traum, who paid $5 per session, "and he had his lessons fairly down pat. There were certain things he'd teach you, and other times he'd play a song and you did your best to keep up. You'd have to stop him to ask, 'How do you play that lick?'"

Everybody, it seemed, was looking to learn how to play like the people on the Harry Smith anthology. "I was at the Washington Square jam sessions from 1956 on," said David Cohen, who grew up in Brooklyn, and who would later play keyboards with Country Joe and the Fish. "I wouldn't miss it even if it was raining, so I really grew up with people like Joshua Rifkin, Stefan Grossman, Danny Kalb. John Sebastian was around, though he was a little younger than us. Happy and Artie Traum. And then there was the older crowd like Dave Van Ronk."

Lots of white folk music fans were discovering the blues. Eric Von Schmidt was born in 1931 and lived in Westport, Connecticut. He was the son of Harold Von Schmidt, a successful illustrator and a regular contributor to the *Saturday Evening Post*, and figured to follow in his father's footsteps. "Then one day," said Von Schmidt, "it was on a Sunday, I was by myself out in the studio, painting a poster for the Senior Football Dance, and I heard this incredible voice coming right out of the radio. . . . It was honey-smooth, but had the bite of a buzz-saw cutting through a cement block. It was Lead Belly, and it changed my life."

Von Schmidt's father bought his son a Gibson acoustic guitar, and he spent hours trying to play along with *Negro Sinful Songs Sung by Lead Belly*. Since he was going out with a girl called Irene, he quickly mastered one of Lead Belly's biggest hits, "Goodnight Irene." Later, he found two books of folk songs by John and Alan Lomax, and noted that the "Folk Song Archives of the Library of Congress" had recorded copies of many of the songs. He visited the archive in 1950. "It was like finding buried treasure," said Von Schmidt. "You could sit all day and listen to these funky records, and they really had good notes and the words and everything. Because I couldn't read music, the songbooks just whetted my appetite. Hearing the actual songs was a feast."

Elsewhere, in the nation's capitol, Dick Spottswood continued to comb used record stores in search of desirable discs. "I'd go hunting records with John Fahey," says Spottswood. "We used to go down to the area around

Tidewater, Virginia, and around Norfolk and Hampton and knock on doors and ask people to sell us old records. We would try to find black neighborhoods, which was about as far as our strategy went."

Fahey, who lived in Takoma Park, Maryland, bought his first guitar from the Sears-Roebuck catalog for $17. As a young musician and collector, he liked country and bluegrass and initially dismissed the blues. Then Fahey and his friend went on a 1956 record-hunting trip and came back to Spottswood's house to listen to their purchases. Fahey was initially dismissive of "Praise God I'm Satisfied" by Blind Willie Johnson. "A couple hours later," said Spottswood, "John calls me up and says, 'Would you play that record again?' So I played it for him over the phone, and he said, 'I've changed my mind—I really like it.'" Fahey later compared his embrace of blues a "conversion experience."

Fahey evolved into an idiosyncratic bluesman playing what he called "American primitive guitar." Joe Bussard, a pal who was in the process of amassing an estimable collection of rare 78s, also had a bare-bones recording studio (complete with a disc-cutting machine) in his parent's Maryland home. Fahey recorded some 78s for Bussard's Fonotone label, and also a full-length album that was credited on one side to Fahey, and on the other to "Blind Joe Death." Fahey pressed up a hundred copies and tried to sell them at the Langley Park gas station where he worked. He also sent a copy to Sam Charters, who had just published the first real history of down-home music, *The Country Blues*. "I still have a letter from 1959," said Fahey, "where I sent Charters a copy of my first record and he wrote me back to tell me how terrible I was and how [Ramblin'] Jack Elliot and so on and so forth were much better than me."

Charters, born in 1929, spent his childhood in Pittsburgh, Pennsylvania, and California. After studying at Harvard, he got a degree in economics from the University of California at Berkeley. By then, Charters had amassed a huge collection of vintage 78s and had spent time in New Orleans studying the city's musical culture. While producing field recordings that were released on Folkways Records, he did research for *The Country Blues*, an ambitious book that he figured would have flaws, but that he hoped would inspire others to hunt for more information about a heretofore arcane subject.

Charters's book gave the "down-home blues" a new name—"country blues"—and he compiled a companion Folkways LP that included fourteen tracks by such musicians as Blind Lemon Jefferson, Sleepy John Estes, Lonnie Johnson, Bukka White, and for the first time on record in twenty-one years, Robert Johnson. While working on his book, Charters also nursed the hope of finding Lightnin' Hopkins, a Texas bluesman who'd all but disappeared after having a handful of R&B hits in the early 1950s. Hopkins, it turned out, was hiding in plain sight.

To help in his search, Charters enlisted the help of Mack McCormick, a record collector and writer who'd known Hopkins, and who also knew his way around Houston. They checked pawnshops and ghetto bars but came up empty; the next day, Charters cruised Dowling Street by himself and stopped at a red light. "A car pulled up beside me," said Charters, "and there was a man with sunglasses saying, 'You lookin' for me?' And I said, 'Are you Lightnin' Hopkins?' And Lightnin' said, 'Yeah.' So he found me. I had been checked out and the decision was that I was safe."

When the talk turned to making a record, Hopkins asked Charters to get him an electric guitar at the pawnshop; instead, the folklorist procured an acoustic and a fresh set of strings. They recorded at Hopkins's rented room at 2803 Hadley Street. Charters used a portable Ampex tape recorder and an Electrovoice microphone, and offered $300 for the afternoon session. Hopkins wanted $100 a song, but also needed the money, so he signed a release. Charters cajoled nine songs out of Hopkins, partly by piquing his interest with well-informed questions about Blind Lemon Jefferson. "I did it all with a hand-held microphone," said Charters. "I would [hold it aloft to] do the vocal and move it down to get the guitar solos . . . As an old folkie myself, I kept insisting that he tune the guitar."

Charters was in the right place to capture a moment in time. "He is one of the last of his kind," Charters wrote of Hopkins in the last paragraph of *The Country Blues*, "a lonely, bitter man who brings to the blues the intensity and pain of the hours in the hot sun, scraping at the earth, singing to make the hours pass. The blues will go on, but the country blues, and the great singers who created from the raw singing of the work songs and the field cries, the richness and variety of the country blues, will pass with men like this thin, intense singer from Centerville, Texas." Shortly after recording for Charters, Lightnin' Hopkins would play his country blues at Carnegie Hall.

THREE BOHEMIAN BLUES AND THE FOLK REVIVAL

Stefan Grossman was a fifteen-year-old Brooklyn kid when he called up the Reverend Gary Davis in 1960 to ask about taking guitar lessons. "Sure," said Davis, "come up and bring your money, honey." The next Saturday, Grossman's parents drove him to a section of the Bronx that he said looked as "bombed out as Dresden." Grossman found his teacher "in a three-room sharecropper's shack behind a burnt-out tenement." It was a revelation to see "a musical genius living in utter poverty." Even before unpacking his guitar, Grossman had learned a lesson in the blues.

Reverend Gary Davis 1896–1972

The Reverend Gary Davis was a guitar virtuoso, arguably the most famous street singer in the history of the blues, and a teacher of enduring renown whose students also included David Bromberg, Ry Cooder, Ian Buchanan, Roy Book Binder, and Woody Mann. His influence spread to such non-students as Bob Dylan, Jorma Kaukonen, and Dave Van Ronk, all of whom were inspired by the snappy syncopations of such Davis instrumentals as "Buck Dance," "Twelve Sticks," and

"Cincinnati Flow Rag." Those guitar players lucky enough to study within the smoky haze of the Reverend's White Owl cigars enjoyed a rare opportunity to literally step into the folk tradition and learn directly from a master instrumentalist. In the early-'60s, folklorists would scour the South in search of forgotten figures of Depression-era blues, some of whom had stopped playing music. New York guitar players had only to take the subway uptown to find a street-singing Segovia who not only had never stopped playing, but had also gotten better.

"Play what you know," Davis told his students. "Play just what you know." Davis knew plenty. Blind since shortly after his 1896 birth in South Carolina, Davis was playing guitar and singing in the Baptist Church by the time he turned eight. He played in string bands as a teenager, but was a loner by nature and spent much of his life as a street performer, settling in Durham, North Carolina, in the early 1930s and relocating to New York City in the 1940s.

Fingerpicking guitarists from the southeast are said to play in the Piedmont style, a term that accommodated such distinct instrumentalists as Blind Blake, Josh White, Blind Willie McTell, and Blind Boy Fuller. Davis had a boisterous, fleet-fingered style that drew upon most every music that had crossed his path, including blues, jazz, gospel, parade marches, and popular tunes. But he probably owed the most to ragtime, the syncopated piano music that was popular in the early twentieth century, and best known to contemporary listeners from "The Entertainer," the Scott Joplin tune used in the 1973 film *The Sting*. Had Joplin played guitar instead of piano, the foremost composer of ragtime might have sounded something like Gary Davis.

Grossman would not just bring his guitar to his lessons but a tape recorder as well. That way, he could study the tunes at home and try to replicate the tricky passages. Grossman also took his recorder to Gerdes Folk City in Greenwich Village, where he taped a week of 1962 Davis performances that were eventually released in 2009. Students brought Davis income and valuable support, with Grossman and others accompanying the Reverend to music gigs both secular and sacred.

"On Friday night, he'd come down to the Village and go to some coffeehouse and earn maybe a hundred bucks passing the hat," said Grossman. "Saturday there might be a Bar Mitzvah, and you'd take him, not to the ceremony, but to entertain your Jewish friends. The parents loved him. Then on Saturday night, there'd be a concert at a college, and you'd find yourself eating with the president of Swarthmore, and the first thing Reverend Davis would do was take out his false teeth and put them on the table. Then he'd eat with his hands. Finally, on Sunday, he'd take us to a storefront church, with maybe fifteen people in the congregation, and you'd have him preaching, and then he'd get into a song and get the spirit. He doesn't get that spirit when he'd sing the song in front of a white audience at Gerdes. But in church, he'd go to places where I've never been."

Dave Van Ronk, who by the early '60s was an established figure on the Greenwich Village folk and blues scene, saw the Reverend play and preach in a storefront church. "His sermons were remarkable," said Van Ronk. "He would set up a riff on his guitar, and then he would chant his sermon in counterpoint to the riff, and when he made a little change in what he was saying, he would make a little change on the guitar. There was this constant interplay and interweaving of voice and guitar, and these fantastic polyrhythms would come out of that—I never heard anything quite like it, before or since."

Davis embodied the psychological conflicts that can confront a musician playing the blues and songs that praised the Lord. After recording a pair of blues during a 1935 recording session, Davis refused to perform anything but religious music. Over the years, he fudged on the pledge like a God-fearing man happy to savor a drink of whiskey; Grossman said Davis and his wife, Annie, would call him the "Devil's Son" because he would always be after his teacher to show him blues songs. The Reverend even showed David Bromberg some naughty blues. "When he taught me the 'Maple Leaf Rag,'" said Bromberg, "he had words to go with it: 'Get it up, get it up, get it up in a hurry.' I also remember him singing, 'Old Aunt Diana, don't you know, used to give her two nickels just to look at her hole. Laid down old Diana on her back, gave me my two nickels back.'"

Van Ronk also taught guitar to supplement his income as a coffeehouse performer and recording artist. "My blues-guitar-artist-to-be-path accelerated with my discovery, at the age of 17, of my mentor, the great Dave Van Ronk," said Danny Kalb, who would later play lead guitar in the Blues Project, an influential blues-inflected rock band. "Dave was a trip, the perfect shock mentor, a grown-up, a bohemian, living in a West 15th Street neo-tenement. An anarcho-syndicalist wise in the ways of the outré left—he gave me the real skinny on the Rosenbergs, a shock to this Westchester Stalinist kid at the time—a pot-smoker iconoclast up the wazoo and more."

Van Ronk worked the same club circuit as Davis, and they once shared a late-night drive from Boston to New York City. The Reverend was sprawled across the back seat idly picking "Candyman," one of his most famous songs.

"By New Haven it was really beginning to bug me," said Van Ronk, "but what could I say? This was the Reverend Gary Davis playing 'Candyman.' Bridgeport, somewhere around Stamford, something inside me snapped. I growled, 'For Christ's sake, Gary, can't you play anything else?' And I turned around, and he was asleep."

Van Ronk called his autobiography *The Mayor of MacDougal Street*, which was metaphorically true, but being a bluesy folkie wasn't a trip down easy street. Recording a folk-blues album for Folkways paid in the low hundreds. The good news was that the records stayed in print, which was important for a walking (or driving) musician, who never expected a record to do much more than promote the next live gig. Prestige Records paid a little better, but it was in a more commercial sphere than Folkways, where Mo Asch's first priority was marketing even the most esoteric music.

Economically, it behooved a folkie bluesman to be flexible. In the late '50s, not long after Britain's Lonnie Donegan launched a skiffle craze in Britain with a version of Lead Belly's "Rock Island Line," Van Ronk aimed for a similar sound with a group called The Orange Blossom Jug Five with guitarist Sam Charters (preparing to publish *The Country Blues*) and his future wife Ann (an accomplished pianist) on washboard. During the early '60s vogue for jug bands, Van Ronk formed the Ragtime Jug Stompers with his former student Danny Kalb on lead guitar.

Greenwich Village was by now crowded with musicians who disparaged the commercial folk music of the Kingston Trio but didn't hate the buzz of tourists it drew to the clubs and coffeehouses located near the intersection of Bleeker and McDougal Street. Albert Grossman had moved from Chicago to New York and approached Van Ronk about joining a trio that would sing folk songs with a male-female vocal blend reminiscent of the Weavers. Van Ronk passed on the offer to join Peter, Paul and Mary, but was thrilled when that best-selling trio recorded one of his tunes. Gary Davis's "If I Had My Way" was also included on the group's debut album.

"Peter, Paul & Mary wanted him to have the publishing royalties to 'If I Had My Way,'" said Ernie Hawkins, who moved to New York from Pittsburgh to study with Davis, "and he and the group and his manager were all gathered in a lawyer's office and they asked him, 'Did you write this song?' And Gary Davis said, 'No.' There was silence and then the Reverend said, 'The Lord gave it to me in 1927.' Coincidentally, that was when Blind Willie Johnson recorded it. So he had loopholes. He was a smart guy." He also now had the money to buy a house in Queens.

Greenwich Village bohemia was transitioning from the era defined by the Beat Generation to that of the hippies. Poet and musician Ed Sanders opened the Peace Eye Bookstore in the East Village and published an avant-garde journal called *Fuck You*. In 1964, he formed the Fugs with Tuli Kupferberg (Stefan Grossman was briefly a member of the group). Harry Smith produced the first Fugs album, and was paid with a bottle of rum. "During the session," said Sanders, "I think perhaps to spur us to greater motivity and energy, he came in from the recording booth where we were singing and smashed the bottle of rum against the wall."

Liquor wasn't the only available intoxicant. "One thing I regret emphasizing in my publications was the defiance in shooting up [heroin]," said Sanders. "I had a bit of a cavalier attitude toward the use of the needle. In some apartments on the Lower East Side a hypodermic needle boiling on a gas ring was almost as prevalent as a folk guitar by the bed. Miriam [his wife] noticed how, just as in later decades a person might ask, 'Do you mind if I smoke a cigarette?' Back in those days it was likely to be 'Do you mind if I shoot up?'"

On any given Village night, Van Ronk, Patrick Sky, Ramblin' Jack Elliott, and whoever else was around would gather to drink at the Kettle of Fish. During the day, they might stop at Izzy Young's Folklore Center to look through the LPs, try out an instrument, or maybe buy a fresh set of guitar strings for a performance at the Gaslight, which was just downstairs from the Kettle of Fish. Bob Dylan got his first break in this Bermuda Triangle of bohemianism when he ran into Van Ronk at the Folklore Center trying out an old Gibson guitar. Dylan asked him how to get a job at the Gaslight. When Van Ronk inquired if he could push a broom, Dylan picked up the Gibson and played an old blues, "Nobody Loves You When You're Down and Out." Van Ronk invited him to come to the Gaslight that night and sing a couple songs during his set.

Dylan soon found his way to the city's premiere folk club. "I spent a lot of time at Gerde's," said Peter Wolf, who was studying painting in New York, and who would later gain fame as the singer of the J. Geils Band. "I got to see John Lee Hooker. Bob Dylan opened for him." The Gerde's gig was still a novelty for Hooker, who was new to the coffeehouse circuit and was now being booked into venues like Boston's Club 47 and the Ash Grove in Los Angeles by Albert Grossman.

For Hooker, the folk clubs meant trading his electric guitar for an acoustic and choosing a repertoire that would appeal to an attentive audience as opposed to a rowdy crowd in a noisy tavern. "He'd sit around and watch me play," said Hooker of Dylan. "He'd be right there every night, and we'd be playing guitars in the hotel. I don't know what he got from me, but he must've gotten something. A lot of guitar players have." Including Pete Townshend of the Who. "Without him there would be no 'power chord,'" said Townshend, describing an abbreviated chord that uses not three notes, but two. "It is time to give credit for that little invention to the man who really created it, John Lee Hooker. Take it from me. I know."

Dylan's second engagement at Gerdes, opening for the Greenbriar Boys, won him a rave review in the *New York Times* that was seen by John Hammond, the legendary Columbia Records talent scout. Hammond met Dylan when he played harmonica on a recording session for Carolyn Hester, and quickly signed him to Columbia. He sent him home with a copy of a soon-to-be-released album, *Robert Johnson: King of the Delta Blues*. Dylan was knocked out by the record, listened to it repeatedly, and wrote down the lyrics to better appreciate the flow of the words and the construction of the songs. If Woody Guthrie was Dylan's yin, then Robert Johnson became his yang. "In about 1964 and '65," said Dylan, "I probably used about five or six of Robert Johnson's blues songs forms, too, unconsciously, but more on the lyrical imagery side of things. If I hadn't heard the Robert Johnson record when I did, there probably would have been hundreds of lines of mine that would have been shut down—that I wouldn't have felt free enough or unpraised enough to write."

Dylan knew Hammond's son, John Jr., who was equally smitten with Robert Johnson. Hammond's parents split up when he was five years old, and his mother brought him up. His father first played him Johnson's "Terraplane Blues" and "Milkcow's Calf Blues" in 1957; two years later, Hammond gave his son a tape of ten unreleased Johnson tunes. Hammond Jr. didn't start playing guitar until he was eighteen, but he caught on fast. In 1961, at Antioch College, he learned the rudiments of country blues guitar from Ian Buchanan, who played on Friday nights at a local bakery. Hammond soon dropped out of school, and went to the West Coast to launch an unlikely career as a white country blues musician. Hammond found work at the Ash Grove, a Los Angeles club that booked folk, blues, and bluegrass acts. His first gig there was opening for the Staple Singers, and over the next few years, he played shows around the country with a wide variety of acoustic bluesmen. But nothing compared to the first time he played the Ash Grove with Howlin' Wolf.

"I was just trembling with the fact that I was on a show with Howlin' Wolf," said Hammond. "I came backstage, and it was just him in the dressing room. He said, 'Come here and sit down. Where the fuck did you learn to play that?' It was a Robert Johnson song, and I said I learned it off the record. He said, 'Play that right now for me!' So I played him the song, and he said, 'Man, that's evil.'" For Hammond, who'd heard complaints that it was inauthentic for a white kid to play country blues, Wolf's support meant the world. "And then," said Hammond, "he picked up my guitar and played [Charley Patton's] 'Stone Pony Blues.' At the end, he flipped the guitar, made three turns, and then hit the last three notes! It was the most slick thing I've ever seen."

Hammond would enjoy a career as a solo performer and occasional bandleader; in 1965, he recorded *So Many Roads* with the Hawks, the group that backed rocker Ronnie Hawkins before working with Bob Dylan and becoming the Band. One night, between shows at the Gaslight, Hammond ducked into the Café Wha? to check out Jimmy James, a guitarist whose real last name was Hendrix. "He was playing a Fender Stratocaster upside down and left-handed," said Hammond, "one of those things that just boggles your mind. I just could not believe it—playing with his teeth, and doing all those really slick techniques that I had seen in Chicago on the South Side on wild nights. But here was this guy doing it, and he was fantastic playing blues."

Bob Dylan had always considered blues as indistinguishable from folk music and recognized that both genres embraced a tradition in which one song was built upon another, with a melody from here, and a lyric from there. That's why the "folk revival" logically fed into the "blues revival" and why it was natural that Dylan's early repertoire was as likely to include a song by Woody Guthrie as Blind Lemon Jefferson. During a trip to Boston, Dylan hung out with the city's premiere white blues singer, Eric Von Schmidt, and learned some of the songs that he sang, including a Blind Boy Fuller tune called "Baby Let Me Lay It on You."

"Later," said Von Schmidt, "somebody said, 'Hey, Bob's put one of your songs on his album.' They were talking about 'Baby, Let Me Follow You Down,' which had a spoken introduction saying he first heard it from me 'in the green fields of Harvard University.' The tune was the same [as 'Baby Let Me Lay It on You'], and the chords were real pretty, but they weren't the same. . . . He also did Van Ronk's version of 'House of the Rising Sun' on that record which pissed Dave off."

The label on the Dylan album listed "R. Von Schmidt" as the composer of "Baby, Let Me Follow You Down," though he never collected any royalties, as Witmark Publishing had registered Dylan as the composer. When Von Schmidt complained, he was told they were honoring a prior copyright. Only later did he figure out that Witmark wasn't talking about a copyright that belonged to Blind Boy Fuller's heirs, but to Dylan. As for "House of the Rising Sun," Van Ronk had the last laugh when the bluesy British rock band the Animals "stole" the song from Dylan and made it into a worldwide hit.

Albert Grossman was now Dylan's manager, which suggests that it might have been more than good taste that led to the inclusion of three Dylan tunes on the second Peter, Paul and Mary album, including the epochal "Blowing in the Wind." Chuck Berry, Willie Dixon, and B.B. King could have used an advocate like Grossman. Before he had a manager, Dylan had signed a contract with Leeds Music Publishing for a $100 advance. Grossman fronted Dylan $1,000 in cash to buy himself out of the contract before he started writing hits.

In 1962 both Bob Dylan and Peter, Paul Mary released their debut albums. The Robert Johnson collection, which was just one of the blues reissues finding an avid audience in a small but influential group of musicians and collectors, also came out that year. Jim McKune, the New York blues collector who'd traveled hours to hear a Skip James record, hated the compilation that Sam Charters had produced to accompany *The Country Blues*, mostly because it didn't include anything by Charley Patton. He encouraged Pete Whelan, a drugstore heir and fellow blues fan, to cull the best recordings from other collectors and start a reissue label.

Whelan's first Origins Jazz Label LP was devoted to Charley Patton; the multi-artist second release alluded to Charters's book with the title, *Really! The Country Blues*. Legally speaking, since Whelan didn't own the rights to these recordings, these LPs were "bootlegs." But since these records were pressed in the hundreds, major labels that technically owned the material either didn't notice or declined to litigate. There was one famous exception: when Columbia Records learned that Whelan was going to produce a record of Robert Johnson tunes, it threatened legal action. Ironically, Columbia couldn't locate some of Johnson's master recordings, and had to reach out to collectors to copy some of the songs from vintage 78s.

Record collectors did more than produce bootleg compilations; they were also a valuable resource for musicians. Stefan Grossman made the rounds of collectors and made tape recordings of their 78s. Dave Freeman turned Grossman on to Blind Boy Fuller, and steered him to Whelan and Bernie Klatzko, who introduced him to the songs of Charley Patton and Skip James. If collectors could be fetishistic about their rare 78s, Grossman was equally fastidious about the music, learning and transcribing each song in painstaking detail.

Grossman was a regular at a Saturday afternoon jam session at Allan

Block's Sandal Shop on West Fourth Street in the Village, and fell into a teenage romance with the owner's daughter, Rory Block, who shared his passion for the blues guitar. When Block was fifteen, she and Grossman recorded an album called *How to Play Blues Guitar* for Elektra Records; because she hated the concept of an instructional record, Block insisted on being billed as "Sunshine Kate." When the couple traveled to Washington, D.C., they stayed with Nick Perls, a well-funded collector thanks to his parents, who owned the Perls Gallery in New York and represented, among others, sculptor Alexander Calder. Perls would soon launch a major blues reissue label, Yazoo Records.

Alan Lomax, who considered the Washington Square folk and blues musicians to be uninspired imitators of the real thing, discovered a significant new blues artist while on a 1959 song collecting trip. Lomax's expedition was bankrolled by Atlantic Records, which provided him with a stereo tape recorder. While recording a ninety-one-year-old fiddler in northern Mississippi, Lomax was approached by a neighbor carrying a guitar. His name was Fred McDowell, and he'd just returned from a day in the cotton fields. When McDowell slipped a bottleneck slide over his ring finger and spun guitar lines around his voice, Lomax said he heard "a silver-voiced heavenly choir answering him from the treble strings. When we played his recording back to him, he stomped up and down on the porch, whooping and laughing and hugging his wife. He knew he had been heard and felt his fortune had been made." Muddy Waters had the exact same reaction when Lomax first recorded him.

McDowell went on to play the folk-blues circuit (where he would influence the slide guitar style of Bonnie Raitt) and was recorded by Chris Strachwitz for his roots music label, Arhoolie Records. Strachwitz was a collector and entrepreneur who'd launched Arhoolie with a field recording of Mance Lipscomb, a singer-guitarist whom he'd found while searching for untapped talent in Texas with blues researcher Mack McCormick. Lipscomb and McDowell were manual laborer and weekend musicians who'd never been recorded. Out of the blue, they found late-life careers touring the folk-blues circuit. Lonnie Johnson was different; he'd played with Louis Armstrong, toured with Bessie Smith, and had a recording career that stretched back to 1925. By the late-'50s, however, he was doing menial work at a Philadelphia hotel. A couple of teenage record collectors, Geoff Muldaur and Joe Boyd, got wind of this and arranged for Johnson to play a house party at the Princeton home of journalist Murray Kempton.

"The party was in 1959," said Muldaur, "and one of the things I remember was that here were these seventeen-year-old kids asking for 'Jelly Roll Baker' and any blues we could think of, and he's trying to sing 'Red Sails on the Sunset' because he's looking out at a room full of middle-aged white people. There was no deal beyond passing the hat, and we might have ended up putting a hundred dollars in his pocket. He couldn't have been sweeter, but there was also a sadness about him, this giant who'd had his own hits and who'd also played with Duke Ellington and Louis Armstrong."

Muldaur's tastes had turned from jazz to blues when he bought a copy of Blind Willie Johnson's "The Rain Don't Fall on Me No More." "That was it for being totally in love with the blues," he said. He and Boyd both ended up going to college in Boston, with Boyd at Harvard (where he was room-mates with singer-guitarist Tom Rush) and Muldaur at Boston University. Boston had a vibrant folk and blues scene that revolved around Club 47, which featured touring acts and local stars like Eric Von Schmidt. Joan Baez was the scene's barefoot Madonna; Albert Grossman had negotiated her recording contract with Vanguard, but she had declined his offer of management, choosing the more mild-mannered Manny Greenhill, who was the preeminent broker of folk talent in New England. When he was a young man, Greenhill had taken a guitar lesson with Josh White, who taught him to play "House of the Rising Sun." His other clients included Gary Davis and Lightnin' Hopkins.

On his first trip to Boston, Hopkins stayed at the Greenhill's home. "My dad liked him more than my mom did," said Mitch Greenhill, a guitarist who eventually took over his father's firm. "My mom found him kind of a prickly house guest, because one time she made him some eggs for break-fast. I guess they were scrambled eggs, and they were too soft or too hard, or something, and he spit them out all over a wall in the kitchen. It didn't endear him to her."

Boyd hired singer-guitarist Sleepy John Estes and harmonica player Hammie Nixon to play a show at Harvard, and traveled with Muldaur to pick up the pair of blind musicians at a music festival in Ithaca, New York. The bluesmen drank bourbon for breakfast and slept on the ride to Boston. Von Schmidt got them more whiskey and brought them to a party where they played music for pretty much anybody who might have gone to the next night's show. The show was a financial bust and taught Boyd a lesson in culture.

"I was beginning to grasp some of the recurring themes in my life," said Boyd. "The tension when artists from a poverty-stricken community confront the spoiled offspring of the educated middle class and the conflict between the latter's desire to hear the 'real thing' and the former's desire to be 'up to date.' Hearing traditional musicians when they first emerge from their own communities is a wonderful experience but impossible to repeat: the music is inevitably altered by the process of 'discovery.'"

Boyd was the promoter and the producer, while others in his circle aspired to musical careers. "One way I learned to become an entertainer," said Jim Kweskin, "was to drop myself off in a city that I'd never been in before in my life like, say, St. Louis, where I didn't know anybody, didn't have any contacts, and . . . go to the nearest guitar shop and find where the places were. Then I'd go and ask if I could play for free. Then, when I got on stage, it was up to me. Could I do it? That was a great education."

Kweskin was, essentially, a walking musician. During his wanderings, he worked in a Chicago music store and played with harmonica player Paul Butterfield, swapped songs with Spider John Koerner in Minneapolis, and performed at the Gaslight in New York with Bob Dylan. Back in Boston, he did a show with a few friends, and Maynard Solomon, the president of Vanguard Records, offered him a record deal. Kweskin said that first he'd get a better band. Geoff Muldaur was his first recruit, and the Kweskin Jug Band was soon the hottest combo in Boston.

Jug bands were as old as the blues, playing a light-hearted mixture of pop tunes, ragtime, string-band songs, and the blues. The term came from the jug that was literally played as a wind instrument in the rhythm section; jug bands were popular in the 1920s, with the Memphis Jug Band and Cannon's Jug Stompers at the head of the class. Thirty years later, right before the Beatles invaded America, jug bands were thought to be the next big thing. With Kweskin and company signed to Vanguard, Paul Rothchild, who'd failed in his attempt to sign the group to Elektra, turned to a New York group, the Even Dozen Jug Band.

Rothchild was fresh off an album project called *The Blues Project*, which was a compilation of white blues singers that included tracks by Muldaur, Dave Van Ronk, Eric Von Schmidt, Tom Rush, Danny Kalb, and Ian Buchanan. "The record took thirteen hours," said Rothchild. "We gave everybody fifty bucks a cut." The final tab was $963. The members of the short-lived Even Dozen Jug Band would later find individual success, including Stefan Grossman, David Grisman (a highly influential mandolin player), Steve Katz (a member of both the Blues Project and Blood, Sweat & Tears), Joshua Rifkin (who seeded a Scott Joplin ragtime revival with his solo piano records), John Sebastian (of the Lovin' Spoonful), and a singer named Maria d'Amato. When the Kweskin band came to New

York to play the Bitter End, the Even Dozen went to check out the highly regarded competition.

"John Sebastian and I were just knocked out when we heard Geoffrey Muldaur sing," said d'Amato. "You can still hear Geoff in John's singing. One night after the show, we were all invited to a party, and I guess I drank a lot . . . at one point, I went over to Geoffrey, and I guess I was trying to tell him how much I liked his singing, but I threw up in his lap." The next day, d'Amato was in the back room of Izzy Young's Folklore Center when she saw Muldaur enter the store and start flipping through the blues LPs. She bashfully hid in the back before finally approaching Muldaur to apologize for soiling his slacks. "He just said, 'It was an honor,'" said d'Amato. A romance was born, and she soon moved to Cambridge to share an apartment with her future husband and Joe Boyd.

Muldaur's friend Phil Spiro was a college deejay at M.I.T. who was also into the blues. "I was sharing an apartment with Al Wilson who later went on to be called 'Blind Owl' in Canned Heat," said Spiro, adding, "It was a time when everybody was just digging in. The Origins Jazz Library records were coming out. We'd just sit around and listen to those and could hardly wait until the next one came out."

The blues animated an otherwise drab dive. "When I moved in with Al," said Spiro, "I didn't quite know what I was getting into. I'm not the world's neatest person, but he was something else. Al cleaned house twice. Once when Bukka White came to stay with us; once when Son House came. His method of cleaning was quite simple. He would bring in three trashcans from outside and start filling them up. He would then take the cans back outside, and the room would be clean."

Wilson might have been a slob, but he knew the blues. "While Bukka was staying with us," said Spiro, "Al talked to him a lot about his music. Al was exceptional in his ability to relate and empathize with older musicians. . . . He had no ego. He was into music for its own sake and that's how he was able to communicate so well. He wasn't interested in finding out what someone had for lunch thirty years ago when he recorded such and such; he was more interested in how he felt about his music."

The Kweskin Jug Band, meanwhile, had gone nationwide after ditching manager Manny Greenhill for Albert Grossman. "Manny was a great guy," said Muldaur, "but we were ambitious and we wanted Big Albert." The Kweskin Band went to Los Angeles for a three-week engagement at the Troubadour and to play on *The Steve Allen Show*. D'Amato found a temporary gig in the box office at the Ash Grove, but soon joined the band as a third lead singer. "We were a family, and we were dedicated to presenting a 'life experience' for people," said Muldaur. "We were trying to get that kid in the fourth row to finally pick up a guitar or take a trip—or just get down."

When Kweskin broke up the band in 1968, Muldaur was devastated. "I realized that I would have to start relating to musicians on a non-family level," he said. "I was going to have to learn the language of music, which meant learning to read. That was the willful act on my part. One day I heard *The Rite of Spring* by Stravinsky and went nuts and started studying. I would play that record every day and read along with the score. The first day I could only follow the first few bars, and the next day I went a little further. I did that every day for a year and learned to read music."

By now, Geoff and Maria had married and were starting a family of their own. "When I went into labor with my daughter, Jenni, I listened to Howlin' Wolf," said Maria Muldaur. "Every time he'd sing, 'Oooooooooo-oooooooooo-weeeee,' I would have a contraction. It was like his visceral, guttural utterances were in synch with the groaning travail of my labor. Geoff was out of town, so I was at a friend's house, and I listened to Howlin' Wolf until it became apparent that I better get to the hospital—and fast!"

FOUR BRITISH BLUES

The name spoke volumes. Three young British musicians—Keith Richards, Mick Jagger, and Brian Jones—were rhythm and blues fans trying to play the American music they loved. Now all they needed was a place to perform, so Jones telephoned *Jazz News* to place a promotional ad seeking work for the band. Jones hesitated when he was asked the name of the combo. "*The Best of Muddy Waters* album was on the floor—and track one was 'Rolling Stone,'" said Keith Richards. "So the band's name was picked for us by Muddy Waters."

In fact, the Muddy Waters collection had an even more central spot in the creation of the Rolling Stones. Richards and Jagger had been childhood acquaintances, but had lost touch until the two teenagers ran into each other on a platform at Dartford Station. "Did we hit it off?" said Richards. "You get in a carriage with a guy that's got *Rockin' at the Hop* by Chuck Berry on Chess Records, and *The Best of Muddy Waters* also under his arm, you are gonna hit it off." Turns out the resourceful Jagger had been mail-ordering hard-to-find LPs directly from Chess

Eric Clapton 1945–

in Chicago, where the future president of Rolling Stones Records, Marshall Chess Jr., processed his requests.

The young Stones studied their favorite records for keys to the sound. "Brian and I started developing this interweaving way of playing two guitars," said Richards, modeling themselves after famous guitar pairs like Jimmy Reed with Eddie Taylor and Muddy Waters with Jimmy Rodgers. "We listened to the team work, trying to work out what was going on in those records; how you could play together with two guitars and make it sound like four or five."

"The main man for me," said Eric Clapton, another aspiring English bluesman, "was Big Bill Broonzy, and I tried to learn his technique, which was to accompany yourself with your thumb, using the thumb to play eighth notes on the bass strings while you pick out a riff or countermelody with your fingers." One guitar sounding like two. Clapton saw Broonzy on British TV in the mid-1950s, and was soon soaking up the styles and techniques of other bluesmen.

Along with Lead Belly and Josh White, Broonzy was one of the first blues musicians to perform in Europe, and he made a big impression. "At three or four or five years old," said Keith Richards, "I was listening to Ella Fitzgerald, Sarah Vaughan, Big Bill Broonzy, Louis Armstrong. It just spoke to me, it was what I listened to every day because my mum played it. My ears would have gone there anyway, but my mum trained them to go to the black side of town without her even knowing it."

In the mid-1950s, British youth was smitten with "skiffle," a rudimentary synthesis of folk and blues that occurred at virtually the same time that Elvis Presley (recorded by Sam Phillips in Memphis) was helping to create rock and roll. Skiffle emerged from Lonnie Donegan's "vocal interlude" during the otherwise instrumental program of the Chris Barber Jazz Band. Donegan typically sang bouncy versions of Lead Belly songs, and during the recording of the group's first Decca album in 1954, Barber and Donegan convinced their reluctant A&R man to let them cut a pair of songs featuring just guitar, string bass, and washboard percussion. When one of those tunes, "Rock Island Line," was released as a single in 1956, it became a huge hit on both sides of the Atlantic and spawned an English fad for the easy-to-play music that had the effect of putting guitars in the hands of such future rock stars as John Lennon, Paul McCartney, Jimmy Page, and Keith Richards. For Eric Clapton and others, skiffle was also a gateway to the blues.

"I started to meet people who knew about Muddy Waters and Howlin' Wolf," said Clapton, speaking of the record collectors who first introduced him to musicians like John Lee Hooker and Little Walter. "These guys would get together in one of their houses and spend the whole evening listening to one album, like *The Best of Muddy Waters*, and then have excited discussions about what they'd heard." Clapton would try to replicate those sounds on his first electric guitar, a thin-bodied, semi-acoustic Kay. "I would take the bits that I could copy from a combination of the electric blues players I liked," said Clapton, "like John Lee Hooker, Muddy Waters, and Big Bill Broonzy and . . . amalgamate them into one, trying to find a phraseology that would encompass all these different artists."

It's little wonder that the African American blues would leave a different impression on white kids in America and Great Britain. In the United States, the economic clout of the teenage consumer was born in the decade of Eisenhower, Elvis, and Joseph McCarthy. While the civil rights movement was having its painful birth, white pop singers like Pat Boone were cashing in with neutered copies of R&B hits by black artists like Little Richard and Fats Domino. For middle-class kids, Elvis was as common as, well, *The Ed Sullivan Show*, while listening to Muddy Waters was akin to going to the other side of the tracks. By the late fifties, rock 'n' roll had lost much of its vigor, with Presley in the army, Buddy Holly dead from a plane crash, and Chuck Berry and Jerry Lee Lewis lost to sexual scandals. Meanwhile, the blues was a waning fixture of black popular music, and far more popular on a Chicago bandstand than on the record charts, which were now dominated by R&B acts like the Drifters and the Coasters.

British kids grew up in the haunted, economically challenged shadow of World War II. When Lonnie Donegan left the Chris Barber Jazz Band to become the superstar of the skiffle fad, he encouraged a taste for American roots music that persisted after the trend had passed. Meanwhile, another member of Barber's band, guitarist Alexis Korner, joined harmonica player Cyril Davis to form a blues duo. They also founded the London Blues and Barrelhouse Club, a society of blues fans that sponsored performances by visiting American performers. In 1962, the pair formed Blues Incorporated, the band that essentially launched the decade's blues boom in the U.K., and whose ever-shifting lineup included such future luminaries as drummer Charlie Watts and bassist Jack Bruce. Blues Incorporated also welcomed such young talents to the stage as Mick Jagger, Keith Richards, and Rod Stewart. The success of Blues Incorporated encouraged John Mayall, a military veteran and blues fan who supplemented his record collection with tapes of music from the Voice of America, to move to London and form a band called the Bluesbreakers.

"You had a sense of being in a clan of people who were sharing information and musical abilities, who were into the blues" said Giorgio Gomelsky, an Italian-born émigré who was an early promoter of the British blues scene. "And that made the whole scene gel." That "the whole scene" consisted of white musicians couldn't help but result in a different approach to a music created by American blacks. In the United States, issues of race inevitably challenged white musicians who chose to play the blues. In Britain, the blues was a musical choice that, like folk music in the States, owed more to bohemian instincts and adolescent rebellion than race.

For Clapton, blues was a musical response to the childhood discovery that his natural mother had abandoned her son, leaving him to be raised by his grandparents. "I felt through most of my youth that my back was against the wall and that the only way to survive was with dignity, pride, and courage," said Clapton. "I heard that in certain forms of music and I heard it most of all in the blues, because it was always an individual. It was the one man and guitar versus the world."

Clapton didn't even recognize the racial aspect of the blues. "In my early teens," he said, "I wasn't sure about what was white and what was black: it all seemed two sides to the same coin. I didn't know Chuck Berry was black. I thought he was another weird-sounding white man [like Elvis]. I had no idea that there was a racial thing involved." To evoke a blues performer's spirit, said Clapton, he tried to imagine "what kind of car he drove and what it would smell like inside." Little wonder that British musicians could be less than purists in their approach to the blues.

British appearances by American blues artists fed the nascent blues movement. In 1962, the first American Folk Blues Festival toured Europe; its only British date was in Croydon, where the posters read "American Negro Blues Festival." Jagger and Richards shared a ride from London with Paul Jones (who would later sing "Do Wah Diddy Diddy" and other songs with Manfred Mann) and Jimmy Page (who'd play guitar with the Yardbirds and Led Zeppelin) to catch a show that featured Howlin' Wolf, Lightnin' Hopkins, Sonny Boy Williamson, and Sleepy John Estes. The next year, the two Stones used Jagger's parents' car to catch the next edition of the folk-blues tour when its headliner was Muddy Waters.

Waters, who'd caught critical hell for the volume of his British concert debut in 1958, left his electric guitar at home and played a set of acoustic blues. Paul Oliver, Britain's best-known writer on the blues, noted the irony that five years had wrought: "Muddy made a typical error when he sang at the Leeds festival, in playing his electric guitar to an audience that couldn't take one from a blues singer. He made another one this time—in playing a bright new Spanish box when he ought to have played electric guitar." A confused Waters could nonetheless tell that tastes were changing: "So far as the groups are concerned, it's beginning to sound like it does in Chicago.... I must tell you I have to feel good about what is happening with the blues in Britain, because there's some of my version in it. If you remember, I got a little criticism last time for playing electric guitar."

Willie Dixon helped to book and organize the Folk Blues tour for a pair of German promoters (Horst Lippmann and Fritz Rau), and traveled with the caravan as its music director and bass player. Playing overseas was an eye-opening experience for the musicians. "Can you imagine," said Lippmann, "you live on the South Side of Chicago, lucky to make it somehow and then you come by plane to Europe and there is something like a red carpet on the floor? That is something strange."

Dixon, already a master at hustling his songs, was more than happy to share his portfolio of tunes with the young British musicians. "I'll never forget," said Gomelsky, "there was Howlin' Wolf, Sonny Boy [Williamson], and Willie Dixon, the three of them sitting on this sofa I had in my living room. Willie was huge, Wolf wasn't exactly small, and Sonny Boy was very towering and lean. These three grand visitors were sitting on this thing and there's like Jimmy Page, Eric Clapton and everybody sitting at their feet. Willie was just singing and tapping on the back of the chair and Sonny Boy would play harmonica and they would do new songs.... I remember '300 Pounds of Joy,' 'Little Red Rooster,' 'You Shook Me' were songs that Willie passed on at that time." Dixon never came empty handed. "I'd make tapes for them and tell them anybody who wants to could go and make a blues song," said Dixon. "That's how the Rolling Stones and the Yardbirds got their songs."

The Rolling Stones' first single in 1963 was an all-Chess affair that paired Chuck Berry's "Come On" with Dixon's "I Want to Be Loved." The sound of the Stones had clicked into gear when they successfully wooed drummer Charlie Watts away from Blues Incorporated. Richards introduced Watts to his favorite blues records, including those by Jimmy Reed. "Brian and I were listening to the two guitars working," said Richards, "and Charlie was listening to Earl Phillips—what a drummer—and hearing how subtle he was. From listening to his playing, Charlie saw his way clear to play a backbeat rock 'n' roll and still swing with his own identity."

In the beginning, the Rolling Stones were on a mission to promote the music they loved, and presumed that a music career was unlikely. Their first real break came when Gomelsky started promoting them every Sunday at the Crawdaddy Club. "There was no space at the Crawdaddy," said Watts. "That's why Mick used to shake his head and all of that, because . . . he had nowhere to dance." The first week, only a handful of people were in the audience, but everybody told their friends, and within weeks, the place was packed.

"They were playing the blues, but they weren't an academic blues band," said Vic Johnson, another London promoter. "The Rolling Stones were more like a rebellion." Within months, the band had moved to larger venues, and Gomelsky was pushed aside when Andrew Oldham became their manager. "Andrew was a publicist for Brian Epstein [the Beatles' manager], although we didn't know that," said Mick Jagger. "He probably said, 'I am the Beatles' publicist'—how about that as a line?" Oldham's strategy was to market the scruffy Stones as the anti-Beatles, and quickly scored them a deal with Decca Records, a company still smarting from failing to sign the Fab Four.

Gomelsky booked the Yardbirds into the Crawdaddy, but as a condition, insisted that he be installed as their manager. As the band played a repertoire of R&B cover tunes not that different from the Stones, Gomelsky encouraged them to feature guitar-harmonica jams that came to be called "rave-ups." A few weeks into the Crawdaddy residency, Eric Clapton joined the group. Clapton would often break a guitar string during a rave-up, and as he restrung his instrument, the audience would encourage him with a leisurely handclap, prompting Gomelsky to give the guitarist an ironic nickname that stuck—"Slowhand."

The Yardbirds were first recorded live while backing Sonny Boy Williamson on a British tour. Williamson, whose real name was Aleck "Rice" Miller, was a hard-drinking Delta veteran who'd hosted the *King Biscuit Time* radio show in Helena, Arkansas, and had hits with tunes like "Help Me" and "Don't Start Me Talking." Miller had assumed his stage name even before the original Sonny Boy Williamson was bludgeoned to death during a South Side Chicago robbery in 1948. (John Lee Williamson, the first "Sonny Boy," had pioneered the harmonica as a lead instrument in blues bands and wrote the enduring standard, "Good Morning School Girl.")

"I couldn't wait to show off," said Clapton, "and tried to impress him with my knowledge, asking him, 'Isn't your real name Rice Miller?' At which point he slowly pulled out a small penknife and glared at me. It went downhill from there." In concert, Williamson would call out one key, play in another, and then blame the band for the dissonance. Other times, he'd make the group get down on their knees in supplication. He famously commented, "Those English kids want to play the blues so bad—and they play the blues so bad."

Sonny Boy Williamson was not the only blues performer to enlist local musicians for British tours. John Lee Hooker's "Dimples" became a pop hit in Britain after he toured with John Mayall's Bluesbreakers in 1964. "You get Hooker on stage and what you know flies out the window," said Mayall. "You feel like rank amateurs." Hooker found more compatible accompanists in a band called the Groundhogs. Tony McPhee, the band's guitarist, recalls his bass player introducing himself to Howlin' Wolf and saying "'Mr. Burnett, we're a band called the Groundhogs and we play your song.' Wolf looked down at him and then looked over him and down at me and said, 'Is this another little groundhog?'"

Ian McLagan, who would soon join the Small Faces, once backed Wolf as a member of the Muleskinners. "We're all anticipating this scary, big man," said McLagan, "and the doors open and he turned up in this huge greatcoat, a big overcoat down to the floor . . . 'My boys!' he yelled. I mean, five little white kids—we were anything but his boys, but we were so happy to be called that."

While British musicians welcomed the opportunity to see and play with American blues players, in a go-go era dominated by the Beatles, they were also anxious to have their own hit records. When the Yardbirds failed to scale the charts with R&B songs, the band recorded "For Your Love," a pop tune written by Graham Gouldman, who would later find success as a member of 10cc. Clapton hated the record, which became a hit, and quit the band in a purist pique. John Mayall was quick to recruit the guitarist for the Bluesbreakers. The Yardbirds ended up enlisting two other influential blues-rock guitarists, Jeff Beck and Jimmy Page. (Page, a successful studio guitarist, initially declined the offer to join the Yardbirds and recommended Beck. He later became a member, and eventually morphed the band into Led Zeppelin.)

Upon joining the Bluesbreakers, Clapton lived for a time with Mayall, his wife, and four children, and studied the bandleader's extensive collection of blues records. Early in his tenure with the band, Clapton also beefed-up his guitar tone. His first move was to swap the Fender Telecaster that he'd used in the Yardbirds for a late-1950s Gibson Les Paul, an instrument that had been discontinued in the early '60s and replaced by the Gibson SG. Clapton was drawn to the Les Paul because it was pictured on one of his favorite albums, *Let's Dance Away and Hide Away with Freddy King*. He also obtained an early version of a Marshall JTM-45 amplifier that powered a cabinet containing four twelve-inch speakers. The thunderous combination would become the de rigueur setup for blues-rock guitarists, prompting Gibson to revive the Les Paul in 1968.

"What I would do," said Clapton, "was use the bridge pickup with all of the bass turned up, so the sound was very thick and on the edge of distortion. I also always used amps that would overload. . . . I would hit a note, hold it, and give it some vibrato with my fingers, until it sustained, and then the distortion would turn into feedback. It was all of these things, plus the distortion, that created what I suppose you could call my sound."

Clapton's powerful, ear-splitting technique inspired perhaps the most famous graffiti (first seen in a London underground station) in the history of rock 'n' roll: "Clapton is God." Clapton had plenty of opportunities to shape his influential sound, as the Bluesbreakers (who were paid a weekly wage of around $50) often played two gigs a day. During Clapton's tenure with the Bluesbreakers, Jack Bruce briefly replaced bassist John McVie. "We had an instant rapport," said Bruce of playing with Clapton, which was more than he had with Mayall. "He was paying terrible money, and we had this gig wagon which was the most undemocratic thing you've ever seen. It was a Thames van with a bed built in the back for Mayall to occupy on the way back from gigs. The rest of the band had to squash into the front. What a nice guy."

While playing with Mayall, Clapton sported a guitar strap that featured the names of three of his blues idols: Buddy Guy, Otis Rush, and Big Maceo (a pioneering Chicago blues pianist). In early 1965, Buddy Guy played London's Marquee and attracted a crowd of musicians. "He had exquisite timing and was delightfully out of key sometimes," said Jeff Beck. "That's what I found so charming. It was just a hair sharp. It wouldn't have ever been right, had it been dead on the note. From there on, I was like a junkie."

Clapton was also in the audience. "His look, everything, was just right," said the fashion-conscious Clapton. "He had this beautiful baggy shark-skin suit. We were used to seeing bluesmen . . . dressed up to be folk-blues musicians, and Buddy came through the way he was. It was such a blast to see him live doing all that pre-Hendrix stuff which he's always done, like playing with his teeth, on the floor and throwing the guitar around."

Seeing Guy perform as part of a trio also left Clapton thinking that he might like such a format. For now, though, he was the principal attraction of a quartet. Still, Clapton could be a reluctant band member. At one point, he set off with some musician friends on a hippie hegira around the world.

They ended up stranded in Greece. During his absence, Peter Green, who later formed Fleetwood Mac, played guitar in Mayall's band; Green was dismissed upon Clapton's return. Another time, Clapton skipped a gig at the Woodhall Community Centre in Hertfordshire. Michael (Mick) Taylor, seventeen, was in the audience with some friends, and their disappointment at the absence of the guitarist prompted them to goad their buddy to get up and jam. "I was very nervous," said Taylor, and "still kind of learning how to play blues guitar—I was really not that good. I played Eric's guitar." Taylor was talented enough, however, for Mayall to take the phone number of a future member of the Bluesbreakers and the Rolling Stones.

Clapton, it turns out, was at the Marquee seeing the British debut of the Lovin' Spoonful, the successful American folk-rock group led by John Sebastian, who'd played with the Even Dozen Jug Band. John Lennon and George Harrison of the Beatles were also in attendance. "I remember we went off to Sebastian's hotel," said Harrison, "and I remember thinking, 'We should have invited that guy [Clapton] 'cause I'm sure we know him from somewhere,' and [he] just seemed, like, lonely." Clapton would soon become Harrison's friend, play lead guitar on his "While My Guitar Gently Weeps," and later, marry his wife.

Clapton's first recording with Mayall was a one-off single for Andrew Loog Oldham's Immediate label that was produced by Jimmy Page. But the producer who would truly capture Clapton's sound was Mike Vernon, a young blues fan who'd gotten a gopher job at Decca in 1963 and got the chance to record blues albums by Otis Spann and Champion Jack Dupree. Vernon was also copublisher of a modestly successful magazine, *R&B Monthly*.

"I thought maybe I should get on to the record side and have my own private little label," said Vernon, "and sell the records though the magazine, so we started Blue Horizon Records. The first record we put out was a single by Hubert Sumlin, Howlin' Wolf's guitar player. We recorded a couple of solo guitar instrumentals in my parents' house and pressed 99 records and whacked them out through the magazine. We sold the lot in two weeks with no effort!" Blue Horizon would eventually become Britain's premiere blues label, but first Vernon would produce England's seminal blues album, *Bluesbreakers: John Mayall with Eric Clapton*.

The LP was recorded over three days in May of 1966 and basically put the band's live set on tape, including songs by Freddie King ("Hideaway"), Otis Rush ("All Your Love"), and Little Walter ("It Ain't Right"). The album also included Clapton's first recorded lead vocal on "Ramblin' on My Mind," a tune by the guitarist's latest blues hero, Robert Johnson. "At first the music [of Robert Johnson] almost repelled me," said Clapton. "It was hard-core, more than anything I had ever heard. After a few listenings I realized that, on some level, I had found the master, and that following this man's example would be my life's work."

Clapton's first task while recording the Bluesbreakers' album, though, was getting the studio personnel to accurately capture the sound of his Les Paul and powerful Marshall amplifier. "Eric absolutely insisted that he wasn't going to play with a tame sound," said engineer Gus Dudgeon, who would later produce Elton John. "Nobody had ever come in wanting to play that loud, not even when I did that [Rolling] Stones audition." Dudgeon waited for Vernon to talk sense to Clapton. "I went to talk to Eric," said Vernon, "and asked . . . 'Can you not turn it down?' And Eric said very politely, 'No, I can't, because if I turn it down, the sound changes. And I can't get the sustain I want. He's the engineer, you're the producer—tell him to engineer it, you produce it. But I'm not turning down.'"

The Bluesbreakers' LP, which is often referred to as "the Beano album" because Clapton is pictured on the cover reading a Beano comic book, was an unexpected hit when it was released in July of 1966, rising to number 6 on the British charts. And while Mayall led the band and was its singer, it was Clapton's guitar that stole the show. Clapton's solos are less unique than uniquely supercharged, as evidenced by his recreation of the guitar lead of Otis Rush's "All Your Love," which had been cut in Chicago a decade earlier. Rush's performance is passionate and raw, and in the small-world department, was produced by Willie Dixon and featured instrumental accompaniment by Ike Turner and his band. Clapton's reinterpretation is not just raw, but volcanic. "All Your Love" was the opening track of the Mayall album, and the first sound one heard was the crude, thunderous squawk of Clapton's Les Paul. Rock music, and the blues, would never again be quite the same.

By the time "Beano" was released, however, Clapton had already left the Bluesbreakers and was rehearsing with Jack Bruce and drummer Ginger Baker. In literal fact, Mayall had fired Clapton when word leaked that he was rehearsing with a band that would become the archetype of the blues-rock power trio: Cream. Mayall's first choice to replace his departed star was Peter Green, who'd briefly played with the Bluesbreakers when Clapton had gone to Greece. At the time, Green was entertaining an offer from Eric Burden to join a revamped version of the Animals.

"When I asked him back," said Mayall, "it was no surprise that he played

CROSSROADS

46

games with me, like I'd played games with him when Eric was away. He definitely wanted to keep me on the hook and make me have a hard time getting him back—so there was a bit of revenge there. He made me sweat for about a week before he accepted the offer." Mayall gave his new guitarist a copy of "Beano" so that he could learn Clapton's leads.

Around the time Clapton was forming Cream, he played on a couple of other recording sessions. Mike Vernon asked him to play a session with Muddy Waters and Otis Spann. "I was absolutely terrified, but not because I felt that I couldn't carry my weight musically," said Clapton. "I just didn't know how to behave around these guys. . . . They had these beautiful baggy silk suits on, and were so sharp. And, they were men. And here I was, a skinny young white boy."

Clapton also recorded with some other skinny white boys in a one-off recording session with a band that included Jack Bruce on bass and Steve Winwood, the gifted singer and keyboard player from the Spencer Davis Group. The sessions were bankrolled by Elektra Records, which wanted English tracks to accompany recordings by two American bands, the Butterfield Blues Band and the Lovin' Spoonful. Joe Boyd, Geoff Muldaur's old Cambridge roommate, oversaw the project; Boyd had moved to Britain to run Elektra's London office after working for George Wein, who promoted the Newport Folk Festival.

What's Shakin'! was designed to be an electric companion piece to Elektra's earlier collection of acoustic folk-blues, *The Blues Project*. The album included three performances by Eric Clapton and the Powerhouse (the billing clearly highlighted the guitarist's British renown), including a Memphis Slim instrumental called "Steppin' Out" (Clapton had cut a different version for the Mayall album), and an interpretation of Robert Johnson's "Cross Road Blues" that was called "Crossroads" and featured vocals by Winwood. Cream, which Boyd tried without success to sign to Elektra, would soon find great success with a hard-rocking live version of "Crossroads" that Clapton would himself sing.

Clapton had yet to set foot in America, the home of the blues. Not so the Rolling Stones and the Yardbirds, who while touring America recorded in the American studios that had produced their favorite records. The Yardbirds cut their version of Bo Diddley's "I'm a Man" and their own "Shapes of Things" at Chess Studios in Chicago. While in Chicago, Giorgio Gomelsky paid a visit to Willie Dixon. "Down in the basement he had this little publishing office," said Gomelsky. "He played me hours of tapes and I picked four or five tunes which the Yardbirds used to do onstage but they weren't meant for our situation. '300 Pounds of Joy'—we didn't have anybody that weighed 300 pounds. We were all . . . skinny English limeys."

"When we got to Chess Records," said Jeff Beck, "I realized I was just copying what already had been done. And then we went from there to Memphis and Sun Records." Beck continued: "We did 'Train Kept A-Rolling' and I remember to this day Sam Phillips' jargon. He goes, 'You're rushing the beginning. The train ain't here yet. . . . The train's a long way off. Make it sound like it's coming from 100 miles away.' Right there I was learning a million things."

The Rolling Stones were also anxious to record at Chess Studios. "It was a milestone event for us to be in an American studio, recording on 4-track," said bass player Bill Wyman. (The Stones' first recordings were done on two-track machines.) "We knew the sound we were getting live in clubs and concerts was not what came across on the records we had cut in England. People were not used to that kind of roughness; a really good, funky American feel was what we were after."

The Stones' two days of recording at Chess were very productive, with four tracks cut in four hours on day one: Irma Thomas's "Time Is on My Side"; the Valentinos' "It's All Over Now"; Muddy Waters's "I Can't Be Satisfied"; and an instrumental called "Stewed and Keefed," named after Richards and Ian Stewart, the piano-playing sixth Stone who was an unofficial member of the band. While at Chess, the Stones also observed a Buddy Guy session and got a taste of down-home sass. "Sonny Boy Williamson and Little Walter were in the studio," said Guy, "arguing about the same young girl they had down in Kentucky." The two bluesmen argued about who best pleased the woman in question, and their banter was blue enough to nearly make the "bad boys of rock" blush.

On their second day at Chess, the Stones tackled two Chuck Berry songs, "Confessing the Blues" and "Around and Around." "Berry himself walked in and stayed a long while," said Wyman, "chatting to us about amps and things. 'Swing on, gentlemen!' he told us. 'You are sounding most well, if I may say so.' This was the nicest I can remember him ever being, but then, we were making money for him!" The Stones then cut seven more tracks: Solomon Burke's "If You Need Me," Tommy Tucker's "High-Heeled Sneakers," Howlin' Wolf's "Down in the Bottom," an original instrumental named after the address of the Chess Studio ("2120 South Michigan Avenue"), and a pair of Jagger-Richards originals ("Empty Heart" and "Tell Me Baby").

Memory seems to have played a peculiar trick on Richards when the Stones recorded at Chess. To this day, the guitarist swears that the band arrived to find Muddy Waters up on a ladder painting the ceiling. Wyman remembers Waters helping the Stones load their equipment into the studio, while Marshall Chess Jr. says the sharp-dressed Waters wouldn't be caught dead pushing a paint brush. Denying all evidence to the contrary, Richards sticks to his story, which invites one to speculate as to what this image of a famous bluesman slopping paint might mean to a British rock star. Does it make Richards feel guilty, privileged, or a little bit of both?

At the time, Jagger and Richards were just starting to get the hang of writing songs, goaded by Andrew Oldham, who wisely advised them that publishing was where the money was in the record business. The first song they wrote was "As Tears Go By," a tune that became a hit for Marianne Faithful, who'd recently left a convent, and who would soon become Jagger's girlfriend. Jagger-Richards compositions appeared on early Stones records, but even they knew their songs couldn't compete with the tunes they were cutting by writers like Berry, Dixon, Bobby Womack, and Buddy Holly.

"It seemed to us it took months and months," said Richards of the effort to write a powerful song for the band, "and in the end we came up with 'The Last Time,' which was basically re-adapting a traditional gospel song that had been sung by the Staple Singers, but luckily the song itself goes back into the mists of time. I think I was trying to learn it on guitar just to get the chords, sitting there playing along with the record, no gigs, nothing else to do."

It wouldn't be the last time that the songwriters would create a hit song from a tune in the public domain. By then, the Stones had studied the masters, and recognized how new blues songs could be fashioned from familiar components. In the case of "The Last Time," they made a gospel song into rock and roll with a memorable guitar lick, driving drums, and a sing-along chorus. Blues musicians had long looked to update tradition; that's what Muddy Waters did when he moved to Chicago and plugged in his Delta blues. Before he bought himself an electric guitar, Waters, looking to be heard in noisy Chicago bars, had positioned a DeArmond pickup across the sound hole of his acoustic. That's the same pickup Richards used to make his first "electric" guitar. But by the mid-1960s, the electric guitar was becoming a whole new animal.

"All the amps were under-powered and screwed up at full volume and always whistling," said Jeff Beck. "It would feed back, so I decided to use it rather than fight it." In the Yardbirds, Beck and Jimmy Page would use volume and distortion to unique effect; Clapton employed similar methods to cultivate an extravagant sound with the Bluesbreakers and cranked it up a notch in Cream. Then in the fall of '66, a game-changing guitarist landed in London from Greenwich Village via Mars.

But before Jimi Hendrix would startle his peers by putting a sonic match to his Stratocaster, Keith Richards woke up after hearing a guitar lick in his dreams. He sang it into a tape recorder, and went back to sleep. In the morning, he listened to a tape of himself humming a catchy riff followed by a lot of snoring. A song was born. Jagger's lyrics echoed an early Muddy Waters song, "I Can't Be Satisfied," but the new title took a different angle—"(I Can't Get No) Satisfaction." The heart of the Rolling Stones' breakthrough hit, of course, was the eight-note guitar theme, but where Muddy played his bluesy lick with a slide, Keith was plugged into a Gibson fuzz box.

When the Stones agreed to play "Satisfaction" on TV's *Shindig!*, they used rock-star muscle to get a guest slot on the same show for Howlin' Wolf. Before the taping of his only appearance on nationwide television, Wolf was astonished to receive a visit from Son House, who'd been lost to history for decades, and who was now in Los Angeles to play a UCLA folk festival. Long ago, Wolf would go to a Delta juke joint and hope for a chance to blow harp behind House. Now Wolf was on a big-time television show thanks to a British rock and roll band that loved the blues. Muddy Waters had an explanation for these unlikely connections; the blues had a baby, he said, and they called it rock 'n' roll.

FIVE OUT OF THE PAST

"John Hurt was dead," said Eric Von Schmidt, sitting in the field at a workshop concert at the 1963 Newport Folk Festival. "Had to be. All the guys on that Harry Smith anthology were dead. . . . But there was no denying that the man singing so sweet and playing so beautifully was *the* John Hurt. He had a face—and what a face. He had a hat that he wore like a halo."

John Hurt was in his thirties when he recorded for Okeh Records in 1928, so it was certainly reasonable to think that he would be alive in 1963. But anybody who cared assumed an old blues singer would have already succumbed to bad luck and an early death. But here they were, coming right from the Delta into the 1960s blues revival: Mississippi John Hurt, Son House, and Skip James. It was as if the record collection of the "blues mafia" had come to life.

Mississippi John Hurt 1893-1966

By 1963, other long-forgotten (or never known) blues singers had already been recorded. Sam Charters, the author of *The Country Blues* who also produced recordings for Folkways, had rediscovered Memphis bluesman Furry Lewis in 1959, around the time that Alan Lomax documented the music of the heretofore-unknown slide guitarist Mississippi Fred McDowell. Other veteran blues performers who surfaced included guitarist Sleepy John Estes, his mandolin-playing partner Yank Rachell, and such never-recorded talents as Robert Pete Williams (discovered in 1959 at Louisiana's Angola prison farm), Texas songster Mance Lipscomb, and a wildly versatile New Orleans guitar player named Snooks Eaglin.

But none of these musicians carried the weight and deep histories of Hurt, House, and James. The gumshoes that found these bluesmen came from the community of record collectors and musicians who had already helped to nurture an audience (albeit tiny) for country blues. Many of them had connections to the District of Columbia, and some of their names have already figured in this text, including Dick Spotswood, John Fahey, and Nick Perls. But it was another D.C. resident, Tom Hoskins, a pot-smoking hipster guitar player, who was the first to find a blues legend.

Hoskins's search was inspired by trying to learn guitar techniques from scratchy old records. "It's too bad we don't have these guys here to show us how it's done," said Hoskins. "I wonder where they are? I began to wonder especially about the singer with the gentle sounding voice and the unique finger style guitar style, who was known only by the name on a couple of rare, old, battered 78s, 'Mississippi John Hurt.'"

The search started after Spottswood came into possession of a tape of John Hurt's 1928 recordings from a collector in Australia. Six 78s of Hurt's recordings had been released in 1928 and 1929, from two different sessions in Memphis and New York City, but they were exceedingly rare, and eight more tracks were never released. Most blues fans were only familiar with the two Hurt songs on the Harry Smith anthology, "Frankie" and "Spike Driver Blues." The song on Spottswood's tape that contained a vital clue was called "Avalon Blues."

"Avalon's my hometown," sang Hurt, "always on my mind." Spottswood listened to this with Hoskins and they wondered, could John Hurt still live in Avalon? Hoskins couldn't find Avalon on a map, but after consulting an atlas published in 1878, discovered that it was a tiny town on a secondary road between Greenwood and Grenada, Mississippi. Hoskins, who didn't have a car, was already anxious to go to Mardi Gras. Now he'd add a stop in Avalon.

At a party at American University, Hoskins flirted with an attractive girl and talked about his plans to go to the Big Easy. Turned out that she had a car and would love to go to New Orleans, so the next day, they left D.C. in a new Dodge. At nightfall, the young travelers checked into a motel and Hoskins went about getting romantic. Deflecting his advances, the girl confessed that she was sixteen, intended to remain a virgin, and that the auto actually belonged to her dad. Long story short, they continued their (platonic) trip, oblivious to an all-points-bulletin put out by the police. "Seventeen states is what I heard," said Spottswood of the dragnet. During that drive through the South in the winter of 1963, Hoskins risked being arrested (like Chuck Berry) under the Mann Act for taking a minor female over state lines for immoral purposes.

After Mardis Gras, Hoskins steered the Dodge from New Orleans to Mississippi and pulled up to Stinson's, a combination general store, gas station, and post office that constituted downtown Avalon. Hoskins inquired about the whereabouts of a blues singer named John Hurt. Was he still alive? As Hurt himself remembered the story, the man replied, "If he ain't died since, he went that way with two sacks of groceries at eleven o'clock this morning." Hoskins followed the directions to Hurt's home.

Hurt was nervous when an unknown white man parked his car in front of his three-room house. "I thought the man was a sheriff or the FBI," said Hurt, "and I was thinking to myself, 'What have I done?'" Apparently nothing. "John," said Hoskins, "we have been lookin' for you for a long time. I want you to come to Washington with me and make some records. Will you go?"

Hurt had not played guitar in a couple of years, and didn't even own an instrument. Hoskins brought in his Gibson J-45, and returned the next day to record an interview and a few songs. Hurt was rusty, but his gift was intact, and at the age of seventy, he traded in minding a herd of cows for performing at folk festivals and urban coffee houses. But he was under no grand illusions about his unexpected change of fortune.

"If you listen to John," said Dick Waterman, who became Hurt's confidante and booking agent, "he said, 'I didn't want for nothing. I had all the milk, and cream, and butter, and the man would slaughter a hog once a year, and slaughter a cow. I had all the pork and beef and ham I wanted. I bought my own tobacco and rolling paper, and I'd go to the store and get some fabric for my wife to make clothes with." But like every sharecropper, Hurt also existed on the edge of poverty.

Hurt's mellifluous guitar style fascinated the folk-blues crowd. "When you think of Mississippi Delta blues," said Stefan Grossman, "you think of a type of music that has nothing to do with John Hurt. He's playing as if the guitar is a piano with a boom-chick in the bass imitating the left hand of the piano player and melody on the treble strings like that played by the right hand. There are no extra notes in his music, there is just the sound, and the sound is rooted in his thumb. Reverend Davis described it as 'old-time picking.'"

Hoskins brought his guitar and tape back to Washington. "When we heard the tape," said Spottswood, "we were almost hysterical with joy but we didn't want the news to leak out. We knew as soon as someone in New York heard about it there would be a plane with someone going down there and beating us to it. We had no signed contract." Within weeks, Hurt was staying in the guest room at the Spottswoods' Arlington, Virginia home. "John was the only Negro for several blocks," said Spottswood. Hurt signed a management contract with Music Research Incorporated, which was owned by Hoskins; Spottswood; and his wife, Louisa. The contract called for a fifty-fifty split between Hurt and MRI, with travel and other expenses coming from Hurt's half. Colonel Tom Parker had a similar deal with Elvis Presley.

The rediscovery of John Hurt caused great excitement in the folk-blues community; it was also pretty thrilling for John Hurt. He took note when a visitor in the Spottswoods' living room played his "Nobody's Dirty Business." "John's eyebrows lifted and his eyes were wide," said Max Ochs. "He realized that, 'Wow! These guys mean business.' John must have been surprised to see and hear a young white man playing his style and . . . over the course of the next few months [Hurt] became better than he had ever been."

Hurt went into the studio for Piedmont Records, a label owned by the Spottswoods. "We recorded in my basement," said Pete Kuykendall, a blue-grass musician and recording engineer. "Part of the deal, since nobody was looking to make money out of this, was that I'd arrange the publishing through Wynwood Music, the company that I'd established to publish the songs I'd written for the Country Gentlemen." Hurt signed a standard publishing deal, which called for a fifty-fifty split between Hurt and Wynwood; Hurt's contract with MRI, however, reduced his share to 25 percent.

In his first months in Washington, Hurt also recorded the bulk of his repertoire for the Library of Congress. "My thought at the time," said Spottswood, speaking like a folklorist, "was, 'Look, this guy could keel over tomorrow. And if he does, it will be a sad and tragic thing. But, it will be a lot less sad and tragic if we have definitive recordings of these songs in place.' I was thinking preservation."

Hurt played his first live gigs outside of the Delta at a coffee house in D.C. called Ontario Place. Hurt and Hoskins also traveled to California for an appearance at the Berkeley Folk Festival. Hurt met Lightnin' Hopkins at the Bay Area home of Ed Denson, a former D.C. resident and blues fan who ran Takoma Records with John Fahey. Mr. Hopkins asked Mr. Hurt if he'd like to meet a Mr. Daniels, opening his jacket to reveal a pint of Tennessee whiskey. The bluesmen went off by themselves to make Jack's acquaintance.

Hurt then played the Newport Folk Festival. "In Chicago, Illinois, and Portland, Oregon," said Pete Seeger by way of introduction, "I met people who treasured, just like they were gold and diamonds, records that came out thirty or thirty-five years ago, and the name of the singer was Mississippi John Hurt." That day, a new kind of star was born: a sweet, seventy-one-year-old songster with a beguiling guitar style. Hurt, smiling from under his felt fedora, was just one of the attractions exciting the young musicians in attendance. "We could not keep up with who was playing," said Geoff Muldaur. "Von Schmidt and I would be running from workshop to workshop. How could you miss those prisoners chopping wood and singing 'Early in the Morning' or Bill Monroe? It was ridiculous."

Dave Van Ronk, who described Newport as "Shriners with guitars," was equally jazzed by the blasts from the past. "John Hurt was the first in 1963," said Van Ronk, "and in 1964 they had Skip James, Sleepy John Estes, Robert Wilkins, and Fred McDowell, and the next year Son House showed up. It was incredible, because we knew these guys from hearing them on old 78s, but it had never occurred to us that they would still be alive and playing, and now they were turning up all over the place. It got to be like the 'Old Blues Singers of the Month Club.'"

"I went to Newport in 1961, '62, '63, so I caught the real stuff," said Taj Mahal, who was one of the few black faces in the audience. Born Henry St. Clair Fredericks, Mahal grew up in Massachusetts and played blues and R&B while in college. "I recognized that these were the people I had to see, and I knew I had to put my energy into acknowledging and giving audience to the masters and the elders of the music. . . . If there was any insight they gave me, I'm sure it was how to communicate with these older men—how to listen."

Hurt played at an evening concert as well as an afternoon workshop that also featured Reverend Gary Davis, John Lee Hooker, John Hammond Jr., Van Ronk, and Brownie McGhee and Sonny Terry. At the time, Newport was run as a not-for-profit festival, with all the performers, including Joan Baez and Peter, Paul and Mary, paid $50 each. Vanguard Records recorded the festival, with artists on the resulting LPs receiving $50 a track. Hurt had four songs on the record of the 1963 festival.

In six months, Hurt had taken an unlikely journey from Avalon to Newport. He was a natural musician, a personable presence, but also something of a mystery. "John Hurt was constantly behind a veil," said Spottswood. "I mean, he wasn't like Uriah Heep, but he was so used to subservience that he found it very hard to get away from that mind-set. And of course that's what gave him a lot of that charm when he performed; to be so cheerful and cordial and humble and everything like that."

A musician plucked from obscurity and brought to an august folk festival could be excused a measure of uncertainty. "Some of the rediscovered bluesmen were exploited," said Geoff Muldaur, "and very few of them made sense of the rediscovery. John Hurt is an example of somebody who did. They rediscovered him, he smiled, and started to play until he died. A lot of those guys were bitter and sad and a lot of them were drunks. But John Hurt was really the quintessential wonderful guy."

After John Hurt was rediscovered in Avalon, blues detectives were quick to check a performer's last known home address. John Fahey and Ed Denson posted a 1963 letter to "Booker White, Old Blues Singer, Aberdeen, Mississippi c/o General Delivery." Scribbled on the back of the envelope: "You could make $100." (White's "Fixin' to Die Blues" had been included on the compilation album Sam Charters produced to accompany his book, *The Country Blues*, and Bob Dylan had covered the song on his first album.) A relative of White's happened to work at the post office, and forwarded the letter to him in Memphis; Fahey also could have found White through his cousin B.B. King. White, who'd been working in factories for the past decade, was happy to unpack his resonator guitar and dust off his locomotive style of slide-guitar blues. He recorded for both Takoma and Arhoolie Records, and became a popular attraction at folk clubs and blues festivals. "I don't play 'em, I stomp 'em," said White of his instrument of choice, a National steel-bodied guitar. "It's loud. I don't need no mike. And I play so rough I would have busted many guitars. This one can stand rain and punishment."

In the summer of 1964, Fahey went searching for Skip James. Interest in the obscure Delta bluesman had increased when three of his Paramount tracks were included on a pair of Origin Jazz Library compilations, *Really! The Country Blues* and *The Mississippi Blues 1927–1940*. Fahey traveled with two other blues-loving guitar players, Henry Vestine (who would soon form Canned Heat) and Bill Barth (who'd play with Insect Trust). From Ishman Bracey, a singer-guitarist who'd recorded in the 1920s, the trio learned that James had lived in Bentonia, Mississippi, where they located the singer's maternal aunt. James had last been seen at the funeral of his father and was now thought to be living in a town called Dunbar. When that address didn't seem to exist, they tried Dundee, where, after more sleuthing, they found a woman who turned out to be James's very suspicious wife. She ultimately led them to her husband's bed at Tunica County Hospital.

Skip James couldn't have been more unlike John Hurt. Where Hurt's music was typically warm and approachable, James played an idiosyncratic style of minor-key blues that was forbidding, if not downright scary. He seemed to carry the burden of the blues, and was forever caught between obliging God or the Devil; significantly, his father, who had abandoned the family when his son was a child, was both a bootlegger and a preacher. James made his records in 1931, and when nothing happened, he reconciled with his father, became a preacher, and sang in a gospel quartet. More recently, he'd worked as a manual laborer.

Lying in his hospital bed, James was less than enamored of Fahey and his crew. The feeling was mutual. Part of the friction came from the fact that Fahey had as much of a musical ego as James; Takoma Records was essentially a vehicle to promote what Fahey called his "American primitive" music, which basically amounted to a highbrow interpretation of country blues guitar. James left the hospital after the three strangers settled his bills. Back home, James, who had not touched a guitar in seven years, made some tentative recordings, and showed Fahey the D-minor tuning that Fahey had been unable to glean from the old recordings. James declined to sign a contract with Takoma Records, but agreed to travel to Washington, D.C. "Bill and John, they just outtalked me," said James. "They talked so fast I could hardly hear a word sideways . . . and then I wasn't feelin' too good noway. I just decided, right after I talked with Baby, that's my wife, she said: 'Well, James, you oughta try it.'"

A month later, James stepped onto the wooden palette that was the workshop stage at the Newport Folk Festival. "Skip sat down," said Dick Waterman, "and put his guitar on his leg. He set himself, doing a little finger manipulation with his left hand, then he set his fingers by the sound hole, sighed, and hit the first note of 'Devil Got My Woman.' He took that first note up in falsetto all the way, and the hairs on the back of my neck went up, and all up and down my arm, the hairs just went right up. Even now I get a reaction to that note when I listen to the recording of it on *Blues at Newport*. It's such an eerie note. It's almost a wail. It's a cry."

James played four songs during his nine-minute set: "Devil Got My Woman," "Sick Bed Blues," "Cypress Grove Blues," and "Cherry Ball Blues." If his unique guitar style had not yet regained its old fluidity, his spooky falsetto made up the difference. James had traveled to Newport with Ed Denson, who'd signed a one-year contract to be his manager, and Bill Barth, who acted as his road manager and made sure that his guitar was in tune. Weeks later, they were joined by Fahey for James's first recording session in thirty-three years. The engineer at the session was Gene Rosenthal, another member of the D.C. blues community who would also become involved in the career of John Hurt. James reprised his old repertoire, singing the songs that he would later record for Vanguard Records. These initial recordings became the object of such bitter litigation that they wouldn't be released until the 1990s. James was soon admitted to a D.C. hospital. The ills that had plagued him in Mississippi had not gone away.

Tape recorders had gotten a lot more portable since Alan Lomax had traveled through the South to record Muddy Waters and Son House, but still, by the time Nick Perls packed his recording equipment into his red Volkswagen beetle, three passengers made for one crowded car. Perls, Dick Waterman, and Phil Spiro drove south from New York City in June of 1964. Their goal was to find Son House, but truth be told, Perls was more interested in finding rare 78s than dealing with living blues musicians. His preference for inanimate works of art perhaps came from his parents, who ran a venerable New York art gallery. Waterman was a photographer and writer who'd been intrigued by the rediscovery of Mississippi John Hurt. Spiro was a blues fan whose interest had been nurtured by his friend Geoff Muldaur and his roommate, Alan Wilson.

Arriving in Memphis, they located Will Shade, who'd been the leader of an influential Depression-era ensemble, the Memphis Jug Band. They recorded Shade in the shabby apartment that he shared with his wife. As the northerners took their leave, Waterman and Spiro pooled their limited cash to give Shade ten bucks. In the car, Perls scolded his traveling companions.

"You just don't get it, do you?" said Perls. "He's an old man with nothing happening in his life. We're the ones who gave him something. What the fuck was he going to do tonight? He was going to do nothing but sit and look at his old hag of a wife. . . . Now his music will live on long after he's dead. . . . He gave us a couple of hours out of his empty life and we have given him eternity."

Waterman and Spiro swallowed their shocked anger and continued their journey into the past. In Memphis, they'd also met Reverend Robert Wilkins, who'd recorded blues in the 1920s but subsequently turned to preaching the gospel and singing religious songs. (Wilkins would soon collect unexpected publishing royalties when the Rolling Stones covered his "Prodigal Son" on *Beggar's Banquet*.) Wilkins, who had once known House, squeezed into the Volkswagen and joined in the search, focusing on the area around Lake Cormorant, Mississippi. Three white Yankees and a black man in a German car with New York plates couldn't help but stand out in the Mississippi Delta. Were they northern college students coming south to register black voters? After many awkward inquiries, a lucky tip led them to knowledgeable sources, reached by phone first in Indianapolis and then Detroit. They finally spoke to Son House on June 21; he was living in Rochester, New York. On that same day, members of the Ku Klux Klan murdered Michael Schwerner, Andrew Goodman, and James Chaney in Philadelphia, Mississippi.

The red Volkswagen headed for Rochester, where on the evening of June 23, the three young men found Son House sitting on the front steps of an apartment building at 61 Greig Street. (Incredibly, this was within days of Fahey's crew finding Skip James.) House had been living in Rochester for about twenty years; he'd also essentially given up playing music after the death of his frequent musical partner, Willie Brown, who had played with him on the recordings made by Alan Lomax. For House, who'd mostly worked at various railroad jobs, music was little more than a memory. He certainly had no idea that his old recordings had been reissued, and that he was considered an important artist among aficionados of country blues.

"When we found Son," said Waterman, "he was a major-league alcoholic. He had no motivation to play. If he had a guitar, he would pawn it. He could still sing, though." House was brought to Boston, where he spent time with Spiro's roommate, Alan Wilson. "Al Wilson taught Son House how to play Son House," said Waterman. "I can tell you flatly that without Al invigorating and revitalizing Son, there would have been no Son House rediscovery. All of Son's successful concert appearances, recordings, and him being remembered as having a great second career; all that was because of Al."

Spiro had a slightly more nuanced view of their interaction. "What really happened was that Al sat down with Son in our apartment playing records," said Spiro. "He played Son his old recordings and also played [songs] for him on guitar. He was reminding Son of what he had done in the past, not teaching him how to play."

As with the other rediscovered bluesmen, all roads led to the Newport Folk Festival, where House was a last-minute booking. Walking onto the festival grounds, House and Waterman were met by Alan Lomax. "How are you, Son?" said Lomax. "Still living by that bridge in Rochester?" Waterman was stunned. "You knew where one of the greatest blues singers of all time was for over 20 years and never told anyone?" said Waterman. "Didn't you think it was important to record him and give him a chance to make some money?" "After I recorded him," said Lomax, sounding a bit like Nick Perls, "it wasn't any of my business what he did with his life. My job was to record him for the Library of Congress. I didn't care what he did after that."

Folklorists leave their discoveries where they find them. Promoters take them to Newport. But before House could perform at the festival, he was hospitalized with abdominal pain. "Son only had about a third of his stomach left," said Spiro, "and he would get seriously plastered on only a drink and a half. And some admirer was always sure to offer him another drink."

The rediscovered bluesmen were strangers in a strange land: Southern black men in a Northern white world. Songs that they once played to rowdy neighbors in a juke joint or at a fish fry were now performed for attentive college kids. At the same time, Hurt, James, and House were wildly different musicians. Hurt's sublime finger picking and soft voice was the epitome of old-time music, a time capsule from the early days of the blues when a musician was as likely to play a folk song or a ragtime tune as the blues. He was a genial man playing gentle music, and seemed to make a seamless transition into his late-life renown.

Son House could not been any more different. He played aggressive, powerful blues, and slammed his National guitar with barely contained fury. "Son House would get himself into a mood of possession and enthusiasm when he was playing and singing," said guitarist Ernie Hawkins, "and that's what it was all about. He was into this intense kind of transport that was just amazing to watch. It was raw and almost painful. His attack seemed like he could just slice himself up on those steel strings."

Skip James played with a subtler kind of intensity, with spidery guitar lines framing his forlorn falsetto voice. Where House confronted the listener with his violently snapped guitar strings, James's unconventional guitar parts wormed themselves into the listener's ear. "I'd rather be the devil," he sang in a voice that seemed to float above his guitar, "than to be that woman's man." His blues came with a shiver.

The young musicians who witnessed these performers couldn't help but be profoundly moved. "These worlds were coming together that nobody could imagine," said Geoff Muldaur. "When I was a kid listening to my brother's record collection, you would hear the occasional strange thing on these jazz compilations, like Blind Willie Johnson or Vera Hall, and it was otherworldly and downright mythical. The land that these people were coming from and singing about doesn't even exist, does it? So for me, fifteen years later, it was a shocking event to find myself hanging out with people like Skip James and John Hurt."

You didn't have to be at Newport to be moved by the music at the festival. Bonnie Raitt, the teenage daughter of John Raitt, the renowned star of such Broadway musicals as *Oklahoma!* and *Carousel*, found her musical soul listening to *Blues at Newport*. Suddenly, she no longer wanted to be Joan Baez. Instead, sitting in her bedroom, Raitt taught herself how to play John Hurt's "Candy Man."

"John Lee Hooker, Brownie McGee, Sonny Terry, Mississippi John Hurt, the great Son House—all those people were just unbelievable to me musically," said Raitt. "I knew that I didn't sound like them—a little 14-year-old white girl. But I wanted to so badly that I played [my guitar] until my fingers bled." But it sure felt good, and day-by-day, Raitt taught her feminine fingers to play the blues.

SIX

UNIVERSITY OF CHICAGO BLUES

James Cotton was playing harmonica with Muddy Waters the first time he saw white faces at Smitty's Corner. "Muddy thought they were the tax people," said Cotton. "He owed some taxes, said, 'Goddamn, they've come to get me. That's got to be them.' Muddy hid in the office between sets." The three visitors—Paul Butterfield, Nick Gravenites, and Elvin Bishop— turned out to be young musicians who were already playing for students at the nearby University of Chicago, the prestigious institution that was surrounded by the black South Side. Waters didn't yet know it, but he'd just been given a clue as to what would give his career a second wind.

Rock and roll, said Muddy Waters, "hurt the blues pretty bad. We still hustled around and made it and kept goin', but we were only playin' for black people when rock and roll came along, and it got so we couldn't play any more slow blues. The people just wanted to 'bug."

The blues is the heart of African American music, but at times, it's also been a motherless child. Church folk had long derided the blues as the "devil's music"; similarly, the faithful railed against gospel singers who turned to secu-

Mike Bloomfield 1943–1981

lar soul music, a transition personified by Sam Cooke. By the start of the 1960s, the blues were in a bad way, for reasons both musical and social. Bluesmen like Waters and Wolf weren't losing their black audience to rock 'n' roll as much as to performers like Ray Charles and James Brown, and later, the pop soul sound of Motown. While their parents might still appreciate a blues singer, black kids who grew up during the struggle for civil rights considered the blues to be old-fashioned, if not downright demeaning.

"Blues represented, at that time, misery," said Bobby Schiffman, who managed New York's Apollo Theater in the 1960s. "Misery and blues were a throwback to slavery, to a time when the black man, intellectually, was at the lower point of his history. And black folks from the street didn't want to hear that shit. They came to the theater to be uplifted, to see the glamour of four-hundred-dollar mohair suits."

B.B. King reflected the pain of being rejected by a young black audience when he said, "Being a blues singer is like being black twice." Wolf and Waters kept busy working in and around Chicago, and mounting the occasional tour, usually down South. B.B. King continued to travel and play most every day of the year. But it was a slow grind for even these extraordinary blues talents. Record sales were negligible, which is why opportunities like the American Folk Blues Festival tours of Europe were such valuable outlets. Waters caught an unexpected break when he played the Newport Jazz Festival in 1960, an appearance that resulted in a memorable live album. Around that time, Chess also compiled early Waters and Wolf tracks and called them "folk-blues" collections to attract the type of white consumer who might go to see music at a coffee house in Greenwich Village.

Now white fans were even showing up at Smitty's Corner. "The University was sort of a pocket of sanity in the midst of Chicago stick-'em-up," said Gravenites, who'd grown up in the neighborhood and went to the university with Bishop, who was from Oklahoma and got a full scholarship for being a National Merit Scholar finalist. Bishop studied physics, but spent a lot of his time playing guitar, often with Butterfield, who studied flute before turning to the blues harmonica. They ran in a crowd that would soon include another harmonica player, Charlie Musselwhite, and a hotshot guitarist from the North Side named Mike Bloomfield.

Musselwhite grew up in Memphis, where he developed a taste for the blues before moving to Chicago. "I got a job as a driver for an exterminator," said Musselwhite, "and I would see posters and pass by bars with signs in the windows that said stuff like 'Elmore James is playing here.' Or Muddy,

Sonny Boy Williamson, and Little Walter. . . . I'd heard all of them on the radio, and I had their records. . . . But here, they were all [playing] in bars."

Bloomfield never went to college, but went to school in those bars. The son of a wealthy businessman—Bloomfield Industries manufactured restaurant supplies, including the first squeezable ketchup bottle—Bloomfield grew up in the wealthy Chicago suburb of Glencoe. In high school, he met Marshall Chess Jr., who swiped one of Muddy's slides for his friend. Bloomfield was a gifted guitarist by his mid-teens, and able to play in a variety of acoustic and electric styles. By the time he started finding his way to the blues bars of the South Side, his musical role models were clear.

"Muddy Waters, he was like a god to me," said Bloomfield. "Well, if he was a god, B.B. King was a deity where I couldn't even imagine ever knowing someone of his magnitude and greatness. But Muddy was in Chicago." By the time he was seventeen, Bloomfield was sharing the stage with his heroes. His dad disapproved of his son's infatuation with the guitar, but he soon found more supportive father figures. "We got to be friends with Muddy and his wife and Otis Spann," said Bloomfield's friend Fred Glaser. "We'd start out at Muddy's house for dinner, and his wife would make, like, gumbo or bouillabaisse or some real hot New Orleans kind of dinner. And then we'd go downstairs to where Spann lived, in the basement, and jam. Michael would play and Muddy would play and Spann would play the piano."

But nothing compared with the excitement of mounting the bandstand. One night, Bloomfield and Gravenites went to the West Side in hopes of sitting in with Howlin' Wolf. They got their wish. "So Michael and I get up there and there's a hushed silence in the crowd," said Gravenites. "And the band launches into 'Killing Floor,' and I play the piano and Michael plays rhythm guitar, doing that riff. Wolf looks like he's six-feet-eight inches tall and at least 300 pounds. I look up and he's wearing a white shirt and a tie, and he's smiling, and Hubert [Sumlin] is smiling with no teeth and we get a standing ovation. . . . My God, man: to be playing that song with Wolf onstage . . . It was like playing baseball in Yankee Stadium with the Yankees."

Bluesmen, of course, don't play stadiums, but in small joints like the Blind Pig. That's where Bloomfield met Big Joe Williams, who played a unique nine-string guitar and wrote the blues standard "Baby Please Don't Go." Williams lived in the basement of the Jazz Record Mart, a Chicago record store owned by Bob Koester, who also ran the Delmark record label. Through Williams, Bloomfield met such Depression-era bluesmen as Tampa Red and Kokomo Arnold. But it was Williams who left the greatest impression.

"Being with Big Joe was being with a history of the blues," said Bloomfield. "You could see him as a man, and you could see him as a legend. He couldn't read or write a word of English, but he had America memorized. From forty years of hiking roads and riding rails he was wise to every highway and byway and roadbed in the country, and wise to every city and county and township that they led to. Joe was part of a rare and vanished breed—he was a wanderer and a hobo and a blues singer, and he was an awesome man."

Bloomfield, a son of privilege, was under no illusion about the nature of his relationship with Williams. In *Me and Big Joe*, a reminiscence of his friendship with the bluesman, Bloomfield recounts a road trip with Williams to visit relatives in St. Louis that included funky food, flophouse accommodations, and an ocean of booze. After starting back to Chicago without Williams, Bloomfield returned to face his friend. How could he not? "To hear him talk about Robert Johnson or Son House or Charley Patton," said Bloomfield, "to hear life distilled from fifty years of thumbing rides and riding rails and playing joints—to hear of levees and work gangs and tent shows; of madams and whores, pimps and rounders, gamblers, bootleggers, and roustabouts; of circuit preachers and medicine-show men—well, it was something. Because to know this man was to know the story of black America, and maybe to know the story of black America is to know America itself."

Williams told his young white friend to return to Chicago without him. Bloomfield took his time before visiting Williams's basement home. Over beers, Williams played a bit of guitar, and handed the instrument to Bloomfield. "'Well, Michael,' he said, 'we really had ourselves a time in that St. Louis, didn't we?' I bent a note or two, high up on the neck. 'We sure did, Joe. Not a doubt about it.' I ran a couple of arpeggios and handed the guitar back to him. But he didn't take it. 'That sound good, Michael,' he said, and gave his head an affirmative little nod. 'You play on some.'

"And I did. There was no way I couldn't. Joe's world wasn't my world, but his music was. It was my life; it would be my life. So playing on was all I could do, and I did it the best I was able. And the music I played, I knew where it came from; and there was not any way I'd forget."

In the early '60s, Bloomfield hired Williams and other blues players when he promoted a weekly blues night at the Fickle Pickle, a club on Chicago's touristy Rush Street. One night, Bloomfield also played with the Texas guitar player Johnny Winter, who'd briefly moved to the city to gig with a Top 40 band in another Rush Street club. But that wasn't Winter's most vivid memory of his brief stay in Chicago. "I went to the South Side to see Muddy Waters," said Winter, "and got beat up and robbed. I took a taxi cab down to Silvio's with a friend from Texas. They let us out of the taxi and said, 'Go right in that door.' We went in that door and got beat up. . . . That was the last time I went down to see if I could find somebody in a blues club." Later in the decade, with his career in ascendance, Winter would jam at the Fillmore East with Bloomfield; in the 1970s, he produced and played on a trio of outstanding albums by Muddy Waters.

Most white musicians had no problem at the blues clubs. Indeed, Nick Gravenites theorized that in a racially polarized city like Chicago, skin color carried a certain amount of protection given the police action and public outrage that would result from a white fan being shot or stabbed. The best musicians, of course, also carried the shield of their talent. Paul Butterfield, a tough, streetwise Irish Catholic, was perhaps the most talented of the white musicians. Butterfield and Gravenites performed as "Nick and Paul," and hung out in the blues clubs looking for chances to perform. "I'd get up and do a couple of Lightnin' Hopkins tunes," said Gravenites, "and people would laugh, like 'Look at this—a white boy singin' the blues!' To them, it was a welcome comic relief. He [Butterfield] was another part of the comic relief in those blues revues, except that he was really good. The black audiences loved this guy. . . . He was a nice kid, and he'd play shuffleboard and pinball with the regulars, and then when it got to be his turn, he'd get up there with his harp and really blow."

Elvin Bishop dropped out of the University of Chicago to focus on the guitar, taking lessons from players who worked with Howlin' Wolf (Otis "Smokey" Smothers) and Muddy Waters (Sammy Lawhorn). He was soon playing with R&B bands as well as with blues players like Hound Dog Taylor and Junior Wells. How Bishop got the gig with Wells speaks to the hustle required of a musical sideman. Lawhorn got an offer to do a Muddy Waters tour that paid a couple bucks more, and told Bishop that Wells would be expecting him to take his place on Tuesday night. "I went down and said, 'Sammy sent me to play guitar for you,' said Bishop. "He hadn't said shit to Junior. Junior took a long look at me, put his arm around my shoulder, took me backstage and started telling me the tunes."

Steve Miller was another white guitarist playing the Chicago circuit. Miller was the son of a pathologist who made live recordings of musicians he invited to his home. That's how the youngster got an impromptu guitar lesson from Les Paul. After the Millers moved from Milwaukee to Texas, T-Bone Walker played a family house party. Miller, who played in bands throughout high school and college, moved to Chicago in the mid-'60s, inspired by hearing Paul Butterfield on an earlier trip to the city. "I joined up with local musician Barry Goldberg," said Miller, "and we competed directly for gigs with Howlin' Wolf, Muddy Waters and Paul Butterfield. There were like five clubs—Silvio's, the Peppermint Lounge, Big John's and a couple of others. It was like graduate school for music—great for your chops, working every day and these guys were adults playing real serious music." (The Goldberg-Miller Blues Band spent a day-and-a-half cutting an album for Epic that went nowhere, but got them an appearance on the television show *Hullabaloo* alongside the Supremes and the Four Tops.)

While in Chicago, Miller also played rhythm guitar in Buddy Guy's band, which had a rule that before each set, the musicians would each have a shot of whiskey. "I had a talk with him on a bar stool one day," said Miller, "and said, 'Well, Buddy, I'm gonna go out to San Francisco and see if I can make it out there.' He was going, 'Steve, let me give you some advice. Call it the Steve Miller Band because you're gonna have lots of different guys come and go in your band. Don't call yourselves the Foghorns or something. Call it the Steve Miller Band and you'll do great.'"

Mike Bloomfield, meanwhile, was making noise not just with his guitar, but also by booking a North Side club called Big Johns. The first weekend featured Big Joe Williams and Bloomfield playing in a band with Gravenites and Musselwhite. Soon, the giants of the South Side were playing to white audiences on the North Side. "Wolf had a regular Monday night gig there," said Gravenites. "It was very homey. He actually had a rocking chair and a little table for his harmonicas. He's sit there and he'd smoke a big meerschaum pipe, like it was his living room, and play his songs. It was the beginning of the blues clubs on the North Side, which is now where they all are."

Bloomfield also caught the attention of John Hammond when he heard his fiery guitar on a forgotten singer's demo tape. (Bloomfield was already friends with John Hammond Jr., having taken him on a blues tour of the South Side: he also played piano on his 1964 album, *So Many Roads*.) Hammond flew to Chicago and arranged for a recording session. "I got him into a studio," said Hammond, "and it was utter chaos. He had absolutely no idea how to run a session. And since rock is not my field, I was not the greatest help I could have been, but I got Epic to sign Mike." The recordings went unreleased.

At Big John's, Bloomfield would sometimes invite Paul Butterfield to join him on the bandstand. The pair had never clicked personally, but had an instinctual musical rapport. With business booming at Big John's, Bloomfield asked for a raise, and when he was turned down, took his band to another club. Butterfield was quickly recruited to lead the house band, which resulted in the first incarnation of the Butterfield Blues Band, with Elvin Bishop on guitar and Howlin' Wolf's rhythm section of Sam Lay on drums and Jerome Arnold on bass. "We was looking at the money part of it," said Lay of joining Butterfield. "We had a guaranteed four nights a week in one place, didn't have to go nowhere. And the money was, like, 20 bucks a night, man—that was a lot of money then. . . . Working with Wolf we were getting, like, $12.50 a night, and we were working just on the weekends."

The Butterfield Blues Band quickly became the talk of the town, filling the club for each performance. Among those who caught their show was Sam Charters, who was now a producer for Prestige Records. (One of the LPs Charters made for Prestige was *Deep Are the Roots*, an album of traditional blues by Tracy Nelson, who was accompanied on harmonica by Charlie Musselwhite. Nelson later gained bohemian fame with the band Mother Earth, named after a Memphis Slim song included on their first album that featured a scintillating Bloomfield guitar solo.) Because Prestige did not record electric bands, Charters passed an enthusiastic recommendation along to Joe Boyd of Elektra, who rang up his boss Paul Rothchild. The next night, they were in the audience at Big Johns, and after the first set, outlined the terms of a contract with Butterfield and Bishop.

Boyd had one reservation. "I told Paul I could see only one problem," said Boyd. "Elvin Bishop was a good rhythm player, a decent singer, a nice guy, a close friend of Butter's and a key to the group's conception and sound. But as a lead guitarist, he was not . . . heroic. I had been telling Paul about the charismatic role a young guitar player for John Mayall's Bluesbreakers named Eric Clapton had in the mythology of English blues bands. To be perfect, the band needed a guitar hero."

The next night, Butterfield and the record men went to see Bloomfield's band, and the harmonica player joined the guitarist to jam on a Freddie King tune. The chemistry was obvious, and after the set, Rothchild quickly convinced Bloomfield to join the Butterfield Blues Band. Back in New York, Rothchild drew up a contract, made plans for a recording session, and alerted Albert Grossman, Bob Dylan's manager, to his latest signing.

Cutting an album by the Butterfield Blues Band proved to be difficult, as the studio engineers, like those who balked at the volume of Eric Clapton's guitar, were still unaccustomed to recording loud, electric bands. Songs from those first sessions were scrapped—they were released in 1995 as *The Original Lost Elektra Sessions*—and plans were made to record the band live at New York's Café Au Go Go. Those recordings were also deemed to be lacking. The Butterfield Blues Band might have been having trouble putting its sound on wax, but it was creating a buzz among musicians, and Bloomfield soon found himself recording with Bob Dylan.

Bloomfield said that when it came to Dylan in particular and recording in general, he was as green as a bean. "I was in Dylan's [Woodstock, New York] house for about three days, learning the songs," said Bloomfield. "I had no identification with the material at all. . . . When the '60s came along and Dick Clark started doing his whole thing, I stopped. By the time we cut the album in 1965, I was into the Beatles, and real into the Stones, but I had no professional session experience, and my ideas about what rock 'n' roll was were pretty uninformed." Dylan gave the guitarist one rule: "I don't want any of the B.B. King shit, man."

Al Kooper, who sang and played keyboards in the Blues Project, had wheedled an invitation to the Dylan session in hopes of playing guitar. "Suddenly Dylan exploded through the doorway," said Kooper, "and in tow was this bizarre-looking guy [Bloomfield] carrying a Fender Telecaster guitar without a case. Which was weird, because it was the dead of winter and the guitar was all wet from the rain and snow. But he just shuffled over into the corner, wiped it off, plugged in and commenced to play some of the most incredible guitar I'd ever heard. . . . I unplugged, packed up, and did my best to look like a reporter from *Sing Out!* magazine." Kooper recouped by sneaking behind a Hammond organ and improvising the famous introduction to "Like a Rolling Stone."

The Blues Project, which played folk-rock as well as blues-rock, featured Danny Kalb on guitar; the group once shared a bill at the Café Au Go Go with Butterfield's band, but couldn't compete with the hard-edged power of the Chicago outfit. The Blues Project also headlined a series of shows at the club dubbed "The Blues Bag" that featured Muddy Waters, Big Joe Williams, Otis Spann, and John Lee Hooker. "I think they picked us to close the show strictly by virtue of the fact that we were unquestionably louder than anyone else on the bill," said Kooper. "It was almost embarrassing, our black heroes having to warm up for us; I guess that's just the American way." Justice was perhaps served when the Blues Project was hired to back Chuck Berry. "We backed up Chuck Berry at his first New York solo concert," said Kooper. "He was a scary guy and a tough leader, and never did he encourage any friendship. He was strictly professional: 'All you do is watch my foot. When it go up in the air, get ready. When it hit the ground, if you playin', stop. If you ain't, start!'"

While in New York working with Butterfield and Dylan, Bloomfield took the opportunity to see Jimi Hendrix play at the Café Wha? "Hendrix knew who I was," said Bloomfield, "and that day, in front of my eyes, he burned me to death. I didn't even get my guitar out. . . . He was getting every sound I was ever to hear him get right there in that room."

The Butterfield Blues Band nailed their studio debut on the third try. The record was an exhilarating shot of Chicago blues with solo space filled by Butterfield's full-bodied harmonica and Bloomfield's soulfully shamanistic guitar. While cutting the disc, which included songs by Willie Dixon, Little Walter, and Muddy Waters, the band added keyboard player Mark Naftlin, a Chicago acquaintance who had moved to New York to study at the Mannes School of Music. While Bloomfield certainly fit the role of the guitar hero, he didn't dominate the record the way that Eric Clapton did on the Bluesbreakers album. Instead, Bloomfield and Butterfield were twin instrumental peaks supported by a powerful blues band (it also helped that Butterfield was a more convincing vocalist than Mayall). The album opened with "Born in Chicago," a hard-hitting shuffle written by Nick Gravenites that might as well have been the story of the Butterfield Blues Band.

The album was completed around the time of the Newport Folk Festival in July of 1965. Invitations to play the not-for-profit festival were extended by a board of directors that consisted of such veteran New York folkies as Alan Lomax and Pete Seeger. In June, Peter Yarrow, another board member and a third of the popular folk group Peter, Paul and Mary, negotiated a last-minute invitation for the Butterfield Blues Band. Was it mere coincidence that Albert Grossman, who represented festival headliner Bob Dylan, also managed Yarrow's group? In any event, by the start of the event, Grossman had a new client, the Butterfield Blues Band.

The Butterfield band was scheduled to close "Blues: Origins and Off-shoots," a Friday afternoon workshop that was emceed by Alan Lomax and included performances by Mance Lipscomb and Memphis Slim with Willie Dixon. Butterfield was last because the band required the stage to be set with microphones, drums, and amplifiers. The galvanizing Delta blues singer, Son House, who'd been rediscovered in 1964, but was unable to perform during that year's festival, immediately preceded them. Paul Rothchild, who was acting as Butterfield's soundman, was stunned by the size of the afternoon crowd. "At workshops, they only expected a few hundred people to show up," said Rothchild, "and thousands of people showed up. The whole area was packed."

Lomax looked upon the band's electric equipment with a disdain reflected in his introduction. "Alan Lomax got up on stage," said Rothchild, "and went into a five or ten minute introduction—like, 'Used to be a time when a farmer would take a box, glue an axe handle to it, put some strings on it, sit down in the shade of a tree and play some blues for himself and his friends. Now here we've got these guys, and they need all of this fancy hardware to play the blues. Today you've heard some of the greatest blues musicians in the world playing their simple music on simple instruments. Let's find out if these guys can play at all.'"

The band subsequently left no doubt. "We were boogying and totally blown out by the Butterfield Band," said Maria Muldaur. "I had heard a lot of blues, but . . . I'd never heard real Chicago electric blues like this, and we loved it." But at show's end, the backstage talk wasn't about the music, but about the fight. "Lomax walked down off the stage," said Rothchild. "And Albert . . . walked up to him and said, 'What kind of fuckin' introduction was that?' and Lomax said, 'What do you know about blues?' Albert said, 'I don't have to know anything about blues to know that was a terrible introduction.' . . . And before anyone knew what was happening there were these two giants, both physically and in the business, wrestling around in the dust!" Some report that Sam Lay, Butterfield's drummer, pulled the men apart. Others say that the two antagonists threw wild haymakers that both missed their mark and sent the pudgy antagonists sprawling to the ground. Everybody agreed that the fisticuffs between Lomax and Grossman were about a lot more than a rude introduction.

"They [Lomax and Grossman] were right in front of the stage, rolling in the dirt while we were playing and I was screaming, 'Kick his ass, Albert!'" said Bloomfield, who rejected Lomax's constricted definition of the blues. "What we played was music that was entirely indigenous to the neighborhood, to the city that we grew up in. There was no doubt in my mind that this was folk music; this was what I heard on the streets of my city, out the windows, on radio stations and jukeboxes in Chicago. . . . That's what folk music meant to me—what people listened to."

Geoff Muldaur, who was scheduled to perform with the Kweskin Jug Band, was "rooting for Albert": "Lomax was known as a pugilistic asshole, and he ripped off black people, and he copyrighted tunes that weren't his. [Lomax claimed composer credit for some eight hundred songs, including "Amazing Grace" and "Stagger Lee."] And yes, he was in the right place at the right time, and got incredible recordings for our country. So I give him credit for that, but not as much as most people. As for Albert, he might take all the money, but he was always in your camp. He enabled anybody who worked with him to become rich if they would apply themselves, which I didn't. I loved the fact that he did that, and that workshop made history. The Butterfield Band smoked the thing.

Joe Boyd, who worked the festival prior to his departure for his job with Elektra Records in London, saw the fight about more than Butterfield. He was also privy to the backstage politics in which, after the scuffle, Lomax demanded that Grossman be banned from the festival grounds. The board demurred when it was pointed out that three of Grossman's clients (Dylan, the Kweskin band, and Peter, Paul and Mary) were yet to play and just might leave with their manager.

"There was a clear generational and cultural gap widening as the weekend went on," said Boyd. "The year before, Dylan had been a pied piper in blues jeans. This year he was in a puffed polka-dotted dueling shirt and there were rumors that they were smoking dope. The old guard—Seeger, Lomax, [Theodore] Bikel—were very upset. They had gotten to the point of having all their dreams comes true two years before, having this gigantic mass movement of politically active kids. And suddenly they could see it all slipping away in a haze of marijuana smoke and self-indulgence. As far as they were concerned, Grossman was the money changer at the gates of the temple."

Bob Dylan, who'd been called "the voice of his generation," was also the point man in this cultural confrontation. In November of 1964, Irwin Silber, the longtime editor of *Sing Out!*, published an open letter to Dylan in the magazine. After reviewing the publication's long-standing support of Dylan, and fretting over the corrupting power of celebrity culture, Silber got to the heart of the matter: "You said that you weren't a writer of 'protest' songs—or any other category, for that matter—but you just wrote songs. Well, okay, call it anything you want. But any songwriter who tries to deal honestly with reality in this world is bound to write 'protest' songs. How can he help himself?

"Your new songs seem to be all inner-directed now, inner probing, self-conscious—maybe even a little maudlin or a little cruel on occasion. And it's happening on stage, too." It famously happened that year at Newport when Dylan performed with a band that included Mike Bloomfield on guitar, Sam Lay on drums, and Al Kooper on the organ. Legend has it that the crowd responded to the music by erupting in boos; others say that people were simply annoyed at Dylan's brief four-song set. (That was the full repertoire of the hastily rehearsed ensemble; Dylan subsequently returned for two acoustic songs, concluding with a defiant "It's All Over Now [Baby Blue].")

"To me, the Butterfield Blues Band was the most important thing to happen at Newport in 1965," said Geoff Muldaur. "Not Dylan going electric, which people have milked for so many years. The thing that happened that changed the world map of music was that an integrated band came in from Chicago to play real Chicago blues. Sure, that model was based on guys like Muddy Waters, but the fact was that this white guy was so good, and had a band that could pull it off and hold their own among the kings, which they did. In the blink of an eye, there would be two hundred thousand blues bands in the world based on that model." In 1965, it was not just the times that were a-changing; it was also the blues.

SEVEN
BALLROOM BLUES

B.B. King's tour bus pulled up to San Francisco's Fillmore Ballroom on February 26, 1967. King's stage act had been recently captured on *Live at the Regal*, a quickie album cut at a venerable Chicago theater with a black clientele; the LP came to be regarded as the perfect encapsulation of King's urban blues, with the ringing, fluid tones of his guitar (nicknamed "Lucille") framing his full-bodied, manly vocals. The live recording also underscored King's easy affinity with his audience.

"I'd like to tell you a little story now if I may," said King over a tinkling piano during the Regal performance, preparing to introduce "It's My Own Fault." From the audience, one can hear "Okay." King continued: "A guy singing about his girlfriend, and he calls his 'Angel,' of course, that's his 'Sweet Little Angel.' But let's think about a guy that loses his girl. Oh, it happens, believe me." "Yeah, I know," exclaims a man from the orchestra seats. King chuckles, and continues: "And then,

B.B. King 1925–

he starts to sing, and you might hear something that sounds like this." Not the sweet sighs of King's voice, but the reverberating cries of Lucille. This magic moment was more than one performer's practiced rapport with his audience; it captured the comfortable conversation of a community.

King had played the Fillmore in the past, but looking out the window of his bus, he did not see his usual black audience, but the longhaired white kids now known as hippies. "I had never seen people wear hair like that around me," said King. "I saw it in papers, books, and the Bible." King figured this had got to be wrong, and dispatched his road manager to find Bill Graham, who was just starting a career that would make him the most famous concert promoter in the history of rock 'n' roll. Graham didn't know B.B. King from Adam, but put him on a bill with the Steve Miller Band and Moby Grape at the recommendation of Mike Bloomfield of the Butterfield Blues Band. Graham came out to the bus and told King that he was at the right place.

"We got to the old dressing room that I had been used to going to," said King, who recognized a familiar couch. "I looked at Bill and I said, 'Bill, I got to have a drink.' He said, 'B, we don't sell liquor here.' 'I don't care. I got to have a drink.' He said, 'Okay. I'll send out and get you one.' He sent out and got me a half a pint of something. They brought it to me and I had a big belt of it."

On stage, Graham handled the introduction: "Ladies and gentlemen, I bring you the Chairman of the Board, B.B. King." Steve Miller watched from the wings: "It was a very emotional night," said Miller. "He had tears in his eyes, because the audience, as soon as B.B. came out on the stage they just stood up and gave him a standing ovation." Carlos Santana, nineteen, was in the crowd and on his feet. "When he hit the note to bring the band in," said Santana, "my whole life was changed. When I saw B.B. and I heard that note for the first time like that, I could see what Michael Bloomfield and Eric Clapton and everybody saw in him. There's a room that you go to if you're pitching a ball or if you're playing basketball like Michael Jordon. There's a certain zone that you get in, to get a note like that."

King said that night at the Fillmore changed his life. "It was a break-through for me," he said. "They didn't seem to look at me as B.B. King, the blues singer. It was B.B. King, the musician." At the time, King kept busy playing big-city joints and the remains of the nation's circuit of black clubs and bars. But now he'd start adding bigger shows at rock halls thanks to blues-rock guitarists like Bloomfield and Clapton who would sing his praises (and cite his influence on their own playing) to the rock press. "Mike

Bloomfield was a special friend," said King. "He was a Jewish boy from a wealthy family with a father who didn't appreciate his son's appreciation of black blues. I believe Mike suffered from that conflict—all sons want Daddy's respect—and poured his pain into his playing."

After playing with Butterfield and Dylan at Newport, Bloomfield was told by Albert Grossman that Dylan wanted him to play electric guitar on his upcoming tour. Bloomfield chose to stick with the Butterfield Blues Band, whose first record would quickly become an influential underground hit. "That [album] left an incredible impact on my mind about a new kind of blues," said Santana, "different than what I was used to hearing. It didn't sound like an old stove where you burn logs. It sounded like a new stove where you burn with electricity . . . And if you couldn't play 'Born in Chicago,' you just couldn't cut it."

The Butterfield Band hit the road in cars and a Ford Econoline stuffed with band members and equipment; the hours on stage both honed the group's musical cohesion, and encouraged experimentation. "I remember one time in Cambridge," said keyboardist Mark Naftalin, "Michael had been given something that was represented as 'Leary acid,' and he took it and spent the entire evening listening to Indian music. The next day . . . the improvisatory mold that came to be known as 'East-West' started to be played."

"East-West" became the title song of the Butterfield Blues Band's second album, released in August of 1966; the LP also included a more traditional, blues-based instrumental, Cannonball Adderley's "Work Song." The album had other highlights, including a transcendent slow blues cut earlier by B.B. King, "Got a Mind to Give Up Living," but the virtuosic instrumental jams are what inspired a generation of blues-rock bands. "'East-West' was a radical departure, melodically, structurally, and chordally, from the rock 'n' roll modes and licks that were being played at that time," said Bloomfield. "Believe me, I knew they were not my scales. They were things I'd heard on John Coltrane records and by guys that played a lot of modal music [including, prominently, Miles Davis]. . . . The idea was not to see how far you could go harmonically, but to see how far you could go melodically or modally." ("Eight Miles High," a song by the Byrds issued in March 1966, also applied modal lessons learned from jazz musicians.)

The Butterfield Blues Band first played the Fillmore in 1966—Jefferson Airplane opened the show—and became highly influential regulars at the Bay Area ballroom. "None of the shows Bill Graham put on were really serious until the Butterfield Band showed up," said Nick Gravenites, who'd relocated from Chicago, "because they were the hotshots from the East, people who were already accomplished electric musicians. Most of the hippie bands that were playing in this area were the result of a lot of acid and not too much expertise. . . . They influenced many musicians, and showed them the way—here's what's happening, here's what's possible. Work at it, apply your musicianship and practice, and you can do this."

Jorma Kaukonen learned Gary Davis tunes from Ian Buchanan at Antioch College before moving to the West Coast in the mid-1960s. Now he was opening for the Butterfield band as the lead guitarist for Jefferson Airplane. "They were the first young virtuosos to come and play here that I'd actually seen," said Kaukonen. "I'd seen the great ones like B.B. King, but this was the first I'd seen of guys who were more or less in my age bracket that were world-class players, and it was really inspirational."

Kaukonen, like most of the San Francisco musicians, was schooled in acoustic folk and blues with maybe a touch of jazz or bluegrass. "I came to the Airplane totally unfamiliar with band playing, or rock and roll," said Kaukonen. "An electric guitar to me was simply an amplified guitar, and I didn't really know any of the stuff that you could do with it." Kaukonen got friendly with Bloomfield, who taught him to bend notes and to use his guitar and amplifier to sustain notes and create feedback. But it was the hard-core Chicago blues and the widescreen improvisations like "East-West" that had the most profound influence on the San Francisco scene; the Grateful Dead, who already played an epic version of Reverend Davis's "Death Don't Have No Mercy," would be soon be fashioning folkie songs into the psychedelic rock that would make them cultural icons.

While the Butterfield Blues Band was wowing the flower children, Bloomfield was having an equally significant effect on Bill Graham. "Nobody held the guitar the way Michael did," said Graham. "He would just dance with it." Graham and Bloomfield clicked both personally and professionally. "He and just a couple of other people were really my teachers as far as who they thought I should expose to the predominantly white audience that came to rock & roll shows," said Graham. "He always had somebody that he was pushing. If it wasn't the Staple Singers, it was Albert King or B.B. King or Otis Redding or Howlin' Wolf."

The result was that over the next few years, the Fillmore West (and its sister venue in New York City, the Fillmore East) presented B.B. King, Muddy Waters, Howlin' Wolf, James Cotton, Albert King, and the Staple Singers, among many others. Graham typically paired the blues acts with rock bands, sending a significant message that rock and the blues belonged on the same stage. As such strategies spread to other hippie-era venues, blues singers found fans that would have never ventured to Smitty's Corner.

Howlin' Wolf played San Francisco's Family Dog ballroom in 1966. "People were running around half-naked, mostly naked, people all painted up," said Gravenites. "This is how the Wolf handled strangeness: He got strange himself. And he could get strange! I saw him just sitting around and lying on the floor and then coming back up and giving looks to the people and making himself look like a monkey or something. . . . People asked, 'Who's that strange guy up there?'"

Steve Miller, who knew that odd bird, went straight from the Chicago clubs to the Fillmore West. "The first night I got to San Francisco," said Miller, "Butterfield was playing at the Fillmore with the Jefferson Airplane. . . . I was living in my Volkswagen bus. Butterfield let me up on stage to jam and announced who I was and that I was moving to San Francisco and starting my band right away." Miller was shocked at the local musicians' relative lack of professionalism. "I thought most of the San Francisco bands were awful," he said. "I mean, the Grateful Dead would play 'In the Midnight Hour' and then stand around for ten minutes and tune." All told, the Steve Miller Blues Band played the Fillmore 109 times, including 1968 shows backing Chuck Berry that were recorded for a live album. (The "Blues" was dropped from the group's name before it cut its debut album.)

Within a year, amid the flurry of record company interest in the so-called "San Francisco Sound," Miller scored a remarkable contract with Capitol Records that guaranteed him total creative control, full ownership of his publishing, a no-cut contract for seven records, and a half million dollars. When Miller had trouble working with the engineers at the Capitol studios in Los Angeles, he brought his band to England and recorded at Olympic Studio with Glyn Johns, who'd already engineered albums by the Rolling Stones and the Kinks.

The Steve Miller Band, which for a time included singer-guitarist Boz Scaggs, became a popular favorite on FM rock stations and at the nation's rock ballrooms. One of their first big gigs was at the Monterey Pop Festival in June of 1967, the famous rock fest that ushered in San Francisco's Summer of Love. Other blues-oriented acts that played at Monterey included Canned Heat, Big Brother & the Holding Company, the Butterfield Blues Band, the Blues Project, the Jimi Hendrix Experience, and the Electric Flag, a new band featuring Mike Bloomfield.

Bloomfield left Butterfield's band shortly after the release of *East-West* for a variety of reasons: to give Elvin Bishop the chance to play lead guitar; to form a band that would play a variety of blues, soul, and jazz; and to get off the road, which was increasingly leaving him a stressed-out insomniac. (Butterfield beefed up his band with a three-man horn section that included

David Sanborn.) Bloomfield's new group, the Electric Flag, was also managed by Albert Grossman and included such Chicago musicians as Harvey Brooks (who'd performed in a band with Steve Miller) and Nick Gravenites (who'd written "Born in Chicago"). Searching for a drummer, Bloomfield was told of a powerful player in Wilson Pickett's band, Buddy Miles.

Pickett was playing a week of New York shows in the spring of 1967 promoted by deejay Murray the K. The package show, dubbed "Music in the Fifth Dimension," presented numerous performers in a revue format that played five times a day at a midtown-Manhattan movie theater. Like the Monterey Festival, the show featured notable blues-rock musicians: Eric Clapton, who was making his American debut with Cream, the trio he joined after leaving John Mayall's Bluesbreakers; Al Kooper and the Blues Project; and Stefan Grossman, who was playing electric guitar behind a one-hit band called the Chicago Loop, whose debut recording featured Bloomfield on guitar. Backstage at the show, Bloomfield advised Grossman to stick to the acoustic guitar. Buddy Miles, smelling fame and fortune, quit Pickett's band to join the Electric Flag.

The Flag's first job was to score a Roger Corman B movie about LSD called *The Trip*, which was written by Jack Nicholson, who starred in it alongside Peter Fonda. The soundtrack included horn licks and rhythm grooves that would find their way into songs on the band's first album. Work on the soundtrack inevitably ate into prep time for the Flag's high-profile debut at Monterey. (The band was so new that the festival's first ads identified them as "The Michael Bloomfield Thing.") The group was scheduled to play at the end of a long day that included Canned Heat, Steve Miller, and the Butterfield band.

Albert Grossman was at the festival courting record executives hungry to sign new acts. "Probably the biggest gig we ever played," said Bloomfield. "And we played rotten, man. . . . And the people loved it. And I could see—oh my God, the hype, the image, the shuck, the jive." Clive Davis of Columbia Records signed the Electric Flag. Davis and Grossman were two of a kind; by the end of the festival, they'd both set their sights on Big Brother and the Holding Company, which was to say, Janis Joplin.

Joplin grew up an outsider in Port Arthur, Texas, and as a teenager, sang folk and blues songs by Lead Belly and Bessie Smith. After a brief stint at college in Austin, she moved to the Bay Area in 1963, and played in a duo with Jorma Kaukonen. Their repertoire included a song by Reverend Davis, "Hesitation Blues," which Kaukonen would later reprise with Hot Tuna. The Joplin gigs encouraged Kaukonen to buy an electric guitar. "I got into playing it," he said, "because whenever I'd play with her, it was just impossible for an acoustic guitar player to compete with her."

Joplin went back to Texas to shake a methamphetamine habit, but was soon back in San Francisco singing with a ramshackle, psychedelic band called Big Brother and the Holding Company. The intimate folk-blues singer quickly became a ballroom belter. "She had to change her vocal style," said Peter Albin, who played bass guitar with Big Brother. "It became much less colored. The range she had when she sang at low volume was fantastic, but she really had to push that range with a rock & roll band. Towards the end of her first year with us she started getting nodules on her throat. You could hear two or three overtones in each note."

Janis Joplin killed at Monterey. She sang and shimmied and became the epitome of the hippie blues mama with her big voice and hair flying everywhere. After Monterey, Janis would forever be identified with Big Mama Thornton's "Ball and Chain," just as ten years earlier, Elvis Presley had taken virtual possession of Thornton's "Hound Dog." Soon managed by Grossman, and signed by Davis to Columbia, Joplin and Big Brother became stars with 1968's *Cheap Thrills*.

Canned Heat, who also played Monterey, was formed with an assist from John Fahey. While performing in Boston, Fahey had met Al Wilson, the guitar player who'd helped Son House relearn his repertoire. "I had two records out at the time," said Fahey, "so he asked me for a guitar lesson. So he comes over to my house and he's got books, you know, everything I'd written and transcribed so he can play everything except for a few short passages that he wanted to make sure he had right."

Fahey encouraged Wilson to come to Los Angeles to help him work on his UCLA master's thesis on the music of Charley Patton. "He [Alan] was fiendishly intelligent and could not only reproduce Patton's music on guitar but explain to you on many levels how it worked," said Fahey. "I still consider Alan the most brilliant musical thinker I've ever known." In L.A., Wilson met Henry Vestine, who'd been with Fahey when he found Skip James in a Mississippi hospital. They were soon jamming with Bob "The Bear" Hite, a husky blues freak who worked in a record store.

Wilson and Hite represented the two sides of Canned Heat. Hite was the vocal shouter of mostly pedestrian up-tempo tunes. Wilson was a much more unique performer, and his feathery falsetto voice and vivid work on guitar and harmonica defined the band's two biggest hits, "On the Road Again" and "Goin' Up the Country." Given Wilson's expertise, it's little surprise that these songs were essentially updates of Depression-era tunes, with "On the Road Again" putting a John Lee Hooker beat to a tune created by pianist Floyd Jones and "Goin' Up the Country" borrowing a melody and flute lick from Henry Thomas's "Bull Doze Blues."

Wilson was quick to credit his source material—Jones gets co-credit for "On the Road Again"—but in an ironic twist, Canned Heat never owned the publishing for these and other hits. That's because after recording its debut album for Liberty Records, the band went on tour and was busted for marijuana possession in Denver. Canned Heat claimed to be set up, but ended up selling its publishing rights to Liberty for the $10,000 in legal fees it took to get the band off the hook.

Country Joe and the Fish also performed at Monterey, and while the political folk-rock band had little to do with the blues, it had connections to significant blues-related personalities. Ed Denson, John Fahey's partner in Takoma Records who'd also worked with Skip James and John Hurt, managed the band. Sam Charters signed the group to Vanguard and produced its records. And finally, Country Joe McDonald played an unlikely role in the success of an important roots music label, Arhoolie Records.

In 1965, McDonald and an early jug-band version of the Fish wanted to record his new antiwar protest song, "I-Feel-Like-I'm-Fixin'-to-Die Rag." Arhoolie owner Chris Strachwitz volunteered to cut the tune in his living room, and when McDonald asked about his fee, Strachwitz said that he'd do if for free if he could handle the song's publishing. That didn't mean diddly until 1969, when McDonald sang the song at the Woodstock festival, a performance that was featured in the subsequent album and movie. Strachwitz's share of the publishing royalties provided the down payment for Arhoolie's headquarters in El Cerrito, California.

Some of the acts who performed at Monterey—including Jimi Hendrix, Janis Joplin, the Butterfield Blues Band, and Canned Heat—also played the Woodstock festival two years later. At Monterey, Hendrix famously climaxed the American debut of his power trio by torching his Stratocaster after dousing it with lighter fluid. But Hendrix was about much more than outrageous showmanship; his incendiary guitar was fueled by rock and funk and feedback, but was also deeply rooted in the blues. With a set list that ran from Howlin' Wolf's "Killing Floor" to Bob Dylan's "Like a Rolling Stone," Hendrix's virtuosity consistently argued that blues was an essential root of popular music. Meanwhile, the stylistic seeds that Hendrix and his peers planted at hippie ballrooms continued to bring new attention to black blues performers.

Albert King, after years working the chitlin' circuit, became a widely known blues star after multiple appearances at the Fillmore. Born Albert Nelson, he'd assumed his stage name following the success of B.B. King's

"Three O'Clock Blues." "Albert was born in Indianola [Mississippi]," said B.B. King, "he called his guitar 'Lucy,' and for a while he went around saying he was my brother. That bothered me until I got to know him and realized he was right; he wasn't my brother by blood, but he was sure my brother in the blues."

Albert King played with various combos during the 1950s, including a stint drumming behind the king of the blues shuffle, Jimmy Reed. His first hit, 1961's "Don't Throw Your Love on Me So Strong," was recorded in St. Louis with the ubiquitous Ike Turner on piano. But King really hit his stride when he signed with Stax Records in 1966 and went into the studio with Booker T. & the MG's to record *Born under a Bad Sign*. The combination resulted in a uniquely soulful style of blues, with songs like the title tune and "Cross Cut Saw" offering a supple showcase for King's lacerating lead guitar.

King's style derived in part from the fact that, like Hendrix, he was left handed, and instead of playing a guitar built for a southpaw, he slung a standard instrument over his shoulder and essentially played it upside down. (When you look at a right-handed guitarist, the high-E string is on the bottom; in King's case, the high-E was facing the ceiling.) This scenario dramatically changed the way King would bend strings, just as his unusual E-minor tuning added another flavor to his uniquely beefy guitar sound. "He was a big strong dude who developed a guitar cry that could cut you in half," said B.B. King. "I liked major scales, and he liked minor. He had his own sound that, far as I can see, had more influence on guys like Jimi Hendrix than I did. Sometimes I'd hear little pieces of myself in bluesmen like Buddy Guy, who I also love, but I think the heavy rockers looked to Albert as a main model."

Albert King was a personable performer who could get the hippies eating out of his very large hand; little wonder that his most famous album, *Live Wire/Blues Power*, was recorded at the Fillmore West. The disc finds King delivering a long discourse on what it means to have the blues, but it was the sound of his guitar that taught a lesson to such players as Eric Clapton (who used King's solo from "Personal Manager" for Cream's "Strange Brew") and a young kid in Texas named Stevie Ray Vaughan. A third King, Freddie, also got a friendly reception in the rock ballrooms. Already popular among blues fans for a series of guitar instrumentals that came in the wake of his 1961 classic "Hide Away," Freddie King was a powerful singer as well, and by decade's end, was signed to Leon Russell's Shelter Records.

Buddy Guy was also finding a more receptive audience in the rock ballrooms. It was around that time, 1970, when Guy ran into B.B. King at Chicago's O'Hare Airport. "Wasn't for these English acts, I'd be playing a bar in Three Mule, Mississippi," said King. "Here I am on my way to Fillmore East in New York City. I think Bill Graham got me booked with the Byrds. Where you off to, Buddy?"

"A traveling hippie festival in Canada. We going by train to four or five different cities. They say it's gonna be bigger than Woodstock."

"Hendrix on it?"

"Don't think so," I said. "But Janis Joplin is."

Guy, who was referring to the Festival Express tour, had by now left Chess Records and been recorded for Vanguard Records by Sam Charters. "I didn't feel that Leonard Chess dealt fairly with me," said Guy. "He didn't release much on me, and the first time I sat down and talked to him was after Cream and Hendrix came out. Before that Muddy and all those guys would bring me in for a session, but Leonard would say that the shit I was playing was too loud, just noise. But then he heard how Eric Clapton and Hendrix were playing [and selling] and he called me in and said he should let me kick his ass."

Turned out things were much the same at Vanguard. "Charters wasn't all that different than Leonard Chess," said Guy, who nonetheless appreciated his pedigree as a blues scholar. "He had his notion of what the blues should be. He wanted that clean sound. . . . I still wanted to explode like I did when I played live." Charters had first worked with Guy when he recorded him with harmonica player Junior Wells for *Chicago/The Blues/Today!*, a series of three 1966 albums that aimed to capture the live sound of blues bands led by J. B. Hutto, Otis Spann, James Cotton, and Otis Rush. Those collections were inspired by an influential 1965 album that Guy recorded with Wells called *Hoodoo Man Blues*, which had itself alarmed blues purists with its overt nods to James Brown and contemporary R&B.

Around that time, Guy started being booked and managed by Dick Waterman, who was by then handling a number of blues revival performers. "Buddy realized that his future didn't lie in playing for black people in Chicago," said Waterman, "but in playing the Fillmore and things like that. That's when he got into more of a rock sound. He would turn around and stop the band, and then in silence, he would begin to play the riff from [Cream's] 'Sunshine of Your Love.' In other words, saying [to Clapton], 'You can play me, well I can play you, too.' And then he'd go back into blues. It was supposed to be an eight- or ten-second interlude, but Buddy liked it so much he stayed with it."

It would still be many years until Guy's records packed the same sonic punch of his blues-rock peers, but live audiences (and fellow musicians) were quick to see the connection. "Buddy Guy was one of the first [players] that turned in an abstract blues," said Carlos Santana. "Almost like what Ornette Coleman did to jazz. He started bending the note beyond the tone you're supposed to hear. He's one of the influences in stepping out, in taking the blues somewhere else but still respecting Muddy Waters."

"Jimi [Hendrix] was very into Buddy," said Linda Keith, who befriended Hendrix before he left Greenwich Village for England. "I think, in a way, Jimi felt he had permission to be flamboyant from seeing and appreciating Buddy. . . . The whole showmanship, that whole distinction from the traditional blues players, was the key to the way Jimi could take the blues and turn them into something else."

The popularity of blues among rock fans encouraged record labels to let veteran artists like B.B. King spend a little more time and money in the studio. King's 1968 album, *Live and Well*, was produced by Bill Szymczyk, who encouraged King to record half of the album with studio musicians (the other half was a live recording with his road band). The studio side produced a funky blues that became a minor hit on FM rock stations, "Why I Sing the Blues." But the true payoff came on the next album, *Completely Well*, which featured the song that would make King a mainstream star, "The Thrill Is Gone."

"The Thrill Is Gone" was originally recorded in 1951 by its author, a piano player named Roy Hawkins. The song's arrangement was created in the studio, and anchored by a hypnotic electric piano track that was the perfect foil for King's clipped, eloquent guitar solos. King left the recording session near dawn; a few hours later, he awoke to a ringing telephone. It was Szymczyk, who had the sudden inspiration to sweeten the track with strings. It was an unusual addition to a blues tune, and the final piece that helped to create an enduring standard. A few years later, Szymczyk would make his fortune producing some of the Eagles' most popular albums. But this would always be his greatest hit.

B.B. King was forty-four years old when he recorded "The Thrill is Gone," and had been making records for twenty years. Suddenly, his future was in fancy nightclubs, concert halls, and on television programs like *The Ed Sullivan Show* and *The Tonight Show*. When King first played the Fillmore West, he said that for the first time he was treated as a musician as opposed to a blues singer. After "The Thrill Is Gone," B.B. King would simply be known as a great American artist.

OUT OF THE PAST AND INTO THE PRESENT

One afternoon before a 1965 performance at the Gaslight Café in Greenwich Village, Mississippi John Hurt and Dick Waterman went to the movies to see a double bill of *A Hard Day's Night* and *Help!* That night at the club, Hurt mentioned his trip to the movies as he tuned his guitar, and somebody asked what he'd seen. Hurt looked to Waterman when he couldn't recall the musical combo who'd been in both films. The blues-revival photographer turned booker-manager sank in his seat; he knew there were folk-blues fans that had no love for rock 'n' roll, even if it was British. Hurt sat on the stage, patiently waiting for an answer. "The Beatles," said Waterman. "Them boys were good," said Hurt. "You should have seen them jumping and playing them guitars when they was in the snow."

The Beatles had almost no musical connection to the blues, though George Harrison later name-checked Elmore James as he played slide guitar on "For You Blues," and the band drew obvious inspiration (and early cover songs) from such bluesy rockers as Chuck Berry and Little Richard. But to picture

Skip James 1902–1969

John Hurt grooving to the Fab Four underscores the surreal nature of his unexpected second career. In 1928, when Hurt had last recorded, movies were silent, and his only gigs were for his Mississippi neighbors. Now rock bands starred in Technicolor movies and he was playing for hippies and college kids in a Greenwich Village club.

John Sebastian, who'd cut his teeth with the Even Dozen Jug Band, found a name for his group in the lyric to Hurt's "Coffee Blues"—the "Lovin' Spoonful." "What I heard in the music of John Hurt," said Sebastian, "was that it was more swinging than a lot of the finger picking that I had heard up to that time. His groove was just deeper, and yet when he'd talk about his playing, he'd make it sound so simple. 'Well, you get your thumb doing this,' he'd tell me, 'and then you got these fingers left over so you can kinda get a little melody going on that.'"

Sebastian was already acquainted with another bluesman, as he'd sometimes carried Lightnin' Hopkins's guitar when the Texan played in New York; Sebastian had first seen Hopkins on a 1960 television special that had also featured his father, also named John, who played classical music on the harmonica. "There's a tradition in this [blues] music," said Sebastian, "that you keep your eye out for the prodigies, the young kids who are musically preoccupied in one way or another, and they can become your lead boy, the incentive being what you can teach, or what they can absorb. But there's also, especially in Lightnin's case, the background of 'If I teach this kid this lick, I may see him across the street from me when I'm trying to fill my hat.'"

Hurt was much more forthcoming, but Sebastian was impressed by more than just his guitar playing. "I remember working with the Spoonful at the Night Owl Café," he said, "and we'd be playing to maybe six beatniks. Then I'd go to see John at the Gaslight and the place would be filled with all these beautiful college girls that we couldn't get down to our little club. All the girls were nuts for John Hurt."

Hurt was a frequent visitor to New York City, and became friendly with many of the other musicians who played the coffeehouse circuit. "I remember one time somebody was passing around a joint," said Dave Van Ronk, "and it came to John. He looked at it for a moment, and said, 'Oh yeah, I remember this. We used to call it "poor man's whiskey." ' And he just passed it on." (Others reported that he enjoyed a toke or two.) Hurt had an especially close rapport with another Southerner, Patrick Sky, who was born in Louisiana and recorded for Vanguard. "One time," said Sky, "I remember telling John that we were going to a place that served 'soul food,' and he said, 'What is that?' Well, when we got there, the menu was filled with stuff like black-eyed peas and collard greens and he said, 'Down home, we just call it food.'"

Like all the other players, Sky was fascinated by Hurt's technique on the guitar. "The thing that made him a giant was the simplicity of the music," said Sky, "and it was a complicated simplicity. When you first hear it you think, that's simple, I can do that, but when you try, you go, 'Forget it.'" Hurt used his thumb to alternate between bass strings in a manner similar to one of country music's most famous guitarists, Merle Travis. The precision of his picking also distinguished him from the other rediscovered bluesmen. "Some of these old guys were hard to play with because they'd do things like playing a twelve-and-a-half-bar blues," said Sky. "But John was steady as a rock."

Hurt charmed the crowd at the 1963 Newport Folk Festival, was included on the live recording of the fest, and then signed to Vanguard Records. Founded in 1950 by Maynard and Seymour Solomon, Vanguard's initial focus was classical music, as Maynard had studied cello and piano. (In the 1960s, Seymour Solomon also ran the go-to Greenwich Village blues-rock club, the Café Au Go Go.) But after recording a successful live Weavers album in 1955, Vanguard increasingly looked to the folk field, and hit pay dirt with the queen of the early '60s scene, Joan Baez.

Hurt stayed in Sky's Greenwich Village apartment when in New York to cut his first Vanguard album, and preferred sleeping in an easy chair to a bed. Sky accepted Hurt's invitation to observe the first session at Vanguard's studio in the Manhattan Towers Hotel. "They had John sitting in this big room at a studio," said Sky, "with a bunch of people in the sound booth. John would try some songs, but he wasn't doing very good, so I walked over to Maynard Solomon and said, 'Do you want to get a good record out of John Hurt? Make me producer.' So the first thing I did as producer was to say, 'Now that I'm the producer, everybody get the fuck out.' So it was just John, the recording engineer, and me. I went outside, got a fifth of Jack Daniels, poured John a drink, we smoked some cigarettes, and it all came out pretty easily after that."

To record John Hurt, all you needed was one microphone for his voice, and another for his guitar. (For the sessions, Hurt played Stefan Grossman's Martin OM-45.) The bigger challenge was choosing songs from the repertoire of a lifetime that included country, pop, folk, and the blues. The obvious starting point was the songs he'd cut in 1928, but he'd now had decades to accumulate additional tunes. "There were some religious things that we decided not to do," said Sky, "and there were a whole bunch of tunes that were regular country songs. I encouraged him to stay closer to home. We went for things that had more of a stamp on it of his playing, his unique style."

Both as a live performer and recording artist, Hurt was more popular than the other rediscovered legends, Son House and Skip James. "He would always draw a good crowd," said musician and blues researcher David Evans. "I remember many times going to see Son House or Skip James and there'd be fifty people or less, often quite a bit less." By all accounts, Hurt was also the most emotionally balanced of the black blues musicians born of poverty who were now performing for white audiences of privilege. "John Hurt had some quality that allowed him to be remarkably free of baggage," said John Sebastian. "I looked at it as a kind of Buddha-like quality, and thought that maybe part of the anger built up in a virtuoso like Lightnin' [Hopkins] or some of the other greats was because they had more of their life invested in their playing. For John, it was something he could do at a party or a way to relax on the porch. It didn't have that self-absorption that performers tend to have. Maybe he had a little lighter dose of that, and a little heavier component of the family and the philosophical."

Jerry Ricks, a black musician, was Hurt's friend during those years. "He wasn't a professional musician and he didn't quit anything to do this," said Ricks. "He had no baggage and no frustrations and he didn't want anything. At big concerts, when introducing a song, he would often twist around the microphone and chat to the people in the front row as if he was sitting in their living room. Maybe that's just how he felt?"

Compared to the thornier personalities (and music) of Son House and Skip James, Hurt had a sly, grandfatherly presence that was somewhat at odds with the charged racial politics of the 1960s. "I remember asking him once whether he was going to vote," said Dick Spottswood. "This was 1964 and he was living in Washington, D.C. And John said, 'You know, if I voted for Mr. Johnson, Mr. Goldwater wouldn't like me, and if I voted for Mr. Goldwater, Mr. Johnson wouldn't like me. In other words, he was telling me, that's your all's business. And that's the way he lived in Mississippi for all those years." (When Spottswood asked James the same question, he got the reply: "I'm voting for Skip.")

It was the business side of Hurt's late-life career, a period during which he moved his wife, Jessie, and two grandchildren to D.C., that caught him unaware. Hurt's music was sweet and winsome, but his business affairs were a web of conflicting interests. The bottom line was the contract Hurt had signed with Tom Hoskins (in partnership with Spottswood and his wife, Louisa) that called for a fifty-fifty split of the money earned by Hurt between the guitar picker and their company, Music Research Incorporated. Albert Grossman, it's worth noting, settled for a 25 percent share of Bob Dylan's income.

Patrick Sky was incensed at Hurt's management deal. "I found out that he was only getting $100 or $150 to play the Gaslight [for multiple nights]," said Sky. "They'd make out the check to the manager, who'd take three-quarters of John's money and say it was because of the money it cost to be on the road. I remember going to Sam Hood at the Gaslight and told him, 'Sam, did you know that they're taking all his money?' So that night he paid John the money direct instead of giving it to the manager, and John almost choked; he'd never seen so much money."

Stories like these made for animated conversations over drinks at the Kettle of Fish. "John never had a bad word to say about anyone," said Dave Van Ronk, "not even people who really did deserve a few bad words. We were sitting around one night, and someone brought up the subject of Tom Hoskins, the guy who had rediscovered him . . . Naturally, we were filled with righteous indignation. . . . [Then] John said: 'Well, you know, if it weren't for Tom, I'd still be chopping cotton in Mississippi.' No way to argue with that."

The real drama wasn't at the Gaslight, but in the courts. "I'm not prepared to discuss any of the details of the legal wranglings between me and Hoskins," said Spottswood, "only that they existed. People who were involved with that are still alive and are kind of lawyer happy." After a few reversals of legal fortune, Spottswood lost his interest in Music Research Incorporated to Hoskins and Ed Denson. At that point, Hurt signed a two-record deal with Vanguard Records, with a guarantee of $2,000 per disc. Which, considering all of the lawsuits, is not exactly Rolling Stones money.

Dick Waterman was by now booking most of Hurt's live shows. After helping to rediscover Son House, Waterman had become his manager (with a handshake deal for 10 percent of House's income) and launched Avalon Productions, a talent agency named after a Hurt tune that handled House and other clients, including Hurt, Skip James, and Bukka White. Waterman's job was to book his musicians into coffeehouses, folk festivals, and every once in a while a college auditorium. "I had a small part of my bedroom with a desk," said Waterman of his Cambridge apartment. "That was my office. We couldn't afford phone calls. I had a manual Underwood typewriter, and I lived on coffee with my money going towards typewriter ribbons, stationary, and postage. And that's what I did all night. I wrote thousands and thousands of letters."

Inevitably, Hoskins and Waterman wound up competing for Hurt's loyalty. "Hoskins I found was an imperfect man," said Fred Bolden, Hurt's nephew, "but any mistakes he made were due to his lack of experience fishing in shark-infested waters. I believe my uncle knew this." Said Bolden of Waterman: "Uncle John and Skip [James] highly respected Dick as an honest man who always gave you a square deal right up front." Hurt nonetheless felt caught between the two men, and he and his family were never at ease living in Washington, D.C. "If this was someone's idea of placing him among his own kind so as to make him more comfortable," said Bolden, "well, it only brought the opposite effect."

Hurt and his family moved back to Mississippi in early 1966, where he turned seventy-four in March. "By all rights," said his wife, Jessie, "John went into this when he ought've been coming out." Three years after moving to Washington, D.C., Hurt bought a house in Granada, Mississippi. Later in the year, while hunting with friends, he suffered a stroke and died in a local hospital on November 2. The amiable guitar player was at peace, but his estate was a whole other story. Around 1970, Hoskins gave Gene Rosenthal the okay to produce a double-LP of Hurt music to be called *Memorial Anthology*. Before it came out, Vanguard released a 1971 double record called *The Best of Mississippi John Hurt*, which was actually a live recording of a 1965 concert at Oberlin College. Vanguard followed that collection with 1972's *Last Sessions*, which featured the remaining studio material produced by Patrick Sky.

After Rosenthal complained to Hoskins that these releases had soured the market for his album, they joined forces to sue Vanguard for issuing four Hurt collections when the agreement with Music Research Incorporated allowed the label to market just two records. The courts upheld the claim against Vanguard, resulting in a 1975 settlement of $297,000. After paying legal fees, Hoskins and Rosenthal each got $107,000. John Hurt had finally turned a serious profit.

But the dust still hadn't settled. In 1993, eleven years after the death of Hurt's wife, Jessie, it was discovered that he had never divorced his first wife, Gertrude, with whom he'd had three children. The courts rule in 1999 that Gertrude and the heirs of their deceased children (more than a dozen) were the rightful inheritors of Hurt's estate. The newly established estate promptly filed suit against Hoskins questioning the efficacy of his management and his share in the ongoing business of John Hurt.

In 2004, Hoskins was found to have a valid interest in Hurt's recordings created during the ten-year tenure of his management contract. But Hoskins was not around to celebrate; he had died in January of 2002 while living a reclusive life in a trailer park in Tallahassee, Florida. Hoskins, sixty-one, liked to drink, and his liver was failing; he died in a local hospital. Cleaning out his trailer, his sister discovered that her brother had been robbed. Gone was his Emory guitar, the instrument that Hurt had played when he first came to Washington and later used to charm the crowd at the Newport Folk Festival.

Lawsuits follow money (or the promise of same), which is why litigation didn't stalk the less lucrative late-life careers of Son House and Skip James. Both men were top-tier blues stars who nonetheless played music that was a little too intense for the coffeehouse crowd comfy with John Hurt. At the same time, their reappearance reaffirmed the historical significance of their Depression-era recordings.

"Cut to 1965," said Rory Block. "I am fifteen and Son [House] is sixty-three. Dick Waterman and Stefan Grossman talk in hushed tones in the background. Dick is trying to hide Son's whiskey bottle, Son is inquiring as to its whereabouts. I am playing a Willie Brown song and Son is asking 'Where did she learn to play like this?' Son House is thin and handsome. His eyes shine with the pain of someone who had recently been crying, or maybe coughing. There is a wildness in his demeanor—you have no idea all the places he has been and the things he's seen. . . . This is the man Robert Johnson idolized."

Johnson, in fact, played an ironic role in helping House become the only rediscovered bluesman to sign with a major label. Dick Waterman had met John Hammond at the Newport Folk Festival and arranged an appointment in New York in hopes of getting House a contract with Columbia Records. The meeting with House went well, with Hammond concluding that since he had always wanted to record Robert Johnson, he might as well make a deal with one of his heroes. Waterman took House to a nearby bar to celebrate his new recording contract, and he proposed a toast to Hammond. House, grasping his glass of bourbon, had another idea. "Here's to Robert Johnson," he said, "for being dead."

House was not exactly well versed in the world of show business. "I'm glad to be back playing now," he said in 1965. "At first I didn't feel like I should fool with it because my memory of all the old songs had gone from me. . . . But then I got to thinking about old man Louis Armstrong. Old Louis is older than I am, and he came back with the 'Dolly' song ["Hello

Dolly"]. Everybody's talking about Dolly, and I said, 'Jesus. If that old guy can come back, maybe I can!'" Armstrong, of course, was a singularly important figure in twentieth-century music that had never left the stage.

When House recorded 1965's *Father of the Delta Blues*, it was just shy of a quarter century since he'd sung into Alan Lomax's microphone. "House's recording session ran over a few days and saw the studio set up like a small club with an invited audience," said Lawrence Cohn, who produced the 1992 reissue that added additional tracks to the original release. "I remember John [Hammond] running around crazed, as was Son's manager, Dick Waterman (a man to whom House owed everything). Al Wilson of Canned Heat was seated alongside Son, and once the recording started occasionally played harp and guitar. He appeared to have a decidedly calming influence on House, who throughout would turn to him to discuss various things. Once things had begun Son was quite nervous, but ever so slowly, as time wore on, the emotional intensity of his performances transported one back to the Mississippi Delta c. 1930."

A Manhattan studio was a far cry from Mississippi, and House was playing for an audience that was not at all like those who patronized a Delta juke. But some things didn't change. House was forever caught between serving the Lord and playing the blues. He sang about it in one of his most famous songs, 1930's "Preachin' the Blues": "Oh, and I had religion, Lord, this very day. But the womens and whiskey, well, they would not let me pray."

For House, the whiskey was the true challenge. "He could not be left on his own all day," said Waterman. "There was an incredible amount of pressure that comes with being with someone who is a total alcoholic and is devious and is looking to find a way to get a bottle to get drunk. And it was up to me to safeguard the gig. . . . If he got out of your sight and found a bottle, there was no 'take a sip' or 'take a swig.' He would simply drink the entire bottle."

House was hardly the only blues musician with a taste for bottled liquor (if not moonshine); booze came with the territory. Roy Book Binder says that when he traveled with the Reverend Gary Davis, one of his jobs was to make sure that he didn't have too much to drink before a performance. "He liked the occasional shot of whiskey," said Book Binder, "and you'd have to be careful to intercept bottles that kids would try to pass along. Of course, I'd give him a glass. He'd say, 'Is there a phone call for me?' That was code for he wanted a drink. I'd go to the bartender and have him put a quarter inch of whiskey in the glass. And I'd come back and say, 'There's a call for you Reverend Davis.' And he'd say, 'Is it long distance or local?'

And I'd say, 'It looks like a local.' And he'd say, 'OK, let me see it.' I never let him get near a long distance call."

When Muddy Waters's doctor said that it was imperative that he quit drinking Chivas Regal, Muddy developed a taste for champagne. Jimmy Reed was a heavy drinker who could neither read nor write; when in the recording studio, he would often forget the words to his songs, which is why his wife would typically be on hand to feed him his lines. During the studio chatter that precedes Reed's "Baby What You Want Me To Do," you can hear the artist, wife, and producer debating the correct title of what would become one of his most famous songs.

House, however, was in a class of his own. "We had to kick him out of our dressing room," said Geoff Muldaur, speaking of a night in Rochester with the Kweskin Jug Band. "Can you imagine that? But he was really disruptive and I said, 'We've got to get this guy out of the dressing room so we can get ready for the show.' He just babbled when he drank; it was just pathetic." Yet House could still produce moments of artistic lucidity. "His head was thrown back," said Paul Oliver of a 1967 British performance, and "his eyes rolled under the lids and he sang loudly and forcefully in a manner that seemed inconceivable after his barely inaudible speech. 'Death Letter,' 'Levee Camp Moan,' 'Empire State Express'—the years rolled away and one was transported by the mesmeric rhythm of the guitar under the flailing fingers, the singing brass ring sliding on the strings and the powerful, musical voice."

If drink could make House unruly, Skip James was naturally ornery. James and John Fahey, who could be equally flinty, butted heads as soon as they met in a Mississippi hospital; Fahey and his comrades got James to D.C. after paying his medical and rent bill. "I bought Skip James for $200," said Fahey. The plan was for James to be as popular a blues revival attraction as John Hurt, but James had another motive for the trip to D.C. Doctors in the hospital had whispered the words "cancer" about his condition, but James was convinced that it was the result of a jealous girlfriend who had cast an evil hex. James had heard of a D.C. practitioner of folk medicine who he figured could break the spell.

"Skip James was dying when I met him," said Dick Spottswood. Months after his rediscovery, and right after his Newport Folk Festival debut, James was hospitalized in Washington, D.C. He wrote "Washington D.C. Hospital Center Blues" about the experience, and although released from the hospital, his medical issues went unresolved. It was during this time that Spottswood, who had lost his business interest in John Hurt, cultivated a professional relationship with James. Everybody, it seemed, wanted his own bluesman.

James was a different sort of performer than House or Hurt. House would lose himself in the music of his past, while Hurt brought a friendly, back-porch sensibility to the coffeehouse stage. James fancied himself a more sophisticated entertainer, and because he had performed a wide variety of songs for whites in the distant past, he mistakenly concluded that he should play more than just the blues that had led to his rediscovery. He was also unnerved by the quiet attention of the white bohemian audience. "Sometimes they look at me," said James, "like I was I don't know what—a bear or somethin.'"

James was generally disdainful of the blues fanatics who populated the revival circuit. "Why don't you take a bath?" he asked Alan Wilson after he'd played a song backstage at Newport in 1964. "You know you ought to lose some weight. You can't play the blues unless you stay in shape." James also dissed such other revival regulars as Stefan Grossman and his girlfriend, Rory Block, whom James once called a "tackhead" (meaning, "brainless female").

But like Hurt and House, James carried the allure of history. Songs like "Devil Got My Woman" and "Special Rider Blues" were as idiosyncratic as blues songs could be, with intricate, minor key guitar lines offering unique support for his haunting falsetto voice. "I'd rather be the Devil," sang James, "than to be that woman's man." Given the notion James had over the cause of his illness, it's little wonder that he would see Satan as a safer bet than a woman.

At the start of 1965, while playing at Ontario Place, James would slip into the men's room and scrutinize the tumor that was disfiguring his penis. "Heap of time I'll be playin'," said James, "I'll be sittin' on stage in misery." He spent $265 on treatments by the native healer, but his health only worsened. He was finally admitted to D.C. General Hospital where it was established that the tumor on his penis was indeed cancerous. Doctors saw only one potential solution—Skip James went under the knife, and was castrated.

Around this time, Spottswood encouraged James to sign a publishing deal with Pete Kuykendall, who then proceeded to copyright all of the songs from the original 1931 Paramount sessions. At the time James first recorded, songs weren't always copyrighted as their future value was thought to be negligible. Such was the case with the songs of Robert Johnson. For Skip James, the lack of such rights would mean that he would have no way to earn publishing money when and if his material was recorded. James's copyrights would prove especially profitable when a tune he recorded in 1931 called "I'm So Glad" was included on the debut album of the British rock trio Cream.

James rerecorded his early songs on a pair of albums (*Today!* and *Devil Got My Woman*) that he made for Vanguard Records. The sessions were produced by label chief Maynard Solomon, who in later years would write biographies of Beethoven and Mozart. "They all developed something special at a single moment of their lives," said Solomon of performers like James and John Hurt, "and they didn't grow beyond that, because what they developed was *them*. That was very true of Skip James."

James, Hurt, and House were not just seen as out-of-time artists by their young white audience, but they also came from a different world than the middle-aged bluesmen that'd been gigging for decades. House was once on a bill with Muddy Waters at Carnegie Hall. Backstage before the show, a member of Muddy's band imitated House's gangly gait. According to Dick Waterman, Waters was quick to scold the musician, saying, "Don't you be mocking that man. When I was a boy comin' up, that man was king. King! If it wasn't for that man, you wouldn't have a job. If it wasn't for that man, I wouldn't be here now."

At the 1966 Newport Folk Festival, Alan Lomax arranged to film a number of the artists, including House and James, performing in a setting dressed to resemble a juke joint, complete with small bags of chips hanging on a rack. "Pro-Tec-Tive Club," read a sign on the wall. "Members only." James had gained weight since his operation, but still looked as if he could be blown over by a breeze as he sat on a square-back chair and pulled the notes of "Devil Got My Woman" out of his guitar. Typical of his performances in the '60s, his featherweight voice was truer to his song than his relatively sketchy accompaniment on guitar. Gathered around him are a group of middle-aged black men, including an imposing figure in a white shirt, a businessman's tie, and black-rimmed glasses: Howlin' Wolf. It's not known whether Wolf ever met James back in their Delta days, though he might have recognized that his haunted blues had an influence on the music of Robert Johnson.

Son House also performed at Lomax's faux juke, and by all appearances, had already taken full advantage of the open bar. Playing a slightly out-of-tune National guitar, House punctuated "Forever on My Mind" with long, woozy swipes of his guitar strings with the metal slide on his left pinky. He shook his head from side to side during the song's pregnant pauses, as if waiting for a cue to continue. It's not a terrible performance as much as one that suggested how dreadful House could be when he really hit the bottle.

House's tune, however, is nowhere near as memorable as his filmed interaction with Howlin' Wolf. Wolf was the clear musical star of the show, with Hubert Sumlin's crackling guitar animating the band as they tore through "Dust My Broom" and "How Many More Years." Wolf is playful between songs, licking his harmonica with lascivious glee, and then chuckling with playful self-awareness. It's during his introduction to "Meet Me in the Bottom" that the camera catches Son House leaning against the bar. He's surrounded by darkness, but easy to identify through the drape of his signature bow tie and the glimmer of light reflected off the metal filling of a tooth.

Wolf sat in a chair and ruminated about the meaning of the blues. "This man got the blues right there," said Wolf, motioning toward House. "See that's where the blues come from. Because he just drank up all of his." House responds, but is inaudible. "You see," said Wolf, "you had a chance with your life, but you ain't done nothing with it. See? And you've got to have the blues." House muttered in protest, trying to offer a defense. "We ain't talking about the womens," said Wolf, "we're talking about the life of a human being. See, now you don't love but one thing, and that's the whiskey. And that's plum out of it." As House incoherently objects, Wolf begins to play his guitar.

In his youth, back in the Delta, Wolf had jockeyed for the chance to accompany House with his harmonica. But that was before he conquered Memphis, Chicago, and the rest of the blues-loving world. House emerged from obscurity to find himself in a strange new environment, and some might have presumed that alcohol was simply an escape. But Wolf was wiser; he knew that the roots of the sadness he saw in House and Skip James were sunk in the soil of Mississippi. Wolf had done his best to leave that behind when he struck out for Memphis. By that time, House and James had both abandoned music, and while they might say otherwise, had let something inside of them die.

For their young fans, the bluesmen offered a cautionary tale. "The Lomax film showed House for what he was," said Geoff Muldaur. "He had his chance. And here you have Howlin' Wolf telling him, 'You could have been the man.' Look at how good-looking he was! Look at his talent! It's the classic case of a failure drunk. We all worshipped that stuff, but it was the part of being a blues guy I never wanted. It was sad, and it also showed how Wolf was so unbelievably intelligent. If he had grown up in a different neighborhood, somebody would have taken him in a different direction.

He could have been like Paul Robeson, a giant of the stage. To me, he had an electricity in the size, the eyes, the intelligence, and the power of that person." If Muldaur's critique of House seems unduly harsh, he speaks from experience; in the early 1980s, he left the music business for fifteen years in a successful attempt to give up drinking.

In the late '60s, life offered diminishing returns for James and House. James never achieved the popularity of John Hurt, whose talents he dismissed; ironically, James abandoned his wife in D.C. and moved to Philadelphia to live with Hurt's step niece. But his health problems lingered; in late 1968, he entered the University of Pennsylvania hospital, where it was determined that he had inoperable cancer. He was sent home to die without taking further treatments. Once more, he addressed the conflict between singing the blues and praising the Lord. "If it please the Lord to restore my health," he said, "I ain't studyin' no more blues whatsoever." James died on October 3, 1969. The money for his medical expenses and burial came from the publishing royalties from Cream's version of "I'm So Glad." Decades later, his heirs would enjoy a fiscal windfall when a cover of his "Hard Time Killing Floor Blues" was included in the hit soundtrack to *O Brother, Where Art Thou?*

Son House performed sporadically through the late '60s, and his shows could be either sad or sublime. One night in 1970, he was discovered passed out in a Rochester snow bank. House was taken to the hospital and treated for exposure and frostbite; his fingers were never quite the same. Around that time, in the early 1970s, Woody Mann, who'd studied guitar with Gary Davis, met House at the home of one of the men who'd found him in Rochester, Yazoo Records owner Nick Perls.

"When I met him, he kind of had the DTs," said Mann. "He was sitting on the couch, and I'd start playing one of his songs and he'd recognize it, and he'd start singing along. Even in that condition, his voice was incredibly loud. I was banging at this National guitar just so it could be heard. We'd get into a tune, but then he'd kind of just drift off. He kept saying, 'I want to go back to Rochester.' I couldn't believe he continued to live for so long. When I met him, I thought there was no way he was going to last out the week."

House gave his last public performance at the Toronto Island Blues Festival in 1974. Two years later, his failing mental state, later diagnosed as the result of both Alzheimer's and Parkinson's disease, prompted his wife, Evie, to move with him to Detroit, where her three children could help with his care. He was eventually moved into a nursing home. Blues fans would occasionally pay him a visit, and sometimes bring a guitar, but House could no longer play, let alone sing. His condition deteriorated until in October of 1988, he died of cancer of the larynx at the age of eighty-six. Smoking had killed House before the booze could put him under. Son House was buried in Detroit's Mt. Hazel Cemetery; his gravestone bears an etching of him playing his National guitar.

House's long, lonely decline gave his intimates time to consider the ramifications of his musical revival. "I'm half inclined to say that if I had to do it all over again, I wouldn't do it," said Phil Spiro, who along with Perls and Waterman, was on that long-ago search through the Delta that led to Rochester. "What did we give them? For the ones who had recorded before, like Son and Skip and Bukka [White], we kept comparing them to their younger selves, and they knew it."

"We also consciously or unconsciously tried to shape the music they played on stage. The same statement could be made for the guys running Paramount during the thirties, but at least their motive was simple profit, which motive the artist shared. Our motivation was a strange combination of ego, scholasticism, and power. . . . In general, we were collectors of people, who we tended to treat as if they were the very rarest of records—only one copy known to exist."

NINE THE CREAM OF (MOSTLY) BRITISH BLUES

When Eric Clapton got together with bassist Jack Bruce and drummer Ginger Baker to form Cream, he figured that the trio would be like the group led by one of his favorite guitar players, Buddy Guy. Those early rehearsals in July of 1966 included Guy's "First Time I Met the Blues" and "Hey Lawdy Mama," a tune from *Hoodoo Man Blues*, the influential album Guy made with Junior Wells.

Clapton and Guy had the blues in common, but operated in worlds that were as different as Chicago, Illinois, and London, England. *Hoodoo Man Blues* was recorded in 1965 for Chicago's Delmark Records in two sessions, totaling seven hours, that essentially documented the live set that singer-harpist Wells played three nights a week at Theresa's, a basement blues bar on the South Side. Where most blues albums used studio musicians and aimed to craft a hit single, *Hoodoo Man Blues* sought to simply reflect the group's live act. Guy worked by day as an auto mechanic; when he was signed to Vanguard Records with a $1,400 advance, he bought himself a Cadillac.

Jimi Hendrix 1942–1970

Cream made its official debut on July 31, 1966, before a crowd of 20,000 at Britain's 6th National Jazz & Blues Festival. Robert Stigwood, whose other primary client was the Bee Gees, managed the group. Cream signed a five-year recording contract with the Reaction label for a reported 50,000 pounds (more than $150,000). In the United States, Cream was signed to Atlantic Records, where label head Ahmet Ertegun was determined to make a star out of the man he considered Cream's chief asset, Eric Clapton. "[We] are tired of having talent that doesn't make any big money," said Clapton, who was twenty-one years old. "Personally, I'd like some big money. I've lived in dingy rooms long enough. I've given all I've had to make music. Now I want something back."

Having become a star with John Mayall's Bluesbreakers, it was his time with Cream that truly defined Clapton's status as a guitar hero. He'd left Mayall's band just as the "Beano" album was released; years later, he would call it one of his proudest accomplishments. "I think the John Mayall album is very powerful," said Clapton, "because I had a definite rebel stance about the whole thing. I was on top of my craft, and I was absolutely confident, and I didn't give a shit about what anyone thought."

Mayall has played the blues for half a century, but his renown has been forever linked to the extraordinary trio of guitarists he recruited for the Bluesbreakers in the 1960s: Eric Clapton, Peter Green, and Mick Taylor. It's the same power-of-three that made the Yardbirds famous for its guitar-playing alumni: Clapton, Jeff Beck, and Jimmy Page. The fact that these blues-rock guitarists became rock stars also had a profound impact on public perception of the blues.

"They got all these white kids now," said Muddy Waters. "Some of them can play good blues. They play so much, run a ring around you playin' guitar, but they cannot vocal like the black man." Waters was certainly painting with a broad brush, but it's true that the image of the guitar hero embodied by players like Clapton and Mike Bloomfield influenced what many white fans looked for in the blues. Among black listeners, B.B. King was known as much for his vocals as his guitar playing, but it was his instrumental skills that eventually attracted the white audience. Conversely, giants like Waters and Howlin' Wolf were instrumentalists supported by great players, but their enduring fame was insured by their deeply moving vocals.

Clapton's notion that Cream would be like Buddy Guy's trio went out the window as soon as he started playing with his new band mates: Jack Bruce, with whom he'd briefly performed in the Bluesbreakers, and Ginger Baker, a jazz-influenced drummer who'd been in the Graham Bond Organization.

"The blues is the basis of everything I do," said Bruce, "but I think Eric thought I was disrespectful about blues music, in the sense that a lot of the British bands would cover blues songs note for note, virtually. But for me, I thought the important thing about the blues is the feeling."

Cream's vision of the blues was expansive, with Willie Dixon's "Spoonful" quickly turning into a twenty-minute jam session. Another constant on Cream's set list was "Toad," a brief guitar instrumental that framed a lengthy drum solo by Ginger Baker. Jack Bruce, who played bass as if it were a lead instrument, also took a long harmonica turn on "Train Time." By featuring such extended improvisations, Cream could sometimes seem like three soloists who just so happened to be in the same group.

Cream's U.S. debut came as a minor attraction within New York deejay Murray the K's package show, "Music in the Fifth Dimension." Cream typically played just "I Feel Free," the single from the group's debut album, *Fresh Cream*. They were offered significantly more freedom when they played two six-day stints at the Fillmore West, sharing a bill the first week with the Butterfield Blues Band, and then the Electric Flag. San Francisco proved to be a whole new trip for Cream.

"This is where we started openly exploring our potential," said Clapton. "We started doing extended solos, and were soon playing fewer and fewer songs but for much longer. We'd go off in our own directions, then hit these coincidental points in the music when we would all arrive at the same conclusion, be it a riff or a chord or just an idea, and we would jam on it for a little while and then go back into our own thing."

Cream became famous for its lengthy jams, but nobody would mistake the trio's thunderous roar for the harmonically sophisticated improvised music played by the groups of jazz masters like Miles Davis or John Coltrane. Similarly, it was a far cry from the extended blues jams of somebody like Muddy Waters, who might add an extra chorus or two to a song like "I Got My Mojo Working," but who made sure his musicians stuck to the tune. By contrast, the sound of Cream was loud and rocking and perfect for a ballroom full of stoned hippies. At the end of their Fillmore engagement, Bill Graham gave the three musicians of Cream gold watches.

The trio's combustible music reflected the personal friction between the players. Derek Taylor, who'd done public relations for the Beatles, accompanied Cream on their first trip to California. "It was the most amazing week I have ever spent," said Taylor, "because they hated each other's guts and would spark one another off all the time. . . . Eric Clapton would play a great break and you could see Jack Bruce thinking, 'OK, I can top that.' . . .

Although I had seen friction in The Beatles, I never witnessed a direct row between John and Paul, so this was mind blowing."

Cream became stars on the concert stage, but it took a little time to capture their act on record. *Fresh Cream* split the difference between rock and blues by mixing original songs by Bruce and Baker with covers of tunes by Muddy Waters ("Rollin' and Tumblin'"), Robert Johnson ("Four until Late"), and Skip James ("I'm So Glad"). By contrast, Cream's second album, *Disraeli Gears*, which was mostly recorded at Atlantic's New York studios, was a rock album that just so happened to be informed by the blues.

Disraeli Gears arrived in 1967 at the peak of the psychedelic age and made Cream rock stars. Unlike Buddy Guy, the band didn't make ends meet working at a garage. Instead, their days were filled with photo shoots, interviews, recording sessions, and special broadcasts on radio and television. It was a well-financed, full-time job. The Fool, a Dutch graphic-arts duo that had given John Lennon's Rolls Royce a psychedelic paint job, also decorated Clapton's Gibson SG guitar with lysergic designs. "Two pressing questions before Cream's concert yesterday," said a Swedish writer. "What happened to their music and how does guitar star Eric Clapton wear his hair?"

Disraeli Gears introduced Cream to two significant collaborators: producer Felix Pappalardi and engineer Tom Dowd. "On the first night," said Clapton, "he [Pappalardi] took home with him the tape we had previously recorded of 'Lawdy Mama,' which was a standard twelve-bar blues, and came back the next day having transformed it into a kind of McCartney-esque pop song, complete with new lyrics and the title 'Strange Brew.'" After working with Cream, Pappalardi would form a successful blues-rock group called Mountain with guitarist Leslie West. In 1983, he was shot and killed by his wife, Gail Collins, who'd written the words to "Strange Brew."

Tom Dowd, who would work on many subsequent Clapton records, was a gifted engineer who put depth and crunch into the sound of *Disraeli Gears*. Clapton's guitar sound was also colored by his use of distortion devices such as the fuzz box and the wah-wah pedal, an oscillating, tone-altering tool that he used to famous effect on "Tales of Brave Ulysses." Still, in form if not exactly sound, a song like "Sunshine of Your Love" was built on a guitar lick and chord progression born of the blues, albeit enriched by Baker's funk-inspired drum pattern. And "Outside Woman Blues," sung by Clapton, was a faithful update of a 1929 Paramount release by Blind Joe Reynolds.

Shortly before the release of *Disraeli Gears*, Cream headlined the 7th National Jazz Pop Ballads & Blues Festival, where only a year earlier the band had made its official debut. The 1967 bill also included the first high-profile appearance of Fleetwood Mac, a new band led by the guitarist who'd replaced Clapton in the Bluesbreakers, Peter Green. "Peter and me," said Stan Webb, guitarist for the blues-rock band Chicken Shack, "were [backstage and] talking about the price of beer—Peter was wearing a white T-shirt and blue jeans—and Eric turned up and came over to us wearing a bed spread, rings on every finger, his frizzy hair sticking out six inches, and said to Peter: 'Pete, you'll never be a star if you dress like that.' Peter just smiled. And that sums it up."

When Peter Green joined the Bluesbreakers, John Mayall gave him a copy of the just-released album that he'd recorded with Eric Clapton so that his new guitarist could learn his predecessor's solos. Green initially struggled to cope with the comparisons to Clapton, but also found a musical mentor in Mayall, and lived for a time with the band leader. "We spent a lot of our free time talking and listening to blues," said Mayall. "I'd been collecting for about ten or fifteen years prior to that—78s and stuff—and Peter more or less wanted to hear everything."

Green's parents had shortened their Greenbaum surname when he was a child. "I remember one time . . . he sobbed as he talked about how painful it was as a little boy being Jewish," said Sandra Elsdon-Vigon, a model who was Green's steady girlfriend when he played with the Bluesbreakers. "He was teased and taunted and quite obviously the scars were still there. I could see then and there how he had absorbed the resentment shown towards his family. And to me those are Peter's blues: the blues to him are Jewish blues."

Bluesbreakers drummer Mick Fleetwood had met Green when they'd both played in a group called Peter B's Looners. "He went immediately for the human touch," said Fleetwood, "and that's what Peter's playing has represented to millions of people: he played with the human, not the superstar touch." The drummer also praised Mayall for teaching Fleetwood and bassist John McVie a valuable musical lesson. "He knew and certainly taught me," said Fleetwood, "that in a good band it's as if each musician plays vicariously through the others. In the short time John McVie and me were together in the Bluesbreakers, that's exactly the attitude he encourage in us: to be a solid backdrop." So was born a world-class rhythm section that would last more than forty years.

Two months after Green joined the Bluesbreakers, the band entered the studio. Producer Mike Vernon and engineer Gus Dudgeon were reportedly surprised at the absence of Clapton. "I was in a shocked state," said Vernon, "but John said, 'Don't worry, we've got someone better.' I said, 'Wait a minute; you've got someone better than Eric Clapton? . . . Then John said, 'He might not be better now, but you wait, in a couple of years he's going to be the best.'"

Green made only one full album with Mayall, *A Hard Road* (1967), and the repertoire consisted of originals and blues covers, including the Otis Rush title tune and both a Freddie King instrumental ("The Stumble") and vocal song ("Someday after a While (You'll Be Sorry)"). Green contributed an eloquent instrumental called "The Supernatural" that was keynoted by reverberating guitar lines that seemed to float in the air. Mayall also encouraged Green to sing his song "The Same Way"—he vocalized with the same stylish restraint that was evident in his guitar playing—and to write more tunes.

"He [Mayall] said that if you really like something, you should take the first lines and make up another song from them," said Green. "So that's what I did with 'Black Magic Woman' [inspired by Otis Rush's "All Your Loving"]. But then it turned out something more like B.B. King's 'Help the Poor.'" Green was no doubt crazy for *Live at the Regal*, and some of his sweetest guitar licks bore King's fingerprints. "The guy who really turns me on is B.B. King," said Green, who traveled to Paris to catch one of his shows. "He's the only modern blues player who really moves me."

When Mayall gave Green a birthday gift of studio time, he got Fleetwood and McVie to help him cut some instrumentals. Green thought that one particularly propulsive shuffle sounded like a train, and he named it after his rhythm section: "Fleetwood Mac." "From then on," said Mayall, "I guess it was a matter of time." Green's original plan upon leaving the Bluesbreakers was to move to Chicago and play guitar with the local bands. That didn't happen, so he formed a group with the encouragement of producer Mike Vernon. The plan was to form a trio like (who else?) Buddy Guy, and Mick Fleetwood, recently dumped from the Bluesbreakers, signed on to play drums. One bass player later, McVie, who was unhappy over Mayall's jazzy inclinations, joined Fleetwood Mac.

Naming the band after its rhythm section suggested that Green was wary of assuming the mantle of the guitar hero, having already suffered under the shadow of Clapton; Green had also been turned off by with the egocentric evolution of Cream. That's why he agreed to Vernon's suggestion to add Jeremy Spencer to the band. Spencer played slide guitar and was a master mimic of Elmore James, whose musical style was defined by his electrifying remake of Robert Johnson's "Dust My Broom." The combination of Green and Spencer would give Fleetwood Mac a somewhat schizophrenic blend of Spencer's up-tempo blues and vintage rock 'n' roll with Green's subtler style of blues and rock. Spencer, who was typically absent from the studio when Green recorded his songs, was himself something of a split personality; he would bring a pink sixteen-inch dildo named "Harold" onto the stage while he performed, but also had a Bible sewn into the lining of his coat.

Fleetwood Mac toured Britain in a van during the fall of 1967; returning to London in the wee hours, Vernon used his key to sneak the band into Decca's studio. Green had agreed to record for Vernon's new label, Blue Horizon, and these sessions created the demos that got the label a distribution deal with CBS. The band's debut, *Fleetwood Mac*, released in February of 1968, contained original songs and covers of tunes by Howlin' Wolf ("No Place to Go"), Sonny Boy Williamson ("Got to Move"), Elmore James ("Shake Your Moneymaker"), and Robert Johnson ("Hellhound on My Trail").

Vernon also hired Green and the rhythm section to spend a day cutting an album with pianist Eddie Boyd, a blues veteran who'd given Muddy Waters one of his first Chicago gigs in the late 1940s, and who'd lately relocated to Europe. The nonchalant ease with which the trio backed Boyd testified to Fleetwood Mac's authentic approach to the blues. Where the players of Cream bounced off each other, the men of Mac cohered. The pianist was impressed by Green's sure, subtle touch on the guitar. "Peter's a great bluesman," said Boyd. "He's a negro turned inside out."

Since Spencer was often lost to the Bible, pot, and Elmore James, Green enlisted another guitar foil, Danny Kirwan, a skinny eighteen-year-old guitarist with shoulder-length blonde hair. He made a dramatic first impression on Mac's second album, *English Rose*, with the jaunty instrumental, "Jigsaw Puzzle Blues," and a powerful blues, "Something Inside of Me." Vernon and Green also experimented with microphone placement to capture the raucous, live sound of "Stop Messing Around," with horns and piano anchoring a hard-swinging blues that would have surely rocked the dance floor at Theresa's.

English Rose also had Fleetwood Mac's first famous songs, "Black Magic Woman" and "Albatross." Guitarist Carlos Santana scored an enduring hit when his band covered "Black Magic Woman," and Green's economical guitar style left a lasting impression on Santana. "Albatross," an elegantly polished instrumental that evoked ocean waves at low tide, had almost nothing to do with the blues; it was a dud when first released as a single, but became a number 1 hit after it was used as incidental music on BBC television.

Forty-plus years later, *Fleetwood Mac* and *English Rose* sound as fresh and vital as when they were released and sit comfortably alongside Junior Wells and Buddy Guy's *Hoodoo Man Blues*. They also represent the pinnacle of British blues and are just as good as the thrilling trio of albums John Mayall made with Clapton, Green, and the gifted guitarist who replaced him, Mick Taylor (heard on *Crusade*). Where Cream could play a succinct blues, they were more inclined to transform a song into a cacophonous roar. By contrast, Fleetwood Mac offered superior vocals, and played with the subtle balance of a true Chicago blues band.

The fact that Green had replaced Clapton in the Bluesbreakers was enough to generate a buzz about Fleetwood Mac in the musical underground. The group first came to the United States in May of 1968; landing in San Francisco, they were met at the airport by an entourage that included Jerry Garcia and Phil Lesh of the Grateful Dead. A long strange trip was about to begin. "We got quite friendly with the Grateful Dead . . . and even let their rambling, jamming acidic style rub off on us," said Mick Fleetwood. "The Dead took good care of Fleetwood Mac, keeping us high, occasionally putting us up in their Haight-Ashbury house, and getting us gigs. We were good friends with their soundman, Augustus Owsley Stanley III, who was always urging us to try some of the superior LSD-25 he was alchemizing. Being nice little English boys at the time, we politely thanked him and said no."

"I will never forget returning to London after recording *Disraeli Gears*," said Eric Clapton, "with all of us excited by the fact that we had made what we considered to be a groundbreaking album, a magical combination of blues, rock, and jazz. Unfortunately for us, Jimi [Hendrix] had just released *Are You Experienced?*, and that was all anyone wanted to listen to. . . . I thought we had made our definitive album, only to come home and find that nobody was interested."

Clapton, who'd first met Hendrix shortly after his arrival in Britain in the fall of 1966, protests too much but also speaks the truth: Jimi Hendrix was an extraordinary talent in an irresistible package; a slim black hippie from Greenwich Village who could squeeze a universe of sounds out of his Fender Stratocaster, especially after he plugged it into a powerful Marshall

100-watt "stack." Like Albert King, Hendrix was a southpaw who played his right-handed guitar upside-down. With his amp and instrument cranked up to the limit, his guitar was quite literally alive to the touch of his long fingers, whether he was picking out a lead line, scratching out a rhythm, manipulating the tremolo bar, or literally striking the Stratocaster to create blasts of perfectly controlled feedback. In his hands, a guitar pick scraped across muffled strings could create a dramatic, even violent impact.

Johnny Allen Hendrix was born in 1942 in Seattle, Washington. One of two sons, he was raised by his father (with the help of relatives) after his parents divorced when he was eight; as a child, his name was legally changed to James Marshall Hendrix. Enlisting in the 101st Airborne as a paratrooper, he was mocked by his mates for his devotion to the guitar he'd played throughout high school. Upon discharge, he found work on the chitlin circuit playing behind acts like Little Richard, the Isley Brothers, and King Curtis. He also played with a club band called Curtis Knight and the Squires, and signed an exclusive recording contract (for an advance of $1) that would come back to haunt him.

Perpetually broke and musically frustrated, Hendrix moved to Greenwich Village and tried singing after figuring that he could do it at least as well as Bob Dylan. In the Village, he was in the uncomfortable position of being a young black man playing the blues alongside the white folkies and the rediscovered bluesmen. He formed a group called Jimmy James and the Blue Flames and played the Café Wha!, a so-called "basket house" that paid the performers by whatever was raised passing the hat. When John Hammond Jr. caught his act, he hired Hendrix and his band to back him on a two-week run at the more upscale Café Au Go Go. During the late shows, Hammond would let Hendrix strut his stuff on a version of Bo Diddley's "I'm a Man." (The Diddley song borrowed its repeated riff and declamatory vocal from Muddy Waters's "Hoochie Coochie Man"; Waters would subsequently turn the Diddley song into his own "Mannish Boy.")

Enter Chas Chandler, a British musician who played bass in the often-bluesy Animals and was looking to become a manager. After acting on a tip from Keith Richards's girlfriend Linda Keith to catch Hendrix's act, Chandler convinced him to try his luck in England. Hendrix figured it couldn't be worse than starving in the Village; he packed his Stratocaster along with a change of clothes and arrived in London in September 1966. On the plane ride, he and Chandler decided he would spell his name "Jimi." A week later, Jimi Hendrix sat in with Cream at one of the trio's earliest shows. "The song Jimi wanted to play was by Howlin' Wolf, entitled 'Killing Floor,'" said Clapton. "I thought it was incredible that he would know how to play this, as it was a tough one to get right. Of course Jimi played it exactly like it ought to be played, and he totally blew me away." A few weeks after playing with Cream, Hendrix sat in with John Mayall's Bluesbreakers, borrowing Mick Taylor's Les Paul and flipping it upside-down.

Auditions were held for musicians to back Hendrix, and while cosmetics were hardly the deciding factors, it didn't hurt that Mitch Mitchell and Noel Redding had elfin, curly-haired looks that complemented the exotic black man from America. Musically, the choices were significant. Redding was a guitarist who tried out on bass, which allowed Hendrix to essentially mold his playing to fit his needs. Mitchell, on the other hand, was a highly developed drummer who could not only rock hard, but also attack his kit with the skill and abandon of a jazz player like Elvin Jones.

The newly christened Jimi Hendrix Experience would become famous as avatars of psychedelic rock, but one of the first numbers the trio rehearsed was "Red House," a showcase for Hendrix's virtuosic touch on a slow blues. The fact that the song would often grace the band's set list underscored the fact that while Hendrix had a voracious musical appetite, his roots were deep in the blues. "In his playing," said Mike Bloomfield, "I can really hear Curtis Mayfield, Wes Montgomery, Albert King. B.B. King, and Muddy Waters. Jimi is the blackest guitarist I've ever heard. His music is deeply rooted in pre-blues, the oldest musical forms like field hollers and gospel melodies. From what I can garner, there was no form of black music that he hadn't listened to or studied."

As the Jimi Hendrix Experience started recording its first album and touring England, people couldn't help but notice how the outrageously clad black man stood out in the white world of British rock. "There was a tremendous sense of him choosing to play in the white arena," said Pete Townshend of the Who, "that he was coming along and saying, 'You've taken this, Eric Clapton, and Mr. Townshend, you think you're a showman? This is how we can do it when we take back what you've borrowed, if not stolen.'"

Statements regarding race can sound particularly tortured in retrospect, especially as in the mid-1960s there were relatively few black people living in England. To wit: "You know English people have a very big thing towards a spade," said Clapton to *Rolling Stone* in 1968. "They really love that magic thing. . . . Everybody and his brother in England still sort of think that spades have big dicks. And Jimi came over and exploited that to the limit." Sometimes, however, a guitar is just a guitar.

Hendrix released three singles while recording his debut album, all of which were British hits and subsequently included in the American release of *Are You Experienced?*: "Hey Joe," "Purple Haze," and "The Wind Cries Mary." Hendrix had been playing "Hey Joe" since his days in the Village; the song of an ill-fated romance that ends in murder was a minor hit for a West Coast band called the Leaves, though Hendrix modeled his version after that of folk singer Tim Rose. "Purple Haze" was built on an epochal two-note riff that employed a flatted-fifth note. Given the role of Satan in blues lore, it's worth noting that during the Spanish Inquisition, composers of religious music were banned from employing this tonal gap, the so-called "devil's interval." "The Wind Cries Mary" was a lovely ballad that, like a later song, "Little Wing," showed that the sultan of psychedelic sounds could also caress guitar strings with a singular sweetness.

Two songs on Hendrix's first album defined the expansive nature of his musical imagination: "Third Stone from the Sun" and "Are You Experienced?" Both songs exploit feedback, with Hendrix using extreme volume to create a wild variety of licks and harmonic twists. "Third Stone" is built on a graceful groove upon which Hendrix plays a melody using octaves in the manner of the influential jazz guitarist Wes Montgomery; elsewhere, waves of spacey sounds push the song to the edge of free jazz. "Are You Experienced?" paints with a similarly wide palette of guitar sounds, but the rhythmic pulse is embedded in the blues, with the muscular, abrasive guitar riff that opens the song emphasizing the highly physical nature of Hendrix's playing.

Are You Experienced? was produced by Chas Chandler, whose primary influence was to encourage Hendrix to keep his tunes to a short, pop-friendly length. Chandler also hired engineer Eddie Kramer to mix the album; Kramer would subsequently be Hendrix's right-hand man in the recording studio. Another important part of the team was Roger Mayer, an electrical engineer who'd built fuzz boxes for Jimmy Page and Jeff Beck, and who created a variety of innovative guitar effects for Hendrix. Chandler also enlisted Mike Jeffery, who'd handled the business affairs of the Animals, to help manage Hendrix. Hendrix's British record deal was with Track Records, which was owned by the managers of the Who. ("I felt threatened," said Pete Townshend, "because I thought, 'Oh God, Kit Lambert has found another guitar player.' He was my Svengali, and he'd found someone else.") In the United States, the band was signed to Warner Brothers with a $150,000 advance. Like many musicians, Hendrix signed contracts with good faith and little understanding. Before long, the financial side of his career would become a legal and fiscal nightmare.

The Jimi Hendrix Experience played the Monterey Pop Festival around the time *Are You Experienced?* was released in the United States. The relatively unknown group got the prestigious booking at the recommendation of Paul McCartney, who was on the festival's board of governors. On the night that Hendrix famously lit his Stratocaster on fire, he and the Experience were introduced to the crowd by Brian Jones of the Rolling Stones. Immediately after his star-making performance at Monterey, Hendrix went to San Francisco to play six nights (two shows per) at the Fillmore West. The original plan was for them to open shows headlined by Jefferson Airplane, but the Bay Area group bailed out after the first night, unable to follow the incendiary guitarist. Bill Graham rewarded his newest stars with a $2,000 bonus and gave them each an antique watch. Less than two years after leaving Greenwich Village as an unknown, Jimi Hendrix had returned to America a star.

Cream was ready to break up almost as soon as it formed. Baker and Bruce had a toxic relationship owing to the fact that the drummer had gotten the bassist fired from the Graham Bond Organization. Clapton, the most famous of the three, acted as the principal mediator. Success helped to paper over the problems. "We are the first group to do what we are doing in America, to go on stage and just improvise," said Bruce, conveniently ignoring the history of jazz. "It works for us because all three of us have got something to say. . . . All of us are leaders of the group."

The popularity of Cream's stage show kept them on the road so much that studio work became something of an afterthought. Cream's third album, *Wheels of Fire*, was a double LP, with one recorded in the studio, and the other cut live. The concert tracks were recorded in San Francisco over three nights (six shows), and while the jacket says "Live at the Fillmore," it was actually captured at the larger Winterland. The highlight of the live set was "Crossroads," a version of Robert Johnson's "Cross Road Blues" which Clapton sang while his lead guitar exploded atop the roiling rhythm section. It didn't hurt that "Crossroads" clocked in at a succinct 4:13 compared to the 16:44 accorded to "Spoonful."

"The way I've always looked upon any interpretation of a great blues musician's material was to take the most obvious things and simplify them," said Clapton. "Like my way of doing 'Crossroads' was to take one musical figure and make that the point, the focal point. Just trying to focus on what the essence of the song was—keeping it simple." It was a lesson that was sometimes lost in the virtuosic thunder of Cream.

While in New York to record the studio tracks for *Wheels of Fire*, Clapton saw B.B. King play at the Café Au Go Go and stuck around for an after-hours jam session. "I met B.B. King," said Clapton, "and when B.B. played I realized it isn't a question of fashion or blues dying or being reborn. It is there all the time whether you play blues or not, and I just realized I want to play blues again." This would not be the last time that Clapton would pledge his fidelity to the blues. For more than forty subsequent years, his recordings would feature a variety of styles—country, reggae, soft rock—but like the return of the swallows, Clapton would periodically cut some blues and declare it his true love. The difference was that this first vow was made when Clapton was playing with one of the most popular and profitable rock bands in the world.

In July of 1968, it was announced that after only a little more than two years, Cream was going to break up. This being big business, however, the group would also embark on a farewell tour of the United States and release a fourth album. While Bruce and Baker would later sustain successful careers, Clapton was virtually guaranteed the life of a rock star. To wit, as Cream's double album climbed the charts, he could also be heard playing lead guitar on George Harrison's "While My Guitar Gently Weeps," which was included on the Beatles' so-called "White Album," the two-LP collection that left no room at the top of the U.S. charts for the number 2 *Wheels of Fire*.

The breakup of Cream was due not only to fractious personalities but also the very nature of its improvised format. Clapton was famously chagrined by a *Rolling Stone* review of Cream that ran in the same May 1968 issue that included an interview with the guitarist by the magazine's editor, Jann Wenner, and a cover photo taken by Linda (not yet McCartney) Eastman. "Clapton is a master of the blues clichés of the last 40 years," wrote Jon Landau, who eight years later would become Bruce Springsteen's record producer and manager. "He knows the music of B.B. King and Albert King like the back of his hand and he didn't play a note that wasn't blues that Saturday night." Landau went on to say that Cream could outplay most every American band before concluding: "When they get over their virtuosity hang-up—which is what I think their sort of virtuosity is—we may really see something. At the moment they're just warming up."

At the time, Clapton was smitten by the subtle vocal and instrumental interplay of *Music from Big Pink*, an album by the group who'd famously backed Bob Dylan and was now called the Band. Clapton traveled to Woodstock, New York, to meet the players whose music made him rethink his own. "These guys were the real thing," said Clapton, "and I was touring with this band of psychedelic loonies."

Cream cleaned up on their farewell tour. Robert Shelton, the critic who had famously championed the career of Bob Dylan, praised their Madison Square Garden show in the *New York Times*. "The Cream has changed the face of rock," said Shelton, "rising from the underground to international popularity. It was a curious reversal that three of the strongest of the group's nine numbers were drawn from the heart of American black folk blues: Skip James 'I'm So Glad,' Robert Johnson's 'Crossroads,' and 'Train Time,' a [blues] harmonica showpiece by Mr. Bruce."

The blues revival had moved from Greenwich Village to Midtown Manhattan. Coincidentally, this future rock critic also saw Cream at the Garden. It was my first concert in an arena—as opposed to a theater like Bill Graham's Fillmore East—and Cream's mountainous stacks of equipment were set up on a revolving stage. As a result, my most vivid memory of the evening is of how my eardrums would literally vibrate when we were lucky enough to be facing the Marshall amplifiers; and how the sound would bounce wildly around the amphitheater as the stage turned. Cream and a few others pioneered concerts in arenas the way the Beatles invented playing a rock 'n' roll show in a ballpark. Neither venue put a premium on high fidelity. The sound quality of mass concerts would only start to improve after the Woodstock Festival confirmed that there was an arena-level demand for live rock 'n' roll.

"Before Woodstock the Jefferson Airplane still played four shows at the Fillmore East and earned $12,000," said Joshua White, who produced psychedelic light shows. "Only really big acts—the Stones and the Doors—played Madison Square Garden. After Woodstock many more played the Garden. I knew—everybody on that stage at Woodstock knew—the future wasn't in rock theaters. The future was in arenas."

Cream played its last two farewell concerts at London's Royal Albert Hall on November 26, 1968. Both shows would be filmed for a subsequent movie, and Cream would release a fourth album, *Goodbye*, that consisted of one original track by each member and more live recordings (subsequent years would also see the release of *Live Cream* and *Live Cream II*). "Badge," written by Clapton and George Harrison, was the hit off *Goodbye*, and confirmed his new status. Clapton was a blues purist when he left the Bluesbreakers to form Cream. Now, two years later, he was a rock star.

TEN
BABY BOOM BLUES

After the Butterfield Blues Band made its dramatic 1965 debut at the Newport Folk Festival, Jim Rooney booked the band for three nights at Club 47 in Cambridge, Massachusetts. "[Butterfield] told me that I should get some of the other bands from Chicago," said Rooney, "starting with Muddy Waters." Peter Wolf, who was studying painting at Boston's Museum School of Fine Arts, and who sang in a band called the Hallucinations, made a beeline to Club 47 when Waters came to town. "Between shows I walked into the men's room of the 47," said Wolf, "and there was [James] Cotton, [Otis] Spann, and S.P. Leary all gathered around a pint. They're all passing it around. They are my idols, so I picked up my cue real good and ran out and scored a couple of pints, and after the next show they were all over me."

Wolf, who was also a jive-talking deejay at Boston's WBCN-FM, opened his nearby apartment as a home away from home for the visiting bluesmen. James Cotton moved right in and cooked soul food for the band. "I could never get over the unlikely sight of Muddy in my own apartment," said Wolf, "shoes off, shirt and suit jacket neatly hung up, wearing a T-shirt and a do-rag (to preserve

Bonnie Raitt 1949-

his carefully straightened and sculpted hair) on his head." The band would play cards, and sometimes Wolf would play Waters some of his early singles, with Muddy requesting tunes that he hadn't heard in years.

By 1970, Wolf would be the lead singer of the J. Geils Band, a hard-rocking group that split the difference between blues and R&B. The band's debut Atlantic album included songs by John Lee Hooker ("Serves You Right to Suffer"), Otis Rush ("Homework"), and Texas guitarist Albert Collins ("Sno-Cone"). Other American rock bands were also covering classic examples of Chicago blues, including the Doors, whose 1967 album included a song Willie Dixon had written for Howlin' Wolf, "Back Door Man." Paul Rothchild, who'd learned how to record electric music when he cut albums with the Butterfield Blues Band, produced the Doors. Around that time, Rothchild also tried to sign Janis Joplin to play in an acoustic blues band with Taj Mahal and Stefan Grossman. She chose to stay with Big Brother and the Holding Company.

While white bands put a modern spin on the blues, black artists were encouraged to produce records that would appeal to fans of bands like Cream. Marshall Chess Jr. grew up not just with the blues, but also listening to rock bands like the Beatles and the Rolling Stones; now he was a young executive at Chess Records. He encouraged Waters and Wolf to reprise some of their signature songs with musicians schooled in jazz and rhythm and blues, and guitarists more likely to use a wah-wah pedal than a bottleneck slide. Purists were outraged at the resulting Waters album, *Electric Mud* (Waters called it "Electric Shit"). Similarly, Wolf was not a fan of his psychedelic side trip, *The Howlin' Wolf Album*. Chess used his disdain as a selling point, illustrating the LP cover with bold-faced copy: "This is Howlin' Wolf's new album. He doesn't like it. He didn't like his electric guitar at first either."

Record producers also tried attracting rock fan by pairing veteran bluesmen with the white blues-rock stars they'd inspired. Norman Dayron had the idea to supplement the Muddy Waters band with Paul Butterfield and Mike Bloomfield, who came up with the title for the 1969 collection, *Fathers and Sons*. The double album paired a studio session with a live recording made at Chicago's elegant Auditorium Theater. *Fathers and Sons* had its moments, but it fell short of either generation's best work. "Bloomfield was so scared of playing with Muddy a couple of times that he took heavy tranquilizers," said Chess, who'd known the guitarist since high school. "He had a lot of soul but he was a troubled, pained person, like a lot of blues singers are. And he liked drugs and alcohol, just like them."

Bloomfield's personal demons aside, he was not the only rock musician inhibited to play with the giants of the blues. Dayron also produced *The

London Howlin' Wolf Sessions, on which Wolf was backed by guitarist Eric Clapton, keyboard player Steve Winwood, and the Rolling Stones' rhythm section of drummer Charlie Watts and bassist Bill Wyman. "Eric Clapton walked in the first day and Hubert [Sumlin] was tuning up his guitar in the corner of the room," said Dayron. "Eric turned around and looked like he was going to leave immediately. He looked at me and said, 'What do you need me for?'" Clapton stuck around and proved to be an effective diplomat when the musicians got ready to record "Little Red Rooster," the Wolf song that had been an early single by the Rolling Stones. Clapton asked Wolf to teach him the song's guitar lick. "Wolf looked at him like he was crazy," said Dayron. "And [Clapton] says, 'No, man. We want to get the right feel for it.' So Wolf picked up his Sears Silvertone guitar, and he started playing slide. The ice was broken, because they had extended themselves to him. Eric did." At the end of the sessions, as a parting present, the British musicians gave Wolf a new fishing rod.

But Hubert Sumlin didn't go home empty handed. After one session, a car pulled up to Sumlin. "It was a chauffeur-driven car, and inside is Clapton," said guitarist Steve Freund. "Clapton says, 'Hubert, get in the car.' . . . They went up to Clapton's mansion. Clapton had one room in this place that was completely devoted to guitars . . . dozens of them there. Maybe even one hundred. Clapton then tells Hubert, 'Go ahead, man. Take any guitar you want. It is my gift to you.'"

"I was a little pre-teenager in L.A. and I just caught the fever," said Bonnie Raitt, whose father John was a celebrated star of Broadway musicals. "I couldn't wait to get old enough to get to Greenwich Village and hang out with John Hammond [Jr.], Dave Van Ronk, Bob Dylan, and Joan Baez. I raced to get to Cambridge in time to hang out with them, and then Club 47 closed my freshman year."

Raitt enrolled at Radcliffe College, but the singer-guitarist was also studying the blues, and like many of her baby boom peers, some of her teachers were British. "The Rolling Stones had a huge influence on my generation getting turned on to the blues," said Raitt. "They and Eric Clapton were very vocal about their influences and cast a lot of attention on people like Muddy, Lightnin' Hopkins, John Lee Hooker, and Howlin' Wolf. And you have to remember; all the great blues-rock that we love came about as a direct result of what was created in the Mississippi Delta. They're all streams from the same tributary."

Raitt was soon performing as a solo at local clubs and attracted the attention, both professional and personal, of blues promoter Dick Waterman. After one coffeehouse performance, she called her father with the news that she'd earned $50. "That's great," said John Raitt. "You're earning $50 a night, and I'm paying $10,000 a year in tuition." He wouldn't for long. Raitt dropped out during her sophomore year to become a full-time musician.

Waterman booked Raitt to open shows for many of his blues acts, and she helped him handle the headliners. "I carried the booze bottles for all those guys," said Raitt. "Like, I knew that Fred McDowell could have two or three gins before he want on; and an hour before the show, Son House could have his bottle of vodka. And if he had any more, he would forget the words. And if he had any less, he would forget the words."

Raitt drank up the music, with her approach to slide guitar particularly influenced by McDowell's highly rhythmic bottleneck playing. "One of the reasons I like to play slide guitar," said Raitt, "what drew me to it in the first place, was the fact that it sounded like a human voice crying—it was very evocative. . . . It's a complimentary way of saying something that you could no longer sing, because it was too emotional."

But Raitt, who was raised as a politically conscious Quaker, learned more than music from the blues musicians. "You have this weird psychological leapfrogging," said Raitt, "where my grandparents passed away when I was 19, but I inherited Sippie Wallace and Muddy and Son House and Fred McDowell, and that's where I got my grand-parenting—from them. And they probably really would have wished that their own children loved their music and took up in their footsteps, but because blues was neglected from around the '30s to the '60s, the only people left to pick it up were the young white kids who romanticized black music and knew of the place in the culture it had."

Touring the blues circuit could be a challenge for a young white woman. Raitt felt self-conscious when her father saw her singing the bawdy Howlin' Wolf song, "Built for Comfort," but said that her folks were supportive if predictably wary of her musical lifestyle. "I was hangin' out with seventy-year-old blues guys who drank at ten in the morning," said Raitt. "My parents were a *little* concerned."

The bluesmen could also bring out Raitt's maternal instinct. At the 1969 Ann Arbor Blues Festival, she worried that McDowell might be lonesome and dragged Waterman to his hotel room. "The door flew open," said Waterman, "and the smell of marijuana, cigarettes and stale beer came rushing out to envelop us. About 40 people were in Fred's hotel room, in full revelry on the beds, beside the beds, between the beds, and under the beds. Fred, surrounded by a bevy of nubile college girls, was sitting on a bed playing guitar. He looked at the door and waved us in."

Raitt soon landed a recording contract with Warner Brothers. Her self-titled 1971 debut included songs by Robert Johnson ("Walking Blues"), Tommy Johnson ("Big Road Blues"), and Sippie Wallace ("Women Be Wise"). She also performed "I Ain't Blue," a tune by Chris Smither, a folk-blues artist Raitt had met in Cambridge who was at the start of his own forty-plus-year career. Raitt was one of a number of musicians recording for Warner Brothers whose critical renown typically topped their sales figures, including Randy Newman, Van Dyke Parks, and a gifted slide guitar player with a taste for American roots music, Ry Cooder.

Ryland Cooder grew up in Los Angeles, the only child of music-loving parents with an interest in leftist politics; little wonder that the first songs he learned on the guitar were by Woody Guthrie and that he was particularly fond of a record by a blues artist who'd successfully charmed New York café society, Josh White. The Harry Smith anthology was also in the family's record collection. Drawn to live music, Cooder spent his teenage years hanging out at McCabe's Guitar Shop and going to shows at the Ash Grove.

"When I was coming up in L.A. it was during this whole folk music revival," said Cooder, "and we were seeing the resurrection of some of these older players, white and black. And they were brought to L.A. and it was an unbelievable opportunity for the people to step out of the grooves of the old records and walk in front of you. And I mean people like the Stanley Brothers or Sleepy John Estes or Mississippi John Hurt. They'd perform and I'd sit ten feet away from 'em. This is when you learn things, because a lot of stuff is transmitted in some molecular way only by being right up against somebody. And people were always nice to me. . . . I'd say, 'Can you show me this sort of thing?' and they always did. I learned an awful lot of shit in a hurry from people like that. Real simple things but important things. How to play, how to make things sound good, how to make tone."

Cooder took lessons with Reverend Davis when he played L.A. "I'd sit there and say 'I like this song' and name one of his tunes—because he had songs," said Cooder. "We'd sit there for an hour or however long he wanted to stay, because when you're in the company of a master, time is not a thing of the clock. . . . I never could play [the song] back to him. A month later, it would come to me, what he had shown me or what he had done."

Cooder's first exposure to the slide guitar came when he was mesmerized by a recording of Blind Willie Johnson's "Dark Was the Night, Cold Was the Ground," though he was at a loss as to how Johnson produced that eerie, whining sound on his instrument. He got the answer from another local musician. "I found out how to use a bottleneck by asking John Fahey," said Cooder, "who had covered the territory looking for records, and he showed me that all you needed was a bottleneck, to tune the guitar to an open chord, and then go for it, sliding it up and down. . . . When I saw somebody like Son House, it was pretty obvious what was going on, and after that, it was just a matter of trying to learn to do it."

Cooder would chase that sound for the rest of his life. Johnson, said Cooder, is "one of those interplanetary world musicians. As for 'Dark Was the Night, Cold Was the Ground,' that's the most transcendent piece in all American music, the way he used his voice and the guitar." As it happened, Johnson did go into space—"Dark Was the Night" was one of the recordings placed in the Voyager spacecraft in 1977, alongside works by Bach, Beethoven, and Chuck Berry's "Johnny B. Goode.")

Open tunings gave Cooder insight into the music of John Lee Hooker and Muddy Waters. "Once I figured out how to play open-G tuning on the guitar," said Cooder, "all of a sudden there were all of John Lee Hooker's chords." As for Waters, Cooder called him "Mr. Microtone" for his deft touch with the slide. "To me, [Waters is] an example of somebody who transcends anything we think we know about the guitar," said Cooder. "When a guy plays like that you don't feel frets and six strings and scale length. . . . He's playing where he knows those notes are, and locking into this spirit thing of playing the movement of the song."

When he was sixteen, Cooder played the Ash Grove in a folk-blues band with singer-songwriter Jackie DeShannon. That's where he met Taj Mahal, who'd relocated to L.A. from Cambridge and gotten a job at the Ash Grove as, said Mahal, "doorman, the chief cook and bottle-washer, announcer, light man, and then sometimes I got to open the shows when the first act didn't show up. . . . For about three years I got to play piano, harmonica, and a little guitar with some really great musicians: Lightnin' Hopkins, Sleepy John Estes, Yank Rachell, Bukka White, Jesse Fuller—all those guys." Mahal was a rarity, a young black musician intent on playing the blues, and his days at the Ash Grove steeled his conviction. "Listen to all these different poets here," said Mahal. "I mean these guys haven't been past the third grade and they write more valuable, alive poetry than nine-tenths of the people who are talked about."

Mahal and Cooder played together in the Rising Sons, which recorded an unreleased album for Columbia, whose executives were perhaps puzzled as to how to promote an integrated roots-music band (the sessions were issued decades later on compact disc). Terry Melcher, who'd produced the

Rising Sons, soon hired Cooder to play sessions by acts like Paul Revere and the Raiders. For a time, he also played guitar with Captain Beefheart and his Magic Band. Beefheart (Don Van Vliet), a protégé of progressive rock musician Frank Zappa, was an accomplished painter and singer with a wide-ranging musical imagination and a bellows of a voice not unlike that of Howlin' Wolf. Cooder helped Beefheart cut his first album, 1967's *Safe as Milk*, but declined to stick with the Magic Band after a disastrous concert in Berkeley during which the singer nearly had a nervous collapse.

Recording sessions kept Cooder busy. "My job," said Cooder, "seemed to consist of taking strange instruments which were not as yet clichéd in the rock field—like mandolin or dulcimer, even bottleneck guitar—and pump 'em up, play 'em hard, and integrate myself into the ensemble as a color or sound effect." When he recorded with Randy Newman, Cooder caught the attention of musician-producer Jack Nitzsche, who brought him to London to help cut the soundtrack for *Performance*, a film starring Mick Jagger and James Fox.

During the soundtrack sessions, Cooder also played in the studio with the Rolling Stones, injecting a slide guitar solo into "Sister Morphine," and playing mandolin on the band's version of Robert Johnson's "Love in Vain." Just as the veteran bluesmen (and Fahey) had taught Cooder, he in turn influenced other musicians, introducing Keith Richards to open-G tuning, and inspiring Duane Allman to take up the slide guitar, a technique that he mastered by the 1969 debut of the Allman Brothers Band.

Cooder's 1970 solo debut included touchstones from his study of guitar, including a ragtime blues by Blind Blake ("Police Dog Blues") and Blind Willie Johnson's "Dark Was the Night, Cold Was the Ground." Cooder reached out to older musicians to play on his early albums; while recording his fourth album, 1974's *Paradise & Lunch*, he planned to record Blind Blake's "Diddy Wah Diddy," and noticed that the famous Chicago jazz pianist Earl Hines happened to be performing in L.A. "I called the club where he was playing," said Cooder, "got his hotel number, called him, told him who I was—which of course meant nothing at all to him—and said, 'There's a little thing we could do on this record I'm doing for Warner Brothers; do you have a spare afternoon? Now here's this guy I grew up listening to in a very ethereal way, thinking, 'Who is this magical person?' Then all of a sudden I'm talking to him on the telephone. That's what used to happen when you went out looking for these old guys—you could find them!"

Cooder wasn't the only white musician playing with veteran artists; in 1970, Canned Heat cut *Hooker 'n' Heat* with John Lee Hooker. Canned Heat's boogie owed everything to Hooker's earliest hits, and he came to have a particularly close rapport with Alan Wilson. "When I got with him," said Hooker of Wilson, "he had my music down like you know your ABCs. He could *follow* me." Hooker, like Lightnin' Hopkins, would stretch his blues on an emotional whim, adding a beat here or a measure there, which can be a nightmare for an accompanist. Wilson was ready, as he'd already had the experience of shadowing Son House.

Hooker was fifty-three and in touch with both the energy of youth and the wisdom of age. Canned Heat was a hippie rock band thrilled to play with the man who'd taught them to boogie; the band also had the good taste to make *Hooker 'n' Heat* essentially a Hooker album, including solo tracks, songs with Wilson adding harp and second guitar, and jams with the entire band. The aim of the three-day session was to tap into the compulsive groove of Hooker's archetypal 1948 song, "Boogie Chillen." The album's liner notes describes how the studio was prepared: "We built a plywood platform for John to sit on while he played. An old Silvertone amp rested a few feet away. One mike on the amp, one for his voice, and one to pick up John's stompin'—he never quits stompin'! Never far away, a bottle of Chivas Regal and a cup of water to smooth it down."

Hooker 'n' Heat was among the bluesman's most successful albums, a latter-day evocation of his influential early work that was highlighted by his solo turns and successful collaborations with Wilson. It would turn out to be Wilson's last recording session, as before the album was even mixed, he was found dead of an overdose of barbiturates. But this wasn't a typical rock star death. Wilson, an ardent environmentalist, regularly eschewed a comfortable bed for a campsite; he was found dead in a sleeping bag on a forested hillside in the bohemian enclave of Topanga canyon. Friends described Wilson as a troubled, lonely soul, and his death was a presumed suicide. He left a musical brief that rested on a couple of hit records, but which was really defined by his sensitive musical rapport with John Lee Hooker and Son House. The cover photo of *Hooker 'n' Heat* shows a funereal, candlelit studio, with the musicians gathered around a photo of the shy, bespectacled musician they called "The Blind Owl."

Young white musicians didn't just meet black blues players in recording studios or folk clubs. In Memphis, where Elvis Presley lived, white kids grew up with the blues living on the other side of town, if not right down the street. Jim Dickinson played in an early-'6os band called Mud Boy and the Neutrons that mixed blues and rock 'n' roll; he'd later record with everybody from Ry Cooder and Bob Dylan to the Rolling Stones. After reading Sam Charters's *The Country Blues*, Dickinson was inspired to meet his neighbors.

"In the summer of 1960, a friend and I followed the trail that Charters left to [jug band musician] Gus Cannon, who was the first one I actually met," said Dickinson. "He was the yardman for an anthropology professor. Gus had told this family that he used to make records and he had been on RCA and they'd say, 'Yeah Gus, sure, cut the grass.'" Cannon showed his teenage visitors a certificate celebrating the sales of "Walk Right In," a song of his that was a hit for the Kingston Trio but for which he received no compensation. He had a copy of the record that he'd recorded with Charters for Folkways, but didn't own a turntable.

Furry Lewis, Bukka White, and other bluesmen were discovered in plain sight. "We would go out in the country and to joints and stuff and run around with these people," said Robert Palmer, who would later become a music critic for the *New York Times*. Palmer would drive out to Como, Mississippi, to pick up Fred McDowell at the Stuckeys, where he pumped gas. "It's something none of us ever got over," said Palmer. "It was really interesting to hear these people doing their individual stuff and not really changing, not giving a shit about trends or fashion or anything like that. And we were very, very devoted to those people."

When Dickinson was coproducing Ry Cooder's *Boomer's Story* in 1972, he invited Cooder to his Tennessee home. Cooder figured it would be fun to record with one of his favorite bluesmen, Sleepy John Estes; Dickinson knew where he lived and arranged for a session. "We got out a tape recorder, and sat up all night playing," said Cooder. "It was quite a nice time—I played mandolin, Dickinson played piano, and Sleepy John sang and played guitar. It was kind of like old Sleepy John records, which was a big thrill for me. He was a great guy, a funny old cat, like some kind of man on a mountain somewhere."

The session produced a tune called "President Kennedy," which was included on *Boomer's Story*. "He [Estes] lived in a shack in Tennessee," said Cooder, "no glass in the window, unbelievable poverty. I'd take royalty money to him . . . and here would come all these people because they heard about white boys coming with money. He knew damn well it wasn't going to do him a damn of good, but he appreciated the fact that he got paid at all. It'd be gone in an hour, people coming over and borrowing money for a new set of tires or a drink. He died so poor that some of us had to send money to bury him."

By now, Cooder was attuned to, and saddened by the hard lives of his musical heroes. "On one side, you've got a group of people indulging their sensibilities in the warm bath of ethnic purity," said Cooder of his folk-blues peers, "and on the other, you've got the guys who actually do it, but who can't afford firewood, and that creates a certain kind of ambivalence that you can never resolve."

But it made for a great learning opportunity. Lee Baker was the guitarist in Jim Dickinson's band and was taught how to play slide guitar in open tunings by Furry Lewis. Baker played with Lewis and others at the Bitter Lemon, the Memphis coffee house that was the focus of the city's folk-blues scene, and the organizational hub of the first Memphis Country Blues Festival in 1966. Baker played the festival with an electric band, but also accompanied Furry Lewis, and later, Bukka White, Gus Cannon, and Sleepy John Estes.

One night in the early '60s, a couple of young white strangers took the stage of the Bitter Lemon. "They played these open-tuned blues guitars, and they went into their act," said John McIntire, who ran the coffee house. "John Fahey was Blind Joe Death. He wore dark glasses and Bill Barth would lead him up onstage, and they would play together." Barth had moved to Memphis from Queens, New York, in search of old bluesmen, and with John Fahey, had rediscovered Skip James. For a time, Barth traveled with James, but the relationship soured soon after James lost Barth's guitar. As a musician, Barth was interested in applying Fahey's acoustic guitar techniques to the electric guitar; while in Memphis, he became friends with Robert Palmer.

"I had been playing professionally since I was about fourteen," said Palmer, "and I thought I could get through a blues progression pretty good. But boy, that first time I tried to play with Bukka [White], I thought, 'Oh! This is a whole other thing!' Barth and I got to jamming with those guys a lot, with Furry and Bukka and so forth, and then later after we moved to New York, Barth and me and Alan Wilson of Canned Heat used to jam together a lot on country blues stuff."

Barth, Palmer, and (future record company executive) Nancy Jeffries started the Insect Trust, a progressive blues-rock band adventurous enough to also play with jazzmen like Pharoah Sanders and Elvin Jones. "Special Rider Blues," a Skip James song, was included on the Insect Trust's first album. "For me," said Barth of the band that folded after two albums, "it was mainly an intellectual exercise, taking traditional musical influences and making them work as pop music, but it was not as visceral or emotionally satisfying as the blues I enjoy playing, and which have deep meaning for me." Barth subsequently bought a juke joint in Clarksdale, Mississippi, that was managed by Ike Turner's cousin Evelyn. He later moved to Amsterdam, where at the age of fifty-seven, he died of a heart attack.

The Memphis Country Blues Festival, organized by the musicians who'd hung out at the Bitter Lemon, fell apart after four years. A Memphis meeting of the National Endowment for the Arts Folklore Panel underscored the different ways in which academic folklorists and local musicians looked at the blues. "You listen to Skip James," said Randall Lyon, who'd helped run the festival, "and then have someone tell you about the folklore of his songs. It was very obnoxious. We figured there was not enough known about class and gender and racism in general for any comment to be made about the aesthetics or the meaning of the music. Other than participating in it and enjoying it as a human fucking being."

The Reverend Gary Davis continued to teach an influential circle of guitar players throughout the 1960s. Roy Book Binder jokes that he was Davis's worst student, but after quitting college to go on the road with him in 1967, he also became one of his closest confidantes. Their first outing was a train trip to Chicago for a four-night stint at the Quiet Knight, a folk club on the North Side. "The guarantee was $400 versus fifty percent of the door," said Book Binder, "and the tickets were $1.75."

"I'd count the money after gigs and he'd tie it up with a string and stick it down his long johns," said Book Binder. "He didn't like to change clothes on the road. I'd say, 'Reverend Davis, this is Tuesday and Mother Davis said to put your brown suit on.' And he'd say, 'Where's Mother Davis?' 'She's back in Queens.' 'When we're on the road,' he'd say, 'we're on the road. I'm wearing the blue suit all week.'" Davis also had his favorite foods. "We'd go out to lunch," said Book Binder, "and he'd say, 'I'll have the pork chops.' And the waitress would say, 'Would you like peas or carrots with that?' And he'd say, 'Are the peas greasy?' And she said, 'Certainly not.' 'OK, then I'll have the carrots.' He liked all that greasy soul food crap."

Traveling can be tough on even the best of friends. "I might not talk to him for two weeks after a road trip," said Book Binder, "because sometimes it was like going on tour with your grandfather. I remember calling up the house, and I'd ask Annie how she was and she'd say, 'Do you want to talk to the Reverend?' And I'd say, 'Not really.' But then I'd say, 'You ask him if he wants to talk to me.' And she'd come back and say, 'He'll talk to you if you want to talk to him.' Then we'd finally talk, and everything would be fine."

Woody Mann still remembers Reverend Davis's phone number—AX1–7609. He first dialed it in 1968, when he was twelve years old. "I was looking for a guitar teacher," said Mann. "I remember asking Van Ronk and he said, 'Get out of here, kid.'" So he called up every Gary Davis in the book, and eventually found the Reverend. His mom drove him from Long Island to his lesson at Davis's home in Queens. "When I arrived, I knew the name Gary Davis and that he'd written 'Candyman,'" said Mann. "So I got there, and he was having dinner, and putting his teeth away, this big ritual, and then he picked up his guitar and started playing in the living room, doing all sorts of amazing stuff. I said, 'What is that?' And he said, 'That's what you call ragtime.' And I said, 'Can I study with you?'"

Book Binder says that Davis instantly recognized Mann as a prodigy; the student remembers his teacher's kind encouragement. "We'd go lick by lick through songs, and then maybe jam on it for an hour," said Mann. "He wouldn't move on before I got a part right. For 45 minutes we'd go over one verse, over and over. The guy had amazing patience." Mann would go home and, having taped his lessons, use the recordings as a study aid. "I'd go back the next week and play it for him," said Mann, "and then he'd play it completely differently. It used to drive me nuts. And that's when I realized that he was really all about improvising. He would play 'Hesitation Blues' for twenty minutes, not repeat himself, make the shit up as he goes, and his timing was always perfect. It was the first time I'd heard a finger style guitar player not playing an arrangement, but improvising."

One Sunday, Mann went with Davis to a church service. "It was like in a condemned movie theater, with all these chairs thrown up in the balcony," said Mann. "The congregation filled the first two rows, and all the women were in their Sunday finery, with white gloves and hats and day-glo colors. And he was up there preaching and playing. And then he turned to me and said, 'Give us a song, boy.' I knew one song I could sing, 'Say No To The Devil.' It was funny, here I was a middle-class white [Jewish] kid, and I'm up there freaking out trying to play and sing. I wasn't even thinking about the lyrics; I was just worried about the guitar. I finally looked up, because my eyes were closed, and I'll never forget it. Nobody was looking at me. They all had their eyes closed, clapping their hands, rolling around in their chairs and singing along with me."

Then Davis came to Mann's house. "I asked Reverend Davis to do a concert at my house and he went, 'Sure, just don't tell my manager.' It was an anti-Vietnam War thing, and he said, 'I'll support that. I'm against war.' My mother made brownies and cookies, and we picked him up, and put him in the living room. We had to pay him $300; I sold tickets and all the kids were on the floor. And he did a concert, and at one point, he even fell asleep."

Reverend Davis once traveled to Pittsburgh to preside over the wedding of a former student. "He had a book with some Braille in it," said Ernie Hawkins, describing the ceremony in his Pittsburgh apartment, "but I didn't know whether he was actually reading it or just making it up. He said some words and gave us a little talk about being married. And then he said, 'OK, you're married.' Then he taught me 'Will There Be Any Stars in My Crown?'—that was my wedding present." (Davis also officiated at the wedding of hippie icon Hugh "Wavy Gravy" Romney. "Dylan was there, [Tom] Paxton, Van Ronk," said the groom, "and they all sang 'Just a Closer Walk with Thee.'")

Davis was a star not just to his students, but also his peers. Ernie Hawkins once booked Davis to play at a blues festival in Pittsburgh. "We had a couple of workshops with guys like Mance Lipscomb and Son House and Fred McDowell," said Hawkins, "and before long everybody was hanging around Gary Davis. He was like the king of these guys. They all respected the way he played, and he entertained them with jokes and stories. Victoria Spivey was there, and they started playing these old songs, with her singing and him playing. His guitar was deep and complex, and you could feel that this was where his heart lived."

Davis went to Europe in 1964 as part of a "Blues and Gospel Caravan" tour that also included Muddy Waters, Sonny Terry and Brownie McGhee, and gospel singer and guitarist Sister Rosetta Tharpe. Joe Boyd had been hired to manage the tour, and he enlisted Tom Hoskins for additional help after Mississippi John Hurt had to bow out due to illness. Boyd initially struggled to create comity among this diverse cast; Tharpe was particularly disgusted after Davis used his hands to eat fried eggs for breakfast. Before long, however, Tharpe was moved to add a mournful descant to Davis's concert rendition of "Precious Lord." "Oh Lord," said Davis, "sing it, girl!"

Reverend Davis left a lasting impression on his students. "He gave me direction and confidence," said Book Binder, "and showed me a way to have a traveling, creative life." For decades, Book Binder literally lived on the road, in a mobile home. These days, he's blessed with a wandering musician's best friend: a wife with a job and a house in Florida. The last time Book Binder saw Davis was in the hospital; the year was 1972, and

Davis was seventy-six. "He weighed maybe 90 pounds," said Book Binder, "and I'm holding his hand, and he didn't have his glasses or his teeth. It was like death. I said, 'Reverend Davis, beside the music, my entire circle of friends, and everybody I know, came from you.' And he said, 'I know.' He knew he was the best. And I believe he was the best because God gave him the ability to convert souls with his music. And in a way, we were all kind of converted."

ELEVEN

ROCKIN'
THE BLUES

Among the 1960s British Invasion rock stars, there was the pop star Beatles, the bluesy Rolling Stones, and everybody else. The Stones became a global sensation upon the release of 1965's "(I Can't Get No) Satisfaction," and that meant both big money and persistent pressure to produce more hits. Allen Klein renegotiated the group's record deal with Decca, and soon took over the band's management from Andrew Loog Oldham and Eric Easton. Klein was a hard-knuckled hustler who'd made his mark in the music business by smoking out an accurate account-ing of Sam Cooke's record royalties, and winning the seminal gospel-soul singer ownership of his own recordings. After Cooke was shot dead in 1964, Klein encouraged his widow to hold on to the singer's assets, including his publishing income; when she decided to cash out four years later, Klein bought out the estate for $350,000.

"With us, Allen was very much like Colonel Tom Parker with Elvis," said Keith Richards. "If you wanted a gold-plated Cadillac, he'd give it to you. . . . It was a paternalistic form of management that obviously doesn't rub anymore these

Jimmy Page 1944–

days. . . . It was rock and roll." And the blues—after all, Chess Records bought Muddy Waters a new car every couple years and deducted the cost from his royalties. And like Leonard Chess, Klein kept a keen eye on the books and the legal letter of a contract.

"We had a company in the U.K. called Nanker Phelge Music," said Richards, "which was a company we all shared in." According to Richards, Klein reorganized the band's finances so that all money would be channeled to a company called Nanker Phelge USA. Long after signing their approval, the Stones discovered that Klein was the sole owner of the new company. "He started out representing us," said Oldham, "and ended up owning us." This sleight of contractual hand meant that Klein controlled all of the band's recordings of the 1960s and shared in the publishing income. The Stones still earned plenty of money, but it was all funneled through Klein, who also got involved in the business of the Beatles. Rock stars, it seemed, were just as likely to sign a bad contract as bluesmen, even one like Mick Jagger, who for a time attended the London School of Economics. But all this came out later; in the '60s, the Stones were too busy making music and mayhem.

Following the release of the Beatles' *Sgt. Pepper's Lonely Hearts Club Band*, the Stones recorded their least representative album, the semi-psychedelic *Her Satanic Majesty's Request*. The relative rejection of the album prompted Jagger and Richards to return to rootsy, blues-related music, resulting in two of the band's most celebrated albums, *Beggar's Banquet* (1968) and *Let It Bleed* (1969). "People would say, 'What you playin' that old shit for,'" said Richards. "Which really screwed me up because that's all I can play." To write new songs, Jagger and Richards would often jam on old country blues tunes until they stumbled on a variation that could be fashioned into an original song. Brian Jones, who'd originally been considered the leader and bluesy soul of the band, was now often absent from the studio, and generally living the life of a stoned rock star without the music.

The biggest change in the Stones' late-'60s music was Richards's use of open tuning, a technique used by blues players in which the guitar is tuned to a major triad (Skip James often used a minor triad). Slide guitar players were particularly fond of this technique, but Richards found that open chords also offered a powerful format for rhythm guitar. He experimented first with an open-D tuning, and used it to create two Stones songs that are regarded as hard-rock classics, "Jumpin' Jack Flash" and "Street Fighting Man." The way these tunes use powerful riffs to frame the song mirrored the construction of many blues songs. Howlin' Wolf's "Smokestack Lightning," for instance, is built upon Hubert Sumlin's twisty guitar lick, just as a repeated musical vamp anchors Muddy Waters' "I Just Want to Make Love to You." Richards applied these principles to the songs he wrote with Jagger, but also had the time, inclination, and studio budget to experiment with their presentation.

The most surprising aspect of both "Jumping Jack Flash" and "Street Fighting Man" is that these epic rockers didn't employ any electric guitars. Richards recorded his guitar parts into a cassette recorder, a strategy that essentially used the primitive machine as a pick-up. "I could get the crispness of an acoustic—which you can never get off an electric guitar—but overloading this tiny little machine so the effect was that it sounded both acoustic and electric," said Richards. After trying in vain to recreate that sound in the studio, he doubled down on his low-tech strategy by plugging the cassette recorder into a speaker, hitting play, and recording the result. "We would all sit back and watch this little microphone record the cassette machine in the middle of the studio at Olympic," said Richards. "Then we'd go back, listen to it, play over it, mash it up and there was the track."

Drummer Charlie Watts could also be experimental; he used a toy drum kit from the 1930s to record "Street Fighting Man." "The snare drum was fantastic," said Watts, "because it had a really thin skin with a snare right underneath, but only two strands of gut." Such are the playful components of powerful rock 'n' roll. Another Stones standard from that time, "Gimme Shelter," also had a blues connection. "Those chords are Jimmy Reed inspired," said Richards of the song's ominous introduction, "the same haunting trick, sliding up the fret board against the drone of the E note."

Ultimately, a different open tuning came to dominate Richards's playing. "Ry Cooder was the first cat I actually saw play the open G chord," said Richards of tuning the guitar to the three notes of a G chord: G, B, and D. "But he was using it strictly for slide playing and he still had the bottom string." By stripping off the bottom string, Richards could slam the open-tuned guitar knowing that the low string was now the root of the G chord. "Five strings cleared out the clutter," said Richards. "It gives me licks and laid on textures. . . . It was like scales falling from your eyes and from your ears at the same time. It broke open the damn."

Richards was experimenting with these techniques in the absence of the Stones' other guitarist, Brian Jones. This posed a real problem in 1969, as the band was planning to tour after a relatively lengthy hiatus due in part to the high-profile drug busts of Jagger, Richards, and Jones. The Stones (minus Bill Wyman) visited Jones at his home, a property once owned by the creator of Winnie the Pooh, A. A. Milne, to tell him of their plans. Jones, who likely felt that Jagger and Richards had essentially taken over his band, and who barely contributed to the recording of both *Beggar's Banquet* and *Let It Bleed*, said that he had another agenda. Jones was given a golden parachute of a hundred thousand pounds a years for life, but didn't live to collect; he was found at the bottom of his swimming pool on July 3, 1969. The coroner's conclusion was "death by misadventure."

By that time, the Rolling Stones already had a new guitar player. While considering possible recruits, Jagger sought the advice of John Mayall, who suggested that he hire Mick Taylor, who'd replaced Peter Green in the Bluesbreakers, and who wasn't happy with Mayall's plan to play without a drummer. When Taylor showed up to audition for the Stones, he was carrying a Les Paul that had once belonged to Richards. "I had met Ian Stewart," said Taylor, "their roadie who also plays piano, and told him I was looking for a Les Paul, because mine had been stolen. And he said, 'Well, we've got one for sale.'" At the time, the Stones were recording *Beggar's Banquet*.

Taylor's first recording session with the Rolling Stones was for "Live with Me," a song that ended up on 1971's *Sticky Fingers*. His first gig with the band was at a free outdoor concert before a crowd of 220,000 in London's Hyde Park; since it was two days after the death of Brian Jones, the show was also cast as a memorial. Taylor "was hired for 150 pounds a week," said Bill Wyman, "until he was confirmed as a fully fledged member of the band when, like all of us, he would receive one-fifth of the band's income from concerts and record sales." But like Jones, Taylor was unable to crack the songwriting monopoly of the Jagger-Richards partnership.

The year was 1969, and the Stones were headed back to America, where during its last concert swing the band played for thirty minutes to screaming fans. "I call that tour 'the Led Zeppelin tour,'" said Watts, "because it was the first time we had to go on and play for an hour-and-a-half. I blame it on Jimmy Page. . . . Two or three hours on stage was what we heard they did, and it became something of a norm for anyone doing a concert."

Jimmy Page built Led Zeppelin with a shrewd pragmatism derived from his experience as a go-to guitarist in the mid-'60s London recording scene. Page was drawn to the guitar during the skiffle fad, and in 1958, appeared on a BBC talent show called *All Your Own* playing Lead Belly's "Cotton Fields." He cut his professional teeth playing with Neil Christian and the Crusaders, but he hated to travel and was happy to find success doing recording sessions with such acts as the Kinks, the Who, and Van Morrison's band, Them. But for every chance to help cut a song like "All Day and All of the Night" or "Gloria," Page played on many more mediocre records that sank without a trace.

When Eric Clapton left the Yardbirds, Page was offered the job, but decided to stick with sessions, and recommended his friend Jeff Beck, who responded by giving Page a 1958 Telecaster. "He came 'round one day, knocked on the door and said, 'It's yours,'" said Page. "It was a really beautiful instrument." It was also the guitar that Page would later use on Led Zeppelin's debut.

Between sessions, Page stretched himself by taking some guitar lessons from John McLaughlin, who worked at a music store before becoming an avatar of jazz-rock fusion with Miles Davis and his own Mahavishnu Orchestra. Page was also drawn to the acoustic style of Bert Jansch, an accomplished finger-style guitarist best known for his membership in Pentangle, a highly regarded folk-rock band. "I watched him playing once at a folk club and it was like seeing a classical guitarist," said Page. "All the inversions he was playing were unrecognizable." That's because, as Page soon discovered, Jansch was playing in a tuning called "DADGAD." Page would subsequently employ that and a host of other alternate tunings.

When Page was asked to join the Yardbirds for the second time, he accepted, as he was now itchy to leave the studio and get back to playing live. He began playing bass, but quickly switched to add a second guitar alongside Beck. When the temperamental Beck abandoned the group during a rigorous U.S. "Caravan of Stars" tour promoted by Dick Clark, Page stepped to center stage. The band soon broke up, but not before its management contract had been sold to record producer Mickey Most and his business partner, a blustery wrestler-turned-manager named Peter Grant. To honor unfulfilled European concert dates, Page assembled a new quartet that was initially called "The New Yardbirds."

Scouting for a singer, Page got wind of a twenty-year-old from the English Midlands named Robert Plant who was in a band called Hobbstweedle. Page traveled to a show in Birmingham and liked what he heard. "I immediately thought there must be something wrong with him personality-wise," said Page, "or that he had to be impossible to work with, because I just could not understand why . . . he hadn't become a big name yet." Page asked him to come to London for a formal audition. Plant, who'd just about given up on a career in music, asked British bluesman Alexis Korner for advice. Korner told him to go to London.

Initially, Page didn't know whether he would steer the group toward hard rock or softer, acoustic music, but when Plant encouraged him to try out a powerful drummer named John Bonham (they'd played together in a group called Band of Joy), the die was cast. Led Zeppelin—the New Yardbirds moniker was quickly abandoned—would specialize in hard rock and blues, although Page would season the repertoire with folk-inspired acoustic music. John Paul Jones, an experienced session player and arranger who ran in the same professional circles as Page, rounded out the quartet, playing both bass and keyboards. Gathered in a rehearsal studio, the quartet tried a run-through of "Train Kept a Rollin'," a '50s rockabilly tune that had been a cornerstone of the Yardbirds' repertoire, and that the band had recorded in Memphis. The walls shook and a major rock band was born.

Page was the band's auteur; he not only had a hand in writing the band's material, but also produced its records. He dipped into his savings to pay for time at Olympic Studios, where he recorded Led Zeppelin's self-titled debut in thirty hours. He applied the lessons borne of his many studio sessions, especially the time he produced a pair of early tracks by John Mayall and Eric Clapton. On that job, the engineer judged Clapton's guitar to be unlistenable. "I told him just to record it . . . and I'd take full responsibility," said Page. "The guy couldn't believe that someone was getting that kind of sound out of a guitar on purpose." He must've loved Led Zeppelin.

For Zeppelin, Page craved immediacy. "The way I see recording," said Page, "is to try and capture the sound of the room live and the emotion of the whole moment." Where most producers would place a single microphone in front of an amplifier, Page would place a second microphone behind the amp, and strike a balance between the two. Page's desire to capture the explosive ambiance of the studio was nothing new; it was the same strategy used by Sam Phillips in the 1950s when he recorded Howlin' Wolf and Elvis Presley at Sun Studios.

Peter Grant took the finished recording to New York and struck a five-album, worldwide deal with Ahmet Ertegun of Atlantic Records. The advance was said to be $200,000, but more importantly, came with a generous royalty rate and the guarantee of artistic control. Executives also capitulated to Page's demand that Led Zeppelin be on the Atlantic label, famous for its rhythm and blues records, instead of Atco, the less prestigious Atlantic subsidiary that had been the home of such rock acts as Cream and Buffalo Springfield.

Led Zeppelin's debut was released in January of 1969 to less than instant acclaim. "The popular formula in England in this, the aftermath era of such successful British bluesmen as Cream and John Mayall, seems to be: add to an excellent guitarist who, since leaving the Yardbirds and/or Mayall, has become a minor musical deity, a competent rhythm section and pretty soul-belter who can do a good spade imitation," said John Mendelsohn in *Rolling Stone*. "The latest of the British blues groups so conceived offers little that its twin, the Jeff Beck Group, didn't say as well or better three months ago, and the excesses of the Beck group's *Truth* album (most notably its self-indulgence and restrictedness), are fully in evidence on Led Zeppelin's debut album."

Jeff Beck had found the singer for his band, Rod Stewart, at a Fleetwood Mac show. "There's this forlorn character sitting nodding his head to Peter Green," said Beck, "and I said, 'Hey, that stuff's happening—it's great, Buddy Guy, the blues. Why don't we form a band and do that?'" Beck recruited Ronnie Wood, who would go on to play guitar with the Faces and, later, the Rolling Stones, to play bass. Like Page, Beck was not averse to plundering the blues songbook, reworking B.B. King's "Rock Me Baby" and calling it "Rock My Plimsoul," and turning Buddy Guy's "Let Me Love You Baby" into "Let Me Love You." After completing *Truth*, manager Peter Grant arranged an American tour for the Jeff Beck Group, where it wowed the crowd at New York's Fillmore East.

Jimmy Page was on hand to catch the show, and visited his old chum to play him some tracks by his new band, including a song that was also on *Truth*, Willie Dixon's "You Shook Me." "He said, 'Listen to this guy called John Bonham that I've got,'" said Beck, "and my heart just sank when I heard it. . . . I looked at him and said, 'Jim, what?' and the tears were coming out with anger . . . and I thought 'Here we go again'—pipped at the post." (John Paul Jones, as it happened, played keyboards on both versions.)

But it was not just one song, but also the different personalities of Page and Beck that determined the future of their respective bands. Page controlled virtually every aspect of Zeppelin's music, whereas Mickey Most, whose calling card was recording succinct pop songs, produced *Truth*. The two bands also had vastly different chemistry. "Before the friendship between Rod and Ronnie cemented," said Beck, "everything was great and we were all over the moon about what was happening. Then they started acting like a couple of girls together." More importantly, Led Zeppelin, like Cream, won its fame on multiple concert tours of the United States. By 1972, Zeppelin was such a powerful concert draw that it could command an unprecedented 90 percent of the gate.

It was while playing the Fillmore West on a 1969 bill with the James Gang that Page bought a 1958 sunburst Les Paul from that band's guitarist, Joe Walsh (later of the Eagles). Page used the instrument on his band's next album, *Led Zeppelin II*, and with that record's monumental hit, "Whole Lotta Love," it became the guitar heard around the world. The aggressive, riff-based tune with its psychedelic middle-section is often cited as an early example of "heavy metal" music. Decades later, after one of his children insisted that he give "Whole Lotta Love" a listen, Willie Dixon sued Zeppelin over the song's similarity to an obscure song of his that had been recorded by Muddy Waters in 1962, "You Need Love."

"Maybe they weren't intending to steal it," said Dixon, "but when you're fooling around, you hear things and you don't hear it at the same time. You put too little of yours and more of somebody else's—that's when you run into trouble." Zeppelin settled with Dixon before the case went to court; the twist is that Zeppelin actually learned the tune from the Small Faces, who called it "You Need Loving," and for a time used it to open its live show.

"We did a gig with the Yardbirds which [Robert Plant] was at and Jimmy Page asked me what that number was," said Steve Marriott, the Small Faces' singer. "'It's a Muddy Waters thing, "You Need Love"' After we broke up, they took it and revamped it. Good luck to them. It was old Percy [Plant] who'd had his eyes on it. He sang it the same, phrased it the same, even the stops at the end were the same; they just put a different rhythm to it."

Dixon, of course, never sued the small-fry Faces. "When these first rock artists came along, guys like Muddy and Wolf and Sonny Boy didn't get a whole lot of money," said Dixon. "The company was telling Muddy they was giving me the money and telling me Muddy was getting the money. Muddy was rolling his eyes at me [saying], 'You oughtta give me some of that money you're making those songs I caused them boys to have.'"

But Dixon, due to his "work-for-hire" contract with Arc Music (via Chess Records), wasn't exactly rolling in publishing royalties. "Prior to my working for Willie in a management capacity," said Scott Cameron, who worked with Dixon in the 1970s, "there were two Willie Dixon songs on *Led Zeppelin* that were properly credited, 'You Shook Me' and 'I Can't Quit You Baby.' When *Led Zeppelin II* came out, Arc Music brought a claim against them claiming that 'Bring It On Home' was Willie's song and that 'The Lemon Song' was Wolf's 'Killing Floor.' They had a settlement on this without Willie's knowledge. . . . I discovered it going through his royalty statements that he kept, and all at once here was this huge amount of money for 'Bring It On Home' out of the middle of nowhere."

Musicians often create new songs from the bones of old ones, but big-money artists have to be extra careful to cover their tracks. "Every one of us has been influenced by the blues, but it's one's interpretation of it and how you utilize it," said Page. "Robert was supposed to change the lyrics, and he didn't always do that, which is what brought on most of our grief. They couldn't get us on the guitar parts or the music, but they nailed us on the lyrics."

That's what can happen when a singer free-associates from the common pool of blues lyrics, a practice that was certainly familiar to Dixon. "Only when I began singing blues," said Plant, "was I able to use the medium [of music] to express what was inside me, my hopes and my fears. I could use several blues lines, well-known blues lines, but they were all related to me that day."

Critic LeRoi Jones (now known as Amiri Baraka) had a unique take on the British style of blues. "Does anybody really think it's weird that all these English 'pop' groups are making large doses of loot?" said Jones. "They take the style of black blues, country or city, and combine it with the visual image of white American non-conformity, i.e., the beatnik, and score very heavily. These English boys are literally 'hipper' than their white counterparts in the U.S. As one young poet said, 'At least the Rolling Stones come on like English crooks.'"

The work of black bluesmen weren't Led Zeppelin's only source material. "Dazed and Confused," from the band's first album, was credited to Page but actually written by Jake Holmes. The guitarist had first heard the song when he was with the Yardbirds and saw Holmes open for Janis Ian at New York's Café Au Go Go. The next day, he bought *"The Above Ground Sound" of Jake Holmes* and, retaining the ominous, descending bass line, refashioned the tune with a different guitar part and rewritten lyrics. The Yardbirds performed the song as "I'm Confused." But by the time it was recorded by Led Zeppelin, it was once more called "Dazed and Confused." Holmes sent Page a letter asking to be credited for the music and to receive due compensation. He got no reply.

Zeppelin's most famous song, "Stairway to Heaven," which became the most played song in the history of album-oriented radio, borrowed its elegant guitar introduction from "Taurus" by Spirit. Zeppelin's first American tour included opening shows for Spirit. Led Zeppelin had no trouble writing an original slow blues, however, and "Since I've Been Loving You" became a concert staple after it was included on *Led Zeppelin III*. The tune's explosive guitar solo underscored the fact that while Jimmy Page was a master of orchestrating pulverizing hard rock songs like "Achilles Last Stand," and could deftly add Middle Eastern elements to a song like "Kashmir," his lead guitar style was often no more than a step or two away from the blues.

Led Zeppelin were the kings of rock during the 1970s, raking in a fortune and developing a lurid reputation for its voracious appetite for sex, drugs, and yes, rock and roll. Like Robert Johnson, there were dark rumors that Zeppelin had made its own pact with the devil, gossip given additional oxygen by Page's well-documented fascination with the dark arts in general, and occultist Aleister Crowley in particular. In any event, bad karma seemed to surround the band. Page became addicted to heroin, which helped to explain the uneven quality of the band's later albums, and in 1977, Plant's five-year-old son, Karac Pendragon, died of a virus. Then, on September 24, 1980, drummer John Bonham, thirty-two, drank heavily before, during, and after a Led Zeppelin rehearsal in preparation for a tour of the United States. Late that night, the sleeping drummer was put to bed. He never woke up. A coroner's report said that in the last twenty-four hours of his life, Bonham had consumed forty shots of vodka. Led Zeppelin died with John Bonham, and despite two records and a tour with Robert Plant in the 1990s, and a celebrated reunion concert in 2007, Jimmy Page's career has been essentially encased in his thunderously influential past. In 2012, both Led Zeppelin and Buddy Guy were recipients of Kennedy Center Honors.

"One day I went out with the ARVN on an operation in the rice paddies above Vinh Long," wrote Michael Herr, "forty terrified Vietnamese troops and five Americans, all packed in three Hueys that dropped us up to our knees in paddy muck. . . . There was a lot of fire coming down from the trees, but we were all right as long as we kept down. And I was thinking, Oh man, so this is a rice paddy, yes, wow! When suddenly I heard an electric guitar shooting right up in my ear and a mean, rapturous black voice singing, coaxing, 'Now c'mon baby, stop actin' so crazy' and when I got it all together I turned to see a grinning black corporal hunched over a cassette recorder. 'Might's well,' he said. 'We ain't going nowhere till them gunships come.'

"That's the first time I ever heard Jimi Hendrix."

Hendrix's "Fire" was like a loud letter from home. Three short years after recording that song, the former paratrooper who could drop bombs and scatter shrapnel with his Stratocaster would play a famously fractured rendition of "The Star Spangled Banner" at Woodstock. Guitar players typically specialize in rhythm (like Keith Richards) or lead (a la Eric Clapton). Hendrix was a master of both, schooled in rhythm from his years of playing

R&B bands led by the likes of Little Richard and the Isley Brothers. Hendrix's rhythm guitar on "Wait until Tomorrow," from his second album, 1967's *Axis Bold as Love*, is as soulfully funky as anything you'd hear on a '60s album by Aretha Franklin or Curtis Mayfield. Similarly, the sophisticated chorded style of songs like "Little Wing" and "The Wind Cries Mary" was derived from soul and gospel music.

Hendrix's cover of Bob Dylan's "All Along the Watchtower," recorded just months after its inclusion on 1968's *John Wesley Harding*, was a thrilling tour de force of both rhythm and lead guitar. For this listener, it's the rarest of overplayed pop songs; one that thrills me every time. The basic track was cut with Hendrix and Dave Mason of Traffic playing dramatically accented acoustic guitars—Mason was on a twelve-string—with Mitch Mitchell on drums. Then electric guitars were added to build a thick bed of rhythm. The solo section passed the baton between four distinct guitar styles: a melodic rock lead; a woozy passage played with a slide on a twelve-string guitar; a barking wah-wah section in which the guitar jumped from speaker to speaker; and a conclusion of soulfully strummed chords punctuated by violent scrapes over muted strings. The result was arguably the most brilliantly realized interpretation of any Dylan song. Indeed, when Dylan returned to the concert stage with the Band in 1974, they played Hendrix's arrangement of "All Along the Watchtower."

The song was on Hendrix's *Electric Ladyland* (1968), his third release within less than two years. The comparatively sprawling two-record set also included two masterpieces that confirmed that the blues lived in his fingertips: "Voodoo Chile" and "Voodoo Chile (Slight Return)." The germ of both performances can be heard on a 1967 BBC broadcast in which Hendrix played "Catfish Blues," a Delta standard with a history as tangled as a fishing line caught in the brush. Robert Petway recorded "Catfish Blues" in 1942; a year earlier, Tommy McClennan, who'd often performed with Petway, cut the similar "Deep Blue Sea Blues." Both songs shared a common verse: "I wished I was a catfish, swimming down in the sea; I'd have some good woman, fishing after me." In the early 1950s, Muddy Waters used the template of "Catfish Blues" to write "Rolling Stone" and "Still a Fool." That's why when Hendrix played "Catfish Blues," he sometimes introduced it as "Muddy Waters Blues."

Hendrix recorded "Voodoo Chile" at Manhattan's Record Plant with Mitch Mitchell on drums, Jack Casady of Jefferson Airplane on bass, and Steve Winwood of Traffic on organ. The musicians arrived from a late-night jam session at a nearby club, The Scene, but by the time the equipment was ready and Hendrix had played the musicians a sketch of the tune, it was after 7 AM. "There were no chord sheets, no nothing," said Winwood. "He just started playing." But according to engineer Eddie Kramer, this wasn't an informal jam. "They may have seemed casual to the outside observer," said Kramer, "but Jimi plotted and planned out nearly all of them. He'd reason that if he had his songs together, if he really wanted to pull out what he heard in his head, he needed [nothing more than] the right people." There were three takes of the tune (Hendrix broke a string on the second), with the last a keeper.

"Voodoo Chile" is a fifteen-minute musical meditation in the key of E, a virtual *Gone With the Wind* of the blues that opened deep in the Delta with Hendrix repeatedly hammering on a single string before casting out long, reverberating lead lines. Hendrix references "Catfish Blues" in the introduction, but by the time the band enters, it's as if the blues had already moved from Mississippi to Chicago, with Hendrix's lyrics suggesting Muddy's "Hoochie Coochie Man": "Well, the night I was born, Lord I swear the moon turned a fire red." As the title suggests, "Voodoo Chile" exists within a catalog of blues songs fitted with references to such native signifiers as a "mojo hand" (a magic charm) and a "black cat bone" (said to grant its owner invisibility). Considering that good Christians looked down on bluesmen, it's hardly surprising that they (and even some good Christians) would look for solace in the charms used by practitioners of the mostly African American folk magic called "hoodoo." Recall that Skip James looked in that direction when he had medical problems.

Hendrix's solos on "Voodoo Chile" referenced the classic urban blues of B.B. and Albert King before he and the band create an explosive, abstract crescendo that approaches the sound of free jazz before collapsing back into a silence interrupted by the solitary sound of Hendrix once more hammering on a single string. All told, the song was a shorthand, round-trip history of the blues, and confirmed Hendrix's significant place in that tradition. And on the subject of "hoodoo," the sound of the hangers-on in the studio was supplemented by other crowd noise to better conjure a late-night (or early-morning) jam session.

"Voodoo Chile (Slight Return)" was performed the next day before a visiting film crew. Recorded with Mitchell and Noel Redding on bass, it pushed the song into the aggressive realm of hard rock while retaining a clear and vital link to its bluesy antecedent. Hendrix carves the introductory guitar riff with his wah-wah pedal before the song explodes into a maelstrom of feedback and feverish guitar licks. "I stand up next to a mountain," sang Hendrix, "chop it down with the edge of my hand." The guitar playing is as brutal as the imagery, but the roaring thunder is nonetheless grounded in a lick derived from "Catfish Blues," except that this particular creature was swimming in a sea of LSD.

"He was the first and last of the space-age bluesmen," said British critic Charles Shaar Murray, "the only one to create an entirely new set of possibilities for the future of the cornerstone of twentieth century popular music, the only one to propose new ways of creating within the blues rather than to heist its treasure and stash them elsewhere. Where his precursors used their instruments to mimic the rural sounds of trains and animals, or the urban clamour of police sirens and traffic jams, Hendrix reproduced bombs and riots, air raids and helicopters, exploding buildings and the screech of tires. In the truest sense of the term, it was modern blues, and the gauntlet is still lying where he left it."

The Rolling Stones added another notch to their antiestablishment image when some radio stations banned the benignly political "Street Fighting Man," which was released in August 1968, the month of the riotous Democratic Convention in Chicago. By the time the band toured the United States in the fall of 1969, they'd released another of their greatest hits, "Honky Tonk Women." Richards's famous guitar lick was played in open-G tuning, but the song was also blessed by a bit of serendipity.

"We've never played the intro to 'Honky Tonk Women' live the way it is on record," said Charlie Watts. "That's [producer] Jimmy [Miller] playing the cowbell and either he comes in wrong or I come in wrong—but Keith comes in right, which makes the whole thing right. . . . It's actually a mistake, but from my point of view, it works."

The Stones, like virtually every rock group in the 1960s, were on a treadmill of recording at least one album per year. By the time *Beggars Banquet* was released in the fall of 1968, the band had already begun recording *Let It Bleed*, which was issued a year later. By that time, Jagger and Richards were writing material for *Sticky Fingers*, some of which was recorded while on the 1969 U.S. tour documented by a celebrated live album recorded at Madison Square Garden, *Get Yer Ya-Ya's Out!* Albert and David Maysles also directed a documentary about the tour, *Gimme Shelter*. Neither the album nor the film included the acoustic portion of the concert where Jagger sang Robert Johnson's "Love in Vain" while Richards played a National steel guitar.

Al Kooper, who famously played on Bob Dylan's "Like a Rolling Stone," also participated in sessions for the Stones' "You Can't Always Get What You Want." "Mick and Keith played the song they wanted to record until everyone had the chord changes and the rhythm accents," said Kooper. "There was a conga player there who could play congas and roll huge hash joints without missing a lick. It was decided I would play piano on the basic track and overdub organ later." Kooper, who also ended up adding a French horn, said he based his piano part on a groove he'd heard on Etta James's version of "I Got You Babe."

The Stones hadn't toured the U.S. since 1966, and had to adjust to the fact that instead of playing to a screaming, inattentive crowd, they were met by an audience ready to listen. "In 1969 the set was getting on for two hours," said Richards. "People had bought the Stones records and now they actually wanted to listen to the music—which we'd been dying for them to do ever since we left the Crawdaddy Club." Watts said it took the band a while to learn how to play longer sets. "We had to learn the shaping of a performance," said Watts. "The start, the finish, and an encore, because we had never, ever done encores."

The Stones brought two opening acts on the 1969 tour, B.B. King and Ike and Tina Turner. "When we played Baltimore," said King, "there was a white lady that came up with her children and she said, 'You're B.B. King.' I said, 'Yes, ma'am.' She said, 'Have you ever made any records?' I said, 'Yes, ma'am.' She said, 'Well, my kids and I like what you did. Can you tell me where I can get one?' I mean, she wasn't joshing me at all, she was serious. And I'm thinking, 'I've been making records since '49.'"

The tour led to an unusual encounter between Richards and Ike Turner. "The open tuning fascinated him the way it had fascinated me," said Richards. "He dragged me into his dressing room [and said] . . . 'Show me that five-string shit.' . . . He got the hang of it in forty-five minutes, picked it up like that. But to me the amazing thing is, I'm showing Ike Turner shit?" Ike and Tina Turner's 1970's album, *Come Together*, employed open tunings, and aimed for rock fans not just with the title tune by the Beatles, but by a cover of "Honky Tonk Women."

At the end of the tour, the Stones spent three days recording at Muscle Shoals Sound Studio in Alabama; the funky facility was home to a celebrated crew of studio musicians who'd famously played on records by Aretha Franklin, Wilson Pickett, and the Staple Singers, among many others. "They [the Stones] were in a position where they could tour but not record and had been prevented from recording in Los Angeles," said Jim Dickinson, the well-connected Southern musician. "They were looking for a place where nobody would care and I told 'em about Muscle Shoals." The band soaked up the studio's unique atmosphere. "You wanted to be there because of all the guys who worked in the same studio," said Watts. "I just placed my drums in the place where Roger Hawkins used to have his kit."

Dickinson ended up playing piano on the ballad "Wild Horses" because Ian Stewart, the so-called "Sixth Stone" who typically played piano with the band, had a peculiar aversion to minor chords. Dickinson also added a lyrical footnote to the sessions' most famous song. "If you listen to the lyrics [of 'Brown Sugar'], he [Jagger] says 'Skydog slaver' though it's always written 'scarred old slaver.' What does that mean? 'Skydog' is what they called Duane Allman in Muscle Shoals, because he was high all the time."

"Brown Sugar" is a terrific rock song with a raucous, open-G rhythm guitar and words that are as politically incorrect as a swastika in a synagogue. Imagine the furor that would ensue today if a major rock band released a tune about a whip-wielding slave trader taking his carnal pleasure with the women he's preparing to sell? To be sure, there were lots of early blues tunes that contained misogynistic and sometimes violent imagery, and it could be argued that the Stones were doing nothing more than taking a cue from the Delta songbook. Except, of course, that they were wealthy white British rock stars. Early feminists had already criticized the Stones over the lyrics to "Under My Thumb," but the uncontested success of the patently offensive "Brown Sugar" is in a league of its own.

A few days after the Stones cut "Brown Sugar," the band flew to California to end the tour with a free concert at the Altamont Speedway on December 6. The concert drew a crowd of 300,000, with the Hells Angels on hand to provide security. "When we went through the backstage area it was full of people," said Watts. "A lot of them were fucked up and the Angels made a razor-sharp line for us to walk through. I felt very worried as we walked the stage. It was an event waiting to go wrong."

And it did. Altamont is typically posited as the dark, flip side of the Woodstock Festival that had proceeded without incident four months earlier. Where Woodstock is painted as a moment of promise, Altamont has come to symbolize the death of the idealistic counterculture. But the "peace and love" of Woodstock was also the sound of a bullet being dodged; in an era marked by political protests and assassination, the potential for disaster as a half-million stoned kids camped out on a muddy field in upstate New York was as clear as the rainy skies were dark. Altamont was even more of a gamble, with a site that had been hastily prepared in a day, and a stage that was barely over a foot high. The Jefferson Airplane played at both festivals.

"Woodstock was a bunch of stupid slobs in the mud," said Grace Slick, "and Altamont was a bunch of angry slobs in the mud."

Other bands played at Altamont, but it wasn't intended as a rock festival as much as the Rolling Stones celebrating its self-proclaimed status as "the greatest rock 'n' roll band in the world." *Gimme Shelter*, however, also revealed the band to be fatuous mortals buffeted by the ill winds of the day. "We could feel the fear in the crowd," said Bill Wyman, "and we were worried ourselves; none of us had ever experienced this level of menace." Hells Angels packed the stage and kept a jaundiced eye on the throng in the pit. "Keep it cool," said Richards to the crowd. He was high on acid, and motioned the band to stop. "If you don't cool it, you' ain't gonna hear no music." A burly Angel immediately grabbed the microphone: "Fuck you!"

The brand-new "Brown Sugar" made its concert debut amid the tumult of Altamont. "I just stood there with my mouth open and hoped for the best," said Mick Taylor. "After about five numbers, there seemed to be fights breaking out everywhere." As the band played, Meredith Hunter, a black man near the front of the stage, was seen to pull a gun, at which point a Hell's Angel lunged at him, and stabbed him to death. The Rolling Stones performed "Under My Thumb" as Hunter bled into the California soil. The Stones fled the stage to a waiting helicopter. The last song in their set was "Street Fighting Man," in which the singer wondered, "What could a poor boy do, but to sing in a rock 'n' roll band?" Mick Jagger flew directly to Switzerland to deposit the $1.2 million payday from the concert tour.

TWELVE

STONED BLUES

"They used to have Sunday matinees at the Fillmore West," said Carlos Santana, "and Paul Butterfield didn't show up for one of those. . . . I think that was my biggest break—there was Jerry Garcia, people from the Jefferson Airplane, Mike Bloomfield and Elvin Bishop, and they were jamming." A friend of Santana's cajoled the musicians into letting his blues-playing friend from Tijuana join the jam. "Michael was very kind," said Santana, "and said, 'Sure, come on up.' He handed me his guitar, because he was playing keyboards."

The Santana Blues Band would soon be a regular attraction at the Fillmore and other Bay Area venues. Bloomfield, meanwhile, soon left Butterfield to form the Electric Flag, which debuted at 1967's Monterey Pop Festival, and was signed by manager Albert Grossman to Columbia Records. Bloomfield and Nick Gravenites, who sang with the Electric Flag, called Grossman "The Cloud." "You could see it," said Gravenites, "huge, gray, and august—but when you went up to touch it, it

Peter Green 1946–

wasn't there." Gravenites reluctantly signed a publishing deal with Grossman after being told that it was the cost for his representation.

The concept behind the Electric Flag was to play blues and Otis Redding–style soul with a twist of jazz and psychedelic rock. Horns, a mainstay of soul music, were new to rock, with bands like Blood, Sweat & Tears (initially led by Al Kooper) and Chicago embracing this broader, instrumental palette. But on the Electric Flag's debut album, *A Long Time Comin'*, the two best songs were both blues: a hard-driving take on Howlin' Wolf's "Killing Floor," and a riveting slow blues called "Texas" that was written by Bloomfield and Buddy Miles, who sang and played drums in the Flag. Bloomfield was a master of such material, for while he had wide-ranging tastes and instrumental talents, he had an especially personal touch on this most emotional style of blues.

The Electric Flag's inconsistent live performances belied the title of one of its songs, "Grooving Is Easy." "I ain't no entertainer," said Bloomfield, "just a musician and a person." By contrast, Miles was not just a showman, but a showboat, wearing colorful clothes (including an American flag shirt), and exhorting the concert audience to clap hands and stomp feet. Bloomfield considered such shuck and jive to be demeaning, but show business strategies weren't the root of the group's troubled existence.

"Michael's problem from 1967 on was junk," said Ira Kamin of Mother Earth. "He told me it started in L.A. when he was putting together the Electric Flag. . . . When he started getting into heroin, he lost himself. He really never came out of that." Albert Grossman took a hands-off approach to the problem. "I just didn't think that Albert was sensitive enough to the problems within the band," said keyboardist Barry Goldberg. "His outlook was, 'Hey, you guys are responsible for yourself.'"

Bloomfield had both a wealthy father and a trust fund from his grandmother, which perhaps contributed to both his limited attention span and his dangerous addiction. Disappointed by meager record sales and less-than-prestigious live gigs, he left the Electric Flag after less than a year. Al Kooper, whom Bloomfield had met while recording with Dylan, and who'd quit Blood, Sweat & Tears and taken an artist and repertory job at Columbia Records, soon approached Bloomfield with a proposition. Kooper figured that since there were loads of jazz albums based on the concept of putting marquee musicians together, they could do the same thing with rock 'n' roll players. Bloomfield agreed, they settled on a rhythm section, and went into a Los Angeles studio.

After one day in the studio, they had half an album in the can. "There was a real comfortable feeling to the proceedings," said Kooper. "I had gotten the best recorded Bloomfield ever and, after all, that was the whole point of the album." The next morning, Kooper awoke to a phone call from a friend of Bloomfield's inquiring if the guitarist had made his plane to San Francisco. After confirming that Bloomfield had indeed flown the coop, Kooper recruited Stephen Stills to record the second half of what would become *Super Session*. The album became an unexpected hit and the best-selling release by either Bloomfield or Kooper. "I think Michael was embarrassed by *Super Session*—not playing-wise but success-wise," said Kooper. "He felt like he was the street, and I was the slick guy."

Super Session, which included memorable Bloomfield guitar turns on "Albert's Shuffle" and "His Holy Modal Majesty," spawned a brief fad for often second-rate rock jams, such as "Apple Jam," which was the third disc of George Harrison's *All Things Must Pass*, and featured Eric Clapton on guitar. It also prompted an inevitable sequel, *The Live Adventures of Mike Bloomfield and Al Kooper*, recorded over three nights at the Fillmore West. When Bloomfield spent the third night in the hospital suffering from extreme exhaustion, he once more left Kooper to hustle for a replacement. Elvin Bishop and Carlos Santana came to the rescue.

"Every time somebody would cancel," said Santana, who had yet to record an album, "Bill Graham would call us, because he knew that we'd keep the audience totally interested." Graham comanaged the Latin-flavored rock band now simply called Santana, and played a vital role in its success, including landing the group a career-making appearance at the Woodstock Festival before the release of its debut LP. While Santana was an unknown artist about to become famous, Bloomfield was an acclaimed musician who increasingly shied away from the spotlight.

Kooper is loath to say that heroin was the singular cause of Bloomfield's problems. "He came from immense wealth," said Kooper. "And I think kicking around the poor side of town and picking up the blues and everything was his rebellion against that. . . . But the ironic thing was: he became famous as a blues singer [frankly, he wasn't much of a singer]. And then the wealth was at his feet, again. . . . It wasn't hellhounds on my trail, it was like, hard cash on my trail." In short, the sorts of trouble of which bluesmen dream.

"Chemical soul," said Tracy Nelson of Mother Earth. "I can't tell you how many times I heard Ray Charles' name invoked in that context. . . . They just didn't get it. Those people weren't soulful because they did heroin. They did heroin because they were in pain. . . . White people doing black music carry a lot of guilt and it might have been a punishment thing as well. But mostly it was, 'How can I be like them? I'll do everything those people do and maybe that'll work.'"

Albert Grossman began managing Big Brother and the Holding company shortly after Janis Joplin and the band brought down the house at the Monterey Pop Festival. He got the band signed to Columbia Records, a deal that required extricating the group from a contract with Mainstream Records to the tune of $200,000. Grossman earned his typical 25 percent commission as manager. "Every time you talk to me you're 10 percent smarter than before," said Grossman. "So I just add that 10 percent on to what all the dummies charge for nothing." Grossman clearly saw Joplin as the star of the show, and perhaps with Bloomfield in mind, insisted that she not do heroin. "I've seen terrible things with it," said Grossman, "and if anybody here is messing with it at all, there's no point in going any further." At the time, none of them were regular users. Grossman eventually took out a life insurance policy in case Joplin died of an accident.

Big Brother moved to the East Coast to tour and record their album for Columbia. Grossman hired John Simon to produce the record; he'd just completed *Music from Big Pink* for another of Grossman's other clients, the Band. Simon was less than impressed by Big Brother's instrumental skills, but still tried to record the band in concert at Detroit's Grande Ballroom. The tapes were terrible, so Simon conspired to create a faux live album by grafting a Bill Graham introduction and crowd noise onto a studio recording. The sessions were less than amicable.

"Here's this dude [Simon] from Princeton with perfect pitch telling this band they're playing their guitars out of tune," said Elliot Mazer, who was involved in the recording, "and telling her [Joplin] that she's singing out of tune, and making them do a million takes." After about two weeks in New York, only three songs were completed; it took another month in an L.A. studio to complete the "live" record, which actually included just one song recorded in concert, "Ball and Chain." Joplin's most intimate performance on the LP was "Turtle Blues," on which Simon accompanied her on piano. "She was planning out every shriek and moan as she went," said Simon, citing her primary vocal models to be Tina Turner, Big Mama Thornton, and Etta James. "We'd do a take. She'd say, 'I like that.' The next take she'd do it the same. It was all planned, like filling up the spaces in a Double-Crostic."

Cheap Thrills was released in August of 1968 and sold a million copies in its first month. Simon, who by then was producing the Band's second album, left his name off the LP, but shared in its profits. "What they [Big Brother] should have had," said Simon, "was an Alan Lomax field recording from San Francisco." *Cheap Thrills* actually did serve as a souvenir of the hippie ballroom culture, complete with a memorable cover by the dean of underground comix, R. Crumb. It established Janis Joplin as a major star, and instantly recast Big Brother as her backing group; tensions couldn't help but mount between the celebrated singer and her critically abused band.

"Big Brother is just a wretched, lame group of cats who she carries for no reason at all," said Mike Bloomfield to Jann Wenner, who was interviewing him for *Rolling Stone*. When Joplin finally dumped Big Brother, Grossman enlisted Bloomfield and Gravenites to find and rehearse a new group. Joplin and the Kozmic Blues Band, which included horns in a move toward soul music, made its debut at a Stax Records show in Memphis, Tennessee, that featured the Staple Singers, Booker T. and the MGs, and Albert King. The under rehearsed hippies wilted before the practiced competition, and famously bombed.

"Janis wanted to emulate Aretha and Otis," said guitarist Sam Andrews, the only musician retained from Big Brother, "but before we even had the repertoire down, we were going to play in front of one of the most demanding audiences in the country, our heroes from Stax. . . . It was intimidating, playing the blues for black people. . . . We just blew it."

The musicians of Stax had honed their craft for years, just as B.B. King had played the country's black venues for decades before performing for hippies at the Fillmore. Janis was a newly minted recording star who, in the interest of striking while the iron was hot, had been rushed into playing with a new band. Between the firing of Big Brother and the troubled start of the Kozmic Blues Band, Joplin was a nervous wreck. A woman left lonely in a man's world, she increasingly took solace in liquor and heroin, which she had previously sniffed, but now took with a needle.

In December of 1968, *Rolling Stone* published a story about the Texas music scene that included the following: "The hottest item outside of Janis Joplin, though, still remains in Texas. If you can imagine a hundred and thirty pound cross-eyed albino with long fleecy hair playing some of the gutsiest fluid blues guitar you have ever heard then enter Johnny Winter." Winter, who'd been playing regionally for nearly ten years, became an overnight sensation, pursued by record labels and managers, including Steve Paul, owner of the Manhattan music business hangout, the Scene. "He said, 'Let's go to New York and I'll show you what I can do,'" said Winter. "And he did. I stayed at his house and he took me to the Fillmore to see Mike Bloomfield and Al Kooper. I sat in with them and played [B.B. King's] 'It's My Own Fault,' and blew everybody away. . . . They'd seen all the stuff in *Rolling Stone* and were waitin' to see what I was like."

Winter had been preparing for this ever since he started playing guitar to records at his comfortable childhood home in Beaumont, Texas. The first single he bought was Little Richard's "Tutti Frutti," but he really liked the blues. "Muddy's records probably are my favorite," said Winter. "I'd play the record, then listen to it, and learn how to do it. I would play note for note when I first learned, but later I'd change it to my own style." Before long, Winter and his albino brother Edgar, a keyboardist, were playing in local combos, and cutting records for regional labels. When Winter was sixteen, he saw B.B. King at the Raven Club, and wheedled his way onto the bandstand. "I said, 'Please, let me sit in, Mr. King; I know your songs,'" said Winter, "and he finally let me play. I played his guitar Lucille. I played 'Goin' Down Slow' [and] got a standing ovation. . . . He said, 'I'll be seeing you down the line; you were great.'"

By the late '60s, Winter was focusing on blues-rock in a Cream-like trio, and had cut *Progressive Blues Experiment*, the best of Winter's recordings to precede his "discovery." He brought those tapes to England and spoke with Fleetwood Mac producer Mike Vernon about signing with Blue Horizon. But before that could happen, the *Rolling Stone* story hit the stands, and Steve Paul orchestrated a bidding war that resulted in a $600,000 contract with Columbia Records. Willie Dixon was a guest on Winter's first album for the label. "Willie Dixon spent most of the time trying to sell Johnny some more of his songs," said drummer John Turner. Around this time, Winter opened for B.B. King at the Fillmore East. "That was the first time I saw him since I played the Raven Club," said Winter. "He said, 'I told you, you were gonna make it.'"

On his way to becoming a rock star, Winter had also picked up a heroin habit. "I remember the Atlantic City Pop Festival vaguely," said Winter. "The festivals were a big blur when you were taking drugs. Sometimes I was tripping . . . but a lot of times the audiences couldn't tell." But you could hear it in the music. Winter played the blues with the amphetamine touch of an amped-up rocker, and was admired more for his fast licks than his shrill guitar tone. Winter might have loved the blues, but he indulged fans that preferred his raucous interpretations of songs by Bob Dylan and the Rolling Stones. The Stones also appreciated Winter; when they played London's Hyde Park in 1969, they opened with his "I'm Yours and I'm Hers."

Winter never knew who he might meet at the next rock show; at the Miami Pop Festival, he ended up jamming with Janis Joplin. "I had taken acid before and Janis and I were drinking Southern Comfort on the stage like it was Kool-Aid," said Winter. "Later on, I got real sick. I threw up on her in the helicopter. . . . It was terrible—it was a mess. She was alright with it; she called me up later on and asked me for another date."

Fleetwood Mac made its American debut at the Carousel Ballroom in San Francisco opening for Janis Joplin and Big Brother. Mac was an instant favorite on the ballroom circuit. "I used to go see the original Fleetwood Mac, and they used to kill me, just knock me out," said Carlos Santana, who jammed with the group, and was influenced by Peter Green's understated guitar style. "It's always been extremely inviting to hear blues executed by English people, because they take the best of the black and the best of the white, like Dionne Warwick or Johnny Mathis, so all of a sudden, blues becomes like water, and can take on any color." Santana's second album, *Abraxas*, included a stunning interpretation of Mac's "Black Magic Woman" that became the band's biggest hit.

Green and Fleetwood Mac were far from household names, but among blues-rock musicians, they were already stars. "He [Peter] first did everything and everyone, like we all did," said Stan Webb, guitarist for the British band Chicken Shack. "[He played] Robert Johnson, Mississippi Fred McDowell, Big Mama Thornton, Buddy Guy, B.B. King and Freddie King; but then Peter developed into the only white player that ended up totally original. That's not praise, it's a fact."

Playing in America, and befriending the San Francisco bands, encouraged Fleetwood Mac to add more extended jams to their live performances, and for Green to write rockier material for the band's third album, *Then Play On*. Still, a tune like "Oh Well," which paired verses framed by intricately syncopated rhythm guitars with raucous, single-note solos, bore the compositional concision of the blues. While touring America in 1969, the band cut *Fleetwood Mac in Chicago*, a double album recorded at Chess Studios with Willie Dixon, Buddy Guy, and Otis Spann. The band also recorded a full album with Spann on vocals and piano, *The Biggest Thing Since Colossus*.

Producer Mike Vernon said Spann liked Green's playing almost as much as he did bourbon. "At first our heroes seemed condescending to us," said Mick Fleetwood. "But Peter Green dazzled the Chicagoans with the sheer feel of his playing. . . . But it was ironic, for these Chess sessions produced the last blues that Fleetwood Mac would record. We were about to mutate into another kind of band altogether."

Fleetwood Mac toured the U.K. with Green's idol B.B. King in 1969. During a show at London's Royal Albert Hall, King broke a string and attributed it to the jitters. "Man, you'd be nervous if you could see what I can see right now," said King, motioning toward the private box where Eric Clapton and George Harrison were seated. "But I've got to say that, I'm sorry, Peter Green is the best." Though King and Green had occasion to trade guitar licks backstage, and jammed on-stage in Manchester, King sensed that his young protégé was in turmoil. One day, Green sat with King on the tour coach. "Around then I was spending a lot of time thinking about religion and faith," said Green, "and I kind of hoped he might have something to tell me—things that we might talk over. But I guess he wasn't comfortable doing that. One thing he did say was that playing guitar I had a sensitive touch."

The rock life was taking a toll on the band in general, and Green in particular. "Here was a young man in his twenties with the world at his feet and he's living at home with his mum and dad," said Paul Morrison, who consulted on Fleetwood Mac's sound equipment. "Now that's not exactly normal and I think the reason is that he felt very vulnerable out in the big wide world. He was never able to cope with being a star: part of him absolutely loved it and part of him was horrified by the whole idea." Taking acid did not help; Green said the drug made him more introspective, but his band mates saw other effects. "A dozen LSD trips had rendered him a spiritually burnt-out case," said Fleetwood. "He had shunted his Jewish heritage aside and became a messianic Christian, which lasted only several weeks." Green let his hair and beard grow long; his wardrobe had changed, with casual T-shirts and jeans replaced with blouses and cloaks.

In January 1970, Fleetwood Mac was on a bill with the Grateful Dead at the Warehouse in New Orleans, and both the audience and the performers were dosed with LSD. "At one point Peter couldn't play anything," said Jenny Boyd, who was married to Mick Fleetwood, "and only Mick was able to perform a bit but to me he looked like a skeleton on stage. Complete madness! Afterwards I remember walking towards Peter and he said, 'Oh no! Stay away from me. I don't want to get caught in your world!'" All things considered, Fleetwood Mac was lucky, for after the acid-laced show, nineteen members of the Dead and their crew were arrested at their French Quarter Hotel. Owsley Stanley, who'd designed the Dead's state-of-the-art sound system and who also manufactured high-quality LSD, ended up spending three years in federal prison. The Grateful Dead's "Truckin'" ("Busted down on Bourbon Street") recounted the bummer in the Big Easy.

Two nights later, the Dead threw themselves a benefit concert at the Warehouse to help defray legal costs. "Towards the end of our set," said Phil Lesh, bass player for the Dead, "Peter Green joined us for 'Turn On Your Lovelight.' Peter's powerful, cogent playing makes our band focus more on leaving room for one another, always a good thing." Ten days later, Green and Fleetwood Mac were involved in another jam session at New York's Fillmore East with members of the Grateful Dead and the Allman Brothers Band.

Memorable musical moments and tremendous success—in 1969, British music fans named Fleetwood Mac best group over the Beatles and the Rolling Stones—didn't stop Green from becoming increasingly disillusioned with his life as a pop star. "I remember how upset he was by the news of starving orphans who were victims of the Nigerian civil war in Biafra," said Mick Fleetwood. "He used to cry in front of the TV news." Green proposed that Fleetwood Mac become a charity band, keeping enough money to cover their expenses, but giving the rest to the poor. "We could still be a band," said Green, "but our lives would be dedicated to something."

"Why Peter Green Wants to Give His Money Away" was the headline of a story in Britain's *New Musical Express*, an article that resulted in numerous appeals to the guitarist's generosity. "Because of all the adoration people were giving him," said his friend, Sandra Elsdon-Vigon, "he was finding it very hard to differentiate between that exalted state and mere mortality— albeit with a God-given talent. . . . As I see it, he wasn't strong enough to contain that power and it soon led to lofty identifications." It was as if the passion that he'd put into his music had pushed him to the edge of madness.

Green's turmoil came to a head when, after a 1970 concert in Munich, Germany, he went to a party with a group of fans that were described as "rich anarchist hippies." Green and Danny Kirwan were accompanied by one of the band's road crew, Dennis Keen. "We were offered a glass of wine," said Keen, "and the next thing I knew all hell broke loose in my head—we'd been drugged." Hours later, Keen found Green in a basement recording studio. "I opened the door and there's Pete playing this guitar with all these other guys. But the sound they were making was awful: this kind of freaky electronic droning noise."

The cacophony reflected Green's recent approach to music, as some tracks on *Then Play On* ("Searching for Madge," "Fighting for Madge") were little more than extracts from longer studio jam sessions. Where Green's early work was rooted in passionate restraint, his new preference for improvisation suggested a reluctance to engage in such musical intimacy. "Peter Green and me," said Danny Kirwan, "we stole the black man's music. What we did was wrong." B.B. King, for one, disagreed. But for Green, like Mike Bloomfield, the fame and fortune that came from their music conspired to alienate them from their art. The bluesmen they idolized struggled to stay in the black, while rock stars felt guilty about a world that offered fabulous fortune. Green soothed his conscious by giving away his money. But the other members of Fleetwood Mac, unlike their leader, were more interested in a career than charity, and the schism finally prompted Green to leave the band.

"Peter Green was never the same again," said Fleetwood of the incident in Munich. "Appealing to his sense of duty, we persuaded him to come with us and finish the tour. But that night, back at the hotel, he told us he was finished. He said he was in a panic, that he couldn't handle the money, that he was just a working-class person."

"The truth about Peter Green and how he ended up how he did is very simple," said Clifford Davis, Fleetwood Mac's manager. "He and Danny Kirwan took what turned out to be very bad, impure LSD. He was never the same again. . . . I've read a lot of articles saying that Peter Green was a religious maniac. I'm afraid that the truth of the matter is different. Sadly, he was suffering from drug induced delusions."

Green left at the end of the European tour. He would soon release a solo record, *The End of the Game*, which collected portions of spontaneous jams that bordered on jazz-rock fusion but added up to much less than a super session. The title was enough to break a Fleetwood Mac fan's heart, for in truth, it was essentially over for the best of the British bluesmen. B.B. King returned to England in 1971 to record an album called *In London* with British musicians. "In the studio he [Green] was quiet and I got the impression that he was very disillusioned with the whole music business," said King. Sadly, for Peter Green, his blues would soon go from bad to worse.

THIRTEEN
EXILES ON STAR STREET

Rock stars, like bluesmen, know how to party, but when success comes calling, playing music can also become a buzz-killing full-time job. The meteoric careers of Janis Joplin and Jimi Hendrix illustrate both the creative and psychological strains of working in the white heat of sudden stardom. Following their splashy debuts at the Monterey Pop Festival, both artists quickly released three albums and engaged in endless concert tours. Joplin and Hendrix were also outsiders in the late-'60s rock world, Janis because she was a woman, and Jimi because he was black.

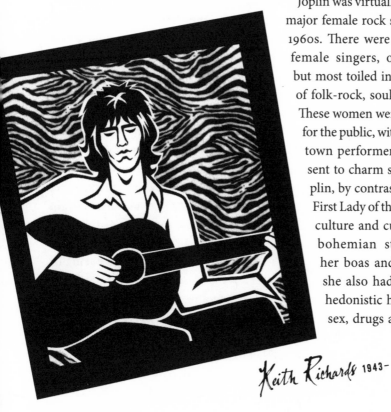

Keith Richards 1943–

Joplin was virtually the only major female rock star of the 1960s. There were plenty of female singers, of course, but most toiled in the fields of folk-rock, soul, or R&B. These women were tailored for the public, with the Motown performers literally sent to charm school. Joplin, by contrast, was the First Lady of the counterculture and cut a vivid, bohemian style with her boas and bangles; she also had as much hedonistic hunger for sex, drugs and booze as any male rock star. Hanging on to her microphone while pulling from a bottle of Southern Comfort, Joplin all but disappeared into her role as a hippie "blues mama."

"The black man's blues is based on the 'have not,'" said Joplin. "'I got the blues because I don't have this. I got the blues because I don't have my baby. I got the blues because I don't have a quarter for a bottle of wine.' . . . Well, you know, I'm a middle class white chick from a family that would love to send me to college and I didn't wanna. I had a job, I didn't dig it. I had a car, I didn't dig it. I had it real easy."

Those weren't the blues of Big Mama Thornton, who wrote the song that Joplin made famous, "Ball and Chain." "Willie Mae was a warmhearted lady," said John Lee Hooker of Thornton, "and a tough, tough lady." Like Hooker, she performed in Greenwich Village clubs during the blues revival, but she was ultimately not much more than a footnote. When she arrived to play a show at Folk City in 1984, the doorman mistook her for a bag lady. "The last thing she said to me," said Robbie Wolliver, who worked at the club, "was 'Here's my number. Call me, don't call my agent. I'll make more money if you just call me.'" She died a few months later.

Joplin had plenty of money, and sometimes fretted that friends and lovers were attracted not to her, but to her fame and fortune. Worse still, some weren't even impressed. Joplin went to her high school reunion in Port Arthur, Texas, at the height of her fame yet was still treated by her class mates as the same oddball they knew as a teenager. Joplin played the man-hungry woman on and off stage, but her most enduring relationships were with women, including Peggy Caserta, who titled her 1973 memoir *Going Down with Janis*. The two shared not just a bed, but a heroin habit. In August of 1969, Joplin and Caserta were backstage at the Woodstock Festival and looking for someplace to shoot up. There was no privacy save wading out into the massive crowd and finding a port-a-potty. "We got there," said Caserta, "and there's a huge line so Janis throws an 'I'm a star' fit and crowds back off and let us in. There's shit piled up so high you couldn't sit down, and I'm gagging from the stench." Few things shuck the glamour from a celebrity like being a junkie.

Joplin tried to stay clean in preparation for making her third Columbia album with Paul Rothchild, who'd produced the Butterfield Blues Band before finding fortune recording the Doors. Rothchild was by far Joplin's most sympathetic producer, and helped to broaden her range in terms of both material and execution. Songwriters naturally coveted placing a track on a Joplin album. "The intense community of musicians at the Chelsea

[Hotel] would often find their way into Janis's suite with their acoustic guitars," said Patti Smith. "I sat on the floor as Kris Kristofferson sang her 'Me and Bobby McGee,' Janis joining in the chorus." The song was destined to be her greatest hit.

During the Los Angeles recording sessions for the collection that would be named *Pearl*, however, Joplin slipped back into her drug habit. Staying at the Landmark Hotel, she ran into a musical acquaintance, Ed Sanders of the Fugs. "She was waiting for a ride and was very upbeat," said Sanders. "She joked about how she was becoming so wealthy she was going to be able to purchase her hometown of Port Arthur, Texas. She talked about two recent lovers, Joe Namath and Dick Cavett. She said Cavett was better. . . . On her arm were about twenty narrow bracelets. I thought later they might have been obscuring her shoot-up marks."

Some time during the night of October 3, 1970, Joplin died of a drug overdose. *Pearl* was released to great, mournful acclaim, with many ruminating over the poignant resignation of a central lyric of "Me and Bobby McGhee": "Freedom's just another word, for nothin' left to lose."

"Those of us who were inspired by Janis," said critic Ellen Willis, "who saw in her an emblem of our own struggle for freedom, have had to live with a kind of survivor's guilt, rooted in questions of whether we somehow collaborated in, or benefited from her self destruction. . . . Yet finally, to invest Janis Joplin's death as an excuse for closing down, playing it safe, would be to trivialize both her life and her art."

The day before Joplin died, her band laid down the instrumental track of a tune by Nick Gravenites; Joplin was scheduled to record her vocal the next day. The song's title was the story of her life: "Buried Alive in the Blues."

Jimi Hendrix was conflicted not by sexual stereotypes, but racial ones. Like Joplin, he was on a lucrative treadmill that provided little time for reflection and artistic development. Since his arrival in England in the fall of 1966, his life had become a blur of live dates, recording sessions, and more concerts. Recording sessions were done on the fly, with two LPs released in 1967 (*Are You Experienced* and *Axis: Bold as Love*) and a double disc in 1968 (*Electric Ladyland*). Predictably, the first album was tight and focused while the third was both brilliant and diffuse.

Hendrix's flamboyant showmanship was grounded in blues tradition; everybody from T-Bone Walker to Guitar Slim and Buddy Guy executed flashy stunts like playing the guitar behind their backs or picking the strings with their teeth. But Hendrix was the only one to do these tricks before a white rock audience new to such novelties, and once fans grew to expect such shtick, Hendrix the musician became increasingly uncomfortable playing the showboat guitarist. With an audience that was almost totally white, Hendrix couldn't help but be fearful of being considered a freakish novelty.

It was as if no place was quite his home. "[Hendrix] was tryin' to fit in on his [black] side of town," said Bobby Womack, "but it wasn't his side of town. . . . When he got to Europe he got with people that was like him, they was his family. . . . And then a lot of blacks started sayin' how it's terrible that he had to go to the white side to make it, 'cause we treated him so bad. . . . All these people would come out of the woodwork: 'He worked for me and I kicked him out.'"

Before Hendrix became a star, he'd signed a three-year contract with producer Ed Chalpin during a recording session with Curtis Knight. "He was so happy to be [treated as] an artist," said Chalpin, "he would have signed anything." After the release of *Are You Experienced?* Chalpin issued a Curtis Knight LP featuring the suddenly famous sideman and sued all the record companies releasing Hendrix's new material for violating his exclusive contract. Warner Brothers, Hendrix's U.S. label, made an out-of-court settlement that gave Chalpin 2 percent of Hendrix's three major albums plus the rights to Hendrix's fourth album (with a $200,000 guarantee).

Hendrix broke up the Experience trio before recording that fourth album, *Band of Gypsies*, with a black rhythm section consisting of his Army buddy Billy Cox on bass and ex-Electric Flag drummer Buddy Miles on drums. Recorded live at the Fillmore East, it's remembered mostly for the funky "Machine Gun," the politically charged standout of an otherwise undercooked repertoire. At the time, Hendrix was catching flack from the Black Panthers, who sought monetary support while also accusing him of being somehow less than truly black. It was an echo of his scuffling days when Hendrix was caught between the black world of slick uptown R&B and the looser blues-rock scene he found in Greenwich Village. All told, it was an odd path by which a black musician came to be a significant figure in the history of the blues.

Hendrix's contract with Chalpin brought fiscal grief, but his management deal with Mike Jeffery was equally fraught. To avoid taxes, all income from the Jimi Hendrix Experience was filtered through Yameta, a holding company incorporated in the Bahamas. Hendrix knew few of the fiscal details, because like most rock stars, his needs were met by a coterie of assistants.

A small fortune was sunk into a state-of-the-art recording studio on Eighth Street in New York City. The aim was to save Hendrix the money he spent at other studios, but between cost overruns and continued litigation with Chalpin, money was tight, and he was always on the road.

Little wonder that Hendrix's many recording sessions failed to produce a proper studio follow up to *Electric Ladyland*. Forever distracted by a busy schedule, he produced fragments of songs rather than completed compositions. The notion that he might be moving toward jazz was sparked by his friendship with Miles Davis, who said that in 1968, he listened not to jazz, but to Hendrix, Sly and the Family Stone, and James Brown. These were the influences that prompted Davis's move into jazz-rock fusion with such landmark albums as *In a Silent Way* and *Bitches Brew*. Hendrix was also said to be planning a recording with Gil Evans, who'd arranged many of Davis's classic recordings. Whatever was to come, however, Hendrix's peers recognized his roots. "Jimi Hendrix came from the blues, like me," said Davis, who was surprised to discover that the guitarist could not read music, but was impressed by his intuitive ear. "Jimi was based in the blues," said B.B. King, "but he went farther out on a limb."

Hendrix's studio, Electric Lady, was finally completed in the summer of 1970. After hosting an opening party, Hendrix flew to England for European concert dates, including a headlining appearance at the Isle of Wight Festival, where Miles Davis was also on the bill. He planned to return to New York to complete an album that he intended to call *First Rays of the New Rising Sun*. There was also talk that he wanted to sever his connection to manager Jeffery. Instead, in the early hours of September 18, 1970, he died in his sleep in London, choking on his own vomit after an evening of wine and too many sleeping pills. Hendrix was known to indulge in both drugs and alcohol—one can hardly imagine his innovative guitar playing without having had the experience of tripping on LSD—but he was neither a junkie nor a drunkard. If anything, he courted danger by having a high tolerance for intoxicants. So his passing was not the clichéd death-by-misadventure rock-star death (though it did inspire conspiracy theories) as much as a stroke of tragically bad luck. Hendrix, fried from the frenzy that was his career, simply went to bed and never woke up.

Hendrix was buried in his hometown of Seattle. Among the mourners at the funeral were Mitch Mitchell, Noel Redding, Miles Davis, Buddy Miles, Johnny Winter, and John Hammond Jr. Death was good for the business of Hendrix, and subsequent years would see the release of a blizzard of recordings, precious few of which came close to the quality of the albums issued in his lifetime. Along with Brian Jones, Janis Joplin, Jim Morrison, Alan Wilson, Kurt Cobain, and Amy Winehouse, he had died at the age of 27. Hendrix, avatar of space-age blues, shared that sad distinction with another man who knew what it was to have a hellhound on his trail: Robert Johnson.

Shortly after the breakup of Cream, Eric Clapton formed a group with Steve Winwood of the band Traffic. Already friends, they'd previously recorded together on the 1966 blues compilation *What's Shakin'*. There was talk that they'd enlist the celebrated rhythm section of Booker T. and the M.G.s, but when Ginger Baker elbowed his way onto the drum stool, everybody expected Cream II (Rick Grech was recruited to play bass). The band was quickly dubbed a "super group" and had high-profile management—Robert Stigwood (for Clapton) and Chris Blackwell (for Winwood)—and a name dreamed up by Clapton, Blind Faith.

Within months, Blind Faith had recorded an album and played before 120,000 at a free 1969 concert in London's Hyde Park. The album met with mixed reviews, with some critics disappointed to find neither the rock bombast of Cream nor the folk-rock charms of Traffic. In the end, the LP was mostly remembered for two songs: a lovely Winwood ballad called "Can't Find My Way Home," which was recorded with just two acoustic guitars and subtle percussion, and "In the Presence of the Lord," a tune by Clapton (but sung by Winwood) that was highlighted by an explosive wah-wah guitar solo. Despite its name, Clapton's tune didn't exactly express religious supplication; with the lyric "I have finally found a place to live," he's literally referring to Hurtwood Edge, the lavish countryside home and estate that he'd just bought.

If it takes a certain amount of rock star hubris to write a song about your new mansion, it takes similar chutzpah for a band with a single album to mount a tour of U.S. arenas. Riots broke out at some of the shows, including a sold-out performance at New York's Madison Square Garden. Critics were largely unimpressed with the band's undercooked live show. "The one Clapton solo that was clearly audible was a marvel of sanity amid the muddle," said critic Robert Christgau, "a forceful electric blues statement that owed something in mood and definition to B.B. King but showed none of King's resignation." This odd use of the word "resignation" was perhaps meant to suggest how a bluesman is different than a rock star.

The biggest story of the tour turned out to be its opening act, Delaney

& Bonnie & Friends, a soulful husband-and-wife team with a band that played a savvy mix of blues, country, and soul. Clapton enjoyed hanging out with the mostly Southern musicians, and frequently joined them on stage to play guitar. By tour's end, Blind Faith was breaking up, and Clapton signed on as a "sideman" with his new friends. Clapton's participation made Delaney and Bonnie instant headliners, with an excellent live album (*On Tour*) documenting the results. Delaney Bramlett encouraged Clapton to sing and write songs, and they collaborated on much of what became the guitarist's first solo album, 1970's *Eric Clapton*. The record was produced by Bramlett and used many of the musicians from his band, as well as Leon Russell, who subsequently took much of the ensemble on the road to back singer Joe Cocker on his celebrated "Mad Dogs and Englishmen" tour. Clapton also enlisted three of Delaney & Bonnie's musicians—keyboardist Bobby Whitlock, bass player Carl Radle, and drummer Jim Gordon—to form his next band, Derek and the Dominoes. The Bramletts never again enjoyed such a high profile. Clapton, by contrast, was about to make one of his most famous records, *Layla and Other Assorted Love Songs*.

In the spring of 1970, Clapton and his new band lived and rehearsed at his estate, Hurtwood Edge. The drugs of choice were cocaine and Mandraz. "'Mandies' were quite strong sleeping pills," said Clapton, "but instead of letting them put us to sleep, we would ride the effect, staying awake by snorting some coke or drinking some brandy or vodka, and this would create a unique kind of high. This became the chemistry of our lives."

The band played concert dates around Britain, and also served as the house band for George Harrison's *All Things Must Pass*, a two-record set that also included a third disc of instrumental jams. Phil Spector, who produced the Harrison collection, recorded the quartet doing its own "Tell the Truth," which was later recut for *Layla*. That album was recorded over three intermittent weeks in the early fall of 1970 in Miami, Florida, by Tom Dowd, who'd worked with Clapton in Cream. Coincidentally, Dowd was also in the process of producing the Allman Brothers Band's second album, *Idlewild South*. Guitarist Duane Allman asked if he could watch a Clapton session, but before that could happen, Dowd took Clapton's quartet to see a nearby concert by the Allman Brothers; after the show, the musicians returned to the studio for a lengthy jam session, during which it was decided that Duane would be added to the recording as the second guitarist.

Duane Allman was a master of the slide guitar, a style he had picked up after hearing the work of Ry Cooder and/or Jesse Ed Davis, who'd both performed with Taj Mahal. "I heard Ry Cooder playing it about three years ago," said Allman in 1971, "and I said, 'Man, that's for me!' I got me a bottleneck and went around the house for about three weeks sayin', 'Hey man, We've got to learn the songs—the blues to play on the stage.'"

Gregg Allman has a slightly different memory, and recalls that when his brother was suffering from a bad cold on his birthday, he'd brought him a bottle of Coricidin for the sniffles along with a gift of the first Taj Mahal album. The next day, Duane excitedly summoned Gregg. "'Man, that record you brought me is out of sight,'" said Gregg, recalling his brother's enthusiasm. "He slips the record on 'Statesboro Blues,' the Coricidin bottle on his ring finger, and a sound was born." ("Statesboro Blues" was also on the then-unreleased Rising Sons album that Cooder recorded with Taj Mahal.) But unlike Cooder or Davis, Allman's style was colored not just by the blues, but also by the pedal steel he heard in country music and the sort of modal improvisations found on Miles Davis's *Kind of Blue*. In the Allman Brothers Band, he played alongside another lead guitarist, Dickey Betts, inspiring a rock trend of twin lead guitars; the band, which included Gregg on vocals and keyboards, also employed two drummers.

Six months after Allman worked on *Layla*, Dowd recorded the Allman Brothers Band's breakthrough album, *At Fillmore East*. Compared to the more navel-gazing explorations of a psychedelic band like the Grateful Dead, or a blues-rock ensemble like Cream, the Allmans' live performances offered a much more organic approach to music making, with the instrumentalists not out to upstage each other as much as to cohere and inspire. The repertoire at the Fillmore included a scorching take on (what else?) Willie McTell's "Statesboro Blues" and an infectious interpretation of Muddy Waters's "Trouble No More." The blues were further represented with tunes by Sonny Boy Williamson ("One Way Out"), Elmore James ("Done Somebody Wrong") and T-Bone Walker ("Stormy Monday"); but it was the expansive originals like "Whipping Post" and "In Memory of Elizabeth Reed" that led many to regard *At Fillmore East* as one of rock's best-ever live albums.

The sound of Derek and the Dominoes was quite different than the Allman Brothers, with Clapton and Allman swapping leads and only rarely executing harmonizing guitar lines. When the sessions began, Dowd was surprised to see that Clapton had traded his Gibson guitar and massive Marshall amplifier for a Stratocaster and a small Fender Champ amp. After the roaring thunder of Cream, Clapton was now playing with the restraint he heard in both his blues heroes and rock contemporaries like Robbie Robertson of the Band. Allman's slide guitar, played on a Gibson Les Paul,

CROSSROADS

provided a perfect complement, and the pair happily traded solos on such blues songs as Big Bill Broonzy's "Key to the Highway," Freddie King's "Have You Ever Loved a Woman," and the Jimmy Cox standard "Nobody Knows You When You're Down and Out."

The original tunes were mostly collaborations between Clapton and Whitlock, including a hard-rocking blues ("Why Does Love Have to Be So Bad") and "Keep on Growing," a gospel-ish song reminiscent of Delaney & Bonnie. "Layla" was written by Clapton, while drummer Gordon composed and played the piano coda that was added at a subsequent recording session. Allman came up with the tune's signature seven-note guitar lick, played in tandem by the two guitarists, by speeding up the first melodic phrase of an Albert King blues ballad, "As the Years Go Passing By." Clapton's lyrics spoke to his unrequited love for the wife of George Harrison, Pattie Boyd. The hard-rock mash note eventually paid off, as Boyd later divorced Harrison and married Clapton.

While the music was inspired, the band's lifestyle haunted the recording sessions. Cocaine and heroin were washed down with Johnny Walker. "We didn't have little bits of anything," said Whitlock. "There were no grams around—let's put it that way. Tom [Dowd] couldn't believe it, the way we had these big bags laying out everywhere . . . It was scary, what we were doing, but we were just young and dumb and didn't know." Dowd raised a red flag, and Ahmet Ertegun of Atlantic Records visited the studio in Miami. "He [Ertegun] told me all about his experiences with Ray Charles," said Clapton, "and how painful it had been for him to watch Ray get more and more caught up in the world of hard drugs. At one point he became very emotional and started to cry. You would think that, because I can recall this with such clarity, it had some effect on me, but the fact is, it didn't make the slightest difference." Ertegun would soon have a similar conversation with Gregg and Duane Allman, who had also become addicted to heroin.

Derek and the Dominos interrupted their recording sessions for a brief tour of England. On an off day, Clapton traveled to Paris to see Buddy Guy and Junior Wells open a show for the Rolling Stones. Backstage, Clapton ran into Ertegun, who had just signed a deal to distribute the next six albums by the Stones. Clapton encouraged Ertegun to sign the bluesmen, and he agreed on the condition that the guitarist would lend his star power by producing the record. In between dates of a U.S. tour by Derek and the Dominos, *Buddy Guy and Junior Wells Play the Blues* was recorded over two days in Miami. Clapton attempted to tamp down his drug use in preparation for his debut as a producer.

"I was three or four days into withdrawal," said Clapton, "and I didn't know the first thing about producing an album. . . . And here I was completely smacked, and no one knew. . . . Tom Dowd said, 'I think you better go home.'" Five years earlier, Clapton had been inspired to form Cream after seeing Buddy Guy front a trio. Now the rock star was unable to shine a light on one of his favorite guitarists. "I was incredibly in awe of [Buddy]," said Clapton, "and I was completely under equipped mentally and emotionally in every way to deal with this situation. I shouldn't have been there. I was sweating and dying inside."

So were the Dominoes. The band played what would be its last concert on December 6, 1970, days before the release of *Layla* (two nights of live recordings made at the Fillmore East would be released in 1973). Clapton, who chronically vacillated between avoiding and basking in the warm bath of fame, was disappointed that *Layla* was initially greeted with lackluster reviews and meager sales. "I know I am just a freak," said Clapton, "an English guy playing the blues. I know that no matter what I play I am not going to get the blues like some of those guys in the States. There is something they are born and raised with; you can't catch up with that if you were born in Surrey." Liquor and drugs, he suggested, were just part of the package. "We're all hooked on something," said Clapton. "We need the drugs to help us, to free our minds and our imaginations from the prejudices and snobbery that have been bred into us."

But Clapton's mind was far from free. "By the end of the tour," said Clapton, "the band was getting very, very loaded, doing way too much. Then we went back to England, tried to make a second album, and it broke down halfway through because of the paranoia and the tension. And the band just . . . dissolved. I remember to this day being in my house, feeling totally lost and hearing Bobby Whitlock pull up in the driveway outside and scream for me to come out. He sat in his car outside all day, and I hid."

Clapton would be a recluse for much of the next two years, lost to heroin and his own tortured relationship to his fame and good fortune. Duane Allman had a much easier relationship with his musical gift than both Clapton and Jimi Hendrix. A reporter once asked him what he was doing to help the revolution. "Every time I'm in Georgia," said Allman, "I eat a peach for peace." It was the fall of 1971, only months after the release of *At Fillmore East*, and Allman was at home in Macon, Georgia. He had his customized Harley-Davidson motorcycle serviced and bought himself a new helmet, which he promptly modified by cutting the chin strap in half. Then, just weeks shy of his twenty-fifth birthday, he swerved the cycle in an attempt to avoid an oncoming vehicle and ran smack into a truck; the impact hurled the Harley into the air before it crashed down on Allman and caused the massive internal injuries that killed him. In a few short years, Allman's virtuosity had helped the Allman Brothers to spark a thriving Southern rock scene, and he had made an album with Clapton that would come to be regarded as a classic. When the Allman Brothers Band subsequently released a two-LP set that included Duane Allman's last studio and concert recordings, they called it *Eat a Peach*.

After Peter Green quit Fleetwood Mac, the remaining four members moved into a communal country home to play music and figure out what was next. By now, John McVie had married the former Christine Perfect, who had sung and played keyboards with Chicken Shack. "I didn't know how to play blues piano very well," said McVie of preparing to audition for that band, "so I rushed out and bought a whole bunch of Freddie King Records. I listened hard to his piano player, Sonny Thompson, and learned to copy his licks. That's where my style comes from." Over the years, she had added piano to a number of Fleetwood Mac tracks, and now joined the band. *Kiln House*, the first Fleetwood Mac album without Peter Green, was a modestly engaging rock 'n' roll record, that began the band's long and tumultuous evolution into one of the biggest pop-rock groups of the late 1970s. But at the time of *Kiln House*, Mac faced an American tour that would challenge Jeremy Spencer and Danny Kirwan to put on a show that would encourage audiences to forget the guitarist who was missing.

Green, meanwhile, was in no hurry to define his musical future. He sat in with bands and made plans to cut a solo album, though his preparations didn't include writing songs. Instead, he took some musicians into the studio and ran the tape. Orchestrating improvisation is a unique gift that requires a killer band and a charismatic leader like Miles Davis. "He [Peter] was in a corner by himself," said guitarist John Morshead, "very much in his own world. There was hardly any talking, just jamming. Some of it was really good and other bits were not." *Melody Maker* called 1970's *The End of the Game* "the most disturbing album release this year." (Carlos Santana released a far more successful example of properly rehearsed rock-jazz fusion with 1972's *Caravanserai*. Jeff Beck recorded a jazz-rock classic in 1975, *Blow By Blow*.)

Fleetwood Mac was in California to start its *Kiln House* tour, and Mick

Fleetwood was concerned about Jeremy Spencer. "He and Danny had taken some mescaline upon arrival," said Fleetwood, "and Jeremy didn't seem to come off it for a long time. . . . He was always a dreamer to begin with; lately he had been immersed in the Bible and all kinds of books on philosophy and changing your life."

In Los Angeles, Spencer left his hotel for a nearby bookstore; hours later, when the band gathered to travel to the evening's concert, he failed to appear. The show was canceled and the police and local radio stations were contacted to help locate the missing guitarist. Four days later, a tip led to a guarded warehouse in downtown L.A. that was the local headquarters for a religious cult called the Children of God. After much negotiation, manager Clifford Davis was permitted to see Spencer. Davis was shocked to see that Spencer had cut off his trademark curly hair, and would now only answer to the name 'Jonathan.'

For three hours, Davis listened as Spencer said that he was convinced that a recent California earthquake anticipated the end of the world, and that he needed to get his soul in order. Spencer showed little concern that the tour would have to be cancelled. "All the while," said Fleetwood, "two disciples were seated on either side of him, rubbing his arm and chanting, 'Jesus loves you.' Other sectarians crowded around, glowered, and told Clifford Davis that he was the devil trying to take Jonathan away from them. . . . His identity and personality had been brainwashed away. The old Jeremy Spencer was . . . gone."

Desperate to avoid the financial ruin that would come with abandoning the tour, Davis reached out to the man who'd founded Fleetwood Mac, and who was now working as a farm laborer. Two days later, Peter Green arrived in L.A. "The fact that Pete played so beautifully made it even sadder," said Fleetwood. "Because we knew we would lose him again. His playing raised gooseflesh on my arms on that tour, and yet at the end he renounced it all once again."

The life of Peter Green then devolved into a Dickensian nightmare. He worked as a groundskeeper in a graveyard and then traveled to Israel to join a kibbutz, where he found himself feeling more of a kinship with the nomadic Arabs he saw wandering the desert. Returning to London, Green's behavior became increasingly erratic until he was hospitalized in 1974. "They took me to the hospital in Epsom," said Green, "the madhouse. . . . I was stuck there and eventually they gave me ECT [electroconvulsive therapy, formerly known as electroshock]. They gave me injections and tranquilizers. I could hardly keep my eyes open."

In 1977, while being treated as an outpatient, Green was arrested after entering his accountant's office while brandishing a shotgun. Green had come seeking to stop payment of 30,000 pounds in royalties due him from his older recordings. "Peter desperately needs help," said Green's father, whose son had bought him and his wife a house after the success of "Albatross." "He must have given away tens of thousands. . . . He lives in an Alice-in-Wonderland of his own." After failing a psychiatric test during a short stay in jail, Green was sent back to the hospital in Epson.

Fleetwood Mac, meanwhile, was transformed when Lindsey Buckingham and Stevie Nicks joined Christine McVie and Mac's namesake rhythm section. The group's 1975 album, *Fleetwood Mac*, was an unexpected hit, selling five million copies. Relatively few people who bought that album knew of Peter Green, and nobody mistook Fleetwood Mac for a blues band. Two years later, as the once-gifted musician got arrested for refusing to collect the bounty of his past, his old band released *Rumours*, a blockbuster album that would eventually sell more than seventeen million copies.

Fleetwood Mac's commercial clout prompted Warner Brother's to offer Green a three-album, $1 million contract. While Green was in Los Angeles, Mick Fleetwood spent $5,000 to buy him a 1959 Les Paul like the one he used to play. Thrilled at being given the instrument, Green promptly gave it to an admiring stranger he met in the hotel elevator (it was recovered at a nearby pawn shop). Then, preparing to sign his record deal, Green balked. "I can't do this," said Peter Green. "It's the work of the devil." Green returned to England and a life dominated by demons of his own. In the late 1990s, friends helped him establish and record with a band called Splinter Group. But his gift was gone, and it was his life, and not his music, that had become Peter Green's most vivid expression of the blues.

In July of 1970, the Rolling Stones severed its ties to Allen Klein and his ABKCO Industries. Klein nonetheless still owned the masters and publishing rights to all of the group's music up to 1971's *Sticky Fingers*. Klein was the last manager of the Rolling Stones; Jagger, with the counsel of Prince Rupert Zu Loewenstein and other advisers, now took care of the business. Marshall Chess Jr., who had sent Chess LPs to a teenage Jagger in the early '60s, was recruited to run their new label, Rolling Stones Records, which signed a $5.7 million distribution deal with Atlantic Records for the band's next six albums. Significantly, two years earlier, Chess Records and its historic catalog of recordings had been sold to the General Recorded Tape company for just $6.5 million.

The Stones' financial brain trust determined that the band should move out of England to avoid its onerous income tax. Southern France became the new, albeit temporary, home of the English hit makers. When the band couldn't find a French recording studio to its liking, it was decided that their mobile recording truck, which had been used by numerous groups, including Led Zeppelin and Fleetwood Mac, would be installed outside of Richards's mansion on the French Riviera.

Richards's home, Nellcote, became legendary in Stones lore, an elegant mansion filled with hard rock and deadly drugs that birthed what is widely regarded as the band's last classic album, *Exile on Main Street* (some argue that this distinction belongs to 1978's *Some Girls*). Between April and November of 1970, Richards's household budget was $7,000 a week, with $1,000 for food, $1,000 for alcohol, $2,500 for rent, and $2,500 for drugs. This was just under a third of the guitarists' weekly income of $25,000.

As the expenditure for drugs suggests, Richards (and his significant other, Anita Pallenberg) were seriously addicted to heroin, a condition that would impact both the art and business of the Stones during the 1970s. Jagger and Richards were now living quite different lives, especially after Jagger married Bianca Perez-Mora Macias during the months in France. "Up until then Mick and I were inseparable," said Richards. "We made every decision for the group. We loved to get together and kick things around, write all our songs. But once we were split up I started going my way—which was the downhill road to dopesville—and Mick ascended to Jetland."

The Stones' sojourn in France turned out to be the band's last instance of sustained musical comity. Richards might have been on a perpetual high, but he was never far from his guitar, or the recording rooms in the basement. Richards played host to Gram Parsons, the musician considered the Godfather of country-rock for his work with the Byrds (*Sweethearts of the Rodeo*), the Flying Burrito Brothers, and a pair of highly regarded solo albums on which he sang with Emmylou Harris. Parsons and Richards would sit around and sing George Jones songs, and Gram taught Keith the distinctions between the country music played in Nashville and the harder-edged Bakersfield style epitomized by Buck Owens. The Stones would soon add more country-flavored songs to their repertoire, an appropriately roots-oriented complement to the band's devotion to the blues and R&B. Parsons would die of a drug overdose in 1973, just shy of turning twenty-seven; he was neither the first nor last to expire in the druggy orbit of the Rolling Stones. "He was my mate, and I wish he'd remained my mate for a lot longer," said Richards. "It's not often you can lie around on a bed with a guy having cold turkey, in tandem, and still get along."

The Stones brought some previously recorded tracks that they wanted to keep from Allen Klein to Nellcote, and later completed the album in Los Angeles. But *Exile* was characterized by the steamy, claustrophobic sound of a song like "Ventilator Blues." This was Delta blues made not in a juke joint, but in the mansion of a decadent rock star. Bluesy rock songs like "Rocks Off," "Rip This Joint," and "All Down the Line" fairly dripped off of Richards's rhythm guitar, which alongside Watts's drums, had always been the heart beat of the band's sound. "It doesn't matter about the B.B. Kings, Eric Claptons, and Mick Taylors," said Richards, "'cause they do what they do but I know they can't do what I do. . . . Everything I do is strongly based on rhythm 'cause that's what I'm best at. I've tried being a great guitar player and, like Chuck Berry, I have failed."

Exile included a couple of blues covers: Slim Harpo's "Shake Your Hips" and Robert Johnson's "Stop Breaking Down." Both songs—the former a swampy boogie, the latter animated by a slashing slide guitar lick—fit comfortably in a collection that also touched upon gospel and country. But not everybody was happy with the record. "*Exile on Main Street* is not one of my favorite albums," said Jagger, who was particularly critical of how it was mixed. "[Producer] Jimmy Miller was not functioning properly. I had to finish the whole album myself, because otherwise there were just these drunks and junkies."

The singer's complaint anticipated the dynamics of the Stones during the 1970s, with Jagger taking care of business and, along with the rest of the band, coping with Richards's erratic behavior. While the *Exile* sessions suggested that Richards was a highly functioning junkie, subsequent subpar albums like *Goat's Head Soup* and *Black and Blue* suggested that this wasn't always the case. Tours also became a logistical and legal challenge for a famous rock group with a junkie guitar player. It helped that the Stones stood to make huge amounts of money on the road; consequently, arrangements could be made, whether it be couriers, local connections, or roadies who carried not guitars, but drugs.

"The reason I made it through was because it was all top quality shit," said Richards of his life as a heroin addict. "When I was into it I was a connoisseur!" All the same, Richards wasn't all that different from every other junkie. "In guys particularly, junk takes the place of everything," said Richards. "You don't need a chick, you don't need music, you don't need nothing. It doesn't get you anywhere. It's not called junk for nothing."

Drugs or no, the 1972 tour captured on the *Ladies & Gentlemen the Rolling*

Stones DVD, saw the group at the peak of its power. In one respect, it was an atypical sound for the Stones, as Richards mostly stuck to rhythm guitar while Taylor did most of the lead work. In the early days, Richards and Brian Jones would aim to integrate their playing so that the two guitarists were all but indistinguishable; that's also been the band's style since Ronnie Wood succeeded Taylor. Taylor was a superb lead guitarist, and arguably the most accomplished musician to ever play with the Stones; he also failed to get any writer's credit on the band's records, even though his influence was clear on songs like "Sway" and "Can't You Hear Me Knocking." Taylor quit the band at the end of 1974, strung out on junk, and bound for a relatively low-profile solo career.

The last date of the Exile tour was at New York City's Madison Square Garden. After the show, Atlantic's Ahmet Ertegun and his socialite wife Mica hosted a party on the Starlight Roof of the St. Regis Hotel to cheer the end of the tour and to belatedly toast Jagger's twenty-ninth birthday. Bill Graham, who'd helped promote the tour, wore a rare jacket and tie. Andy Warhol took Polaroid pictures; Bob Dylan, at his request, had his photo taken with Zsa Zsa Gabor. The tables were crowded with bold-faced celebrities, from Woody Allen to Oscar de la Renta, and from Carly Simon to Dick Cavett and Tennessee Williams. "The party is an Ertegun affair," said Truman Capote. "It had little relationship to the Stones." Suzy wrote in the *Daily News* that it was "the wildest craziest best party of the year—so far."

Ertegun was a connoisseur of great black music, and had hired both Count Basie and Muddy Waters to play the party. Something is wrong, thought jazz fan Charlie Watts, about Basie playing *his* soiree. After Basie's big band, Waters took the stage with his group. "It's so wonderful bein' here playin' for them Rollin' Stones," said Waters, "and especially Marshall Chess. I worked for his father for twenty-five years an' I wanna dedicate this next song to him." Marshall Chess Jr., whose father had suffered a fatal heart attack in 1970, and who had become addicted to heroin during his years with the Stones, smiled as Waters sang "Seventh Son."

But no one was listening as Muddy sang, said writer Robert Greenfield. "It [was] a party for people who go to parties, for whom the world of music is an amusing, temporary, and bizarre source of pleasant conversation." It was an event that showed just how much had changed for a rock 'n' roll band that had once dreamed of seeing Muddy Waters play the blues on the South Side of Chicago. "Right now," said Keith Richards, "is when you realize you're a product." Richards, it seemed, hadn't been paying attention.

FOURTEEN

FATHERS, MOTHERS & SONS

In 1964, Little Walter, the most influential harmonica player in the history of the blues, was playing England with pickup bands. Ian McLagan, a future member of the Small Faces, had been hired to play with Walter, and was waiting outside the Ricky Tick Club in Guildford when a gray Ford Contina pulled up to the curb. "I saw Little Walter Jacobs in the shadow of the back seat, apparently asleep," said McLagan. "When he stepped out into the bright sunlight of middle class England, he was clutching a pint bottle of whiskey, his bug-eyes not yet fully open." The gig was a disaster, but McLagan left with an autograph: "To my pal from Little Walter." Little Walter subsequently played London's Marquee with Long John Baldry and the Hoochie Coochie Men. Rod Stewart was also on the bill. "He was great at the rehearsal at the Marquee," said Geoff Bradford, who played guitar in Baldry's group, "but he got horribly drunk before the gig and tried to stick Rod Stewart with a knife."

Howlin' Wolf 1910–1976

For Little Walter, it had been a long hard fall from the mid-1950s, when he was one of the biggest names in blues. Born in Louisiana in 1930, he came to Chicago with Dave "Honeyboy" Edwards in 1945. "We had heard all about Maxwell Street—they called it Jewtown, too—and we wanted to go there because that was where the happening was," said Edwards of the commercial strip that attracted street singers. Edwards returned south in September to avoid the Chicago winter. "Next thing I know, I heard Little Walter on a record with Muddy Waters."

Walter was to the harmonica what Jimi Hendrix was to the guitar, a musician who used amplification to shape the sound of his instrument. Instead of producing a typically reedy harmonica tone, Walter would use volume and distortion to create rich, sustained tones and sharp, emotional cries. His technique made the harmonica into a lead instrument, and Walter shined in the Muddy Waters band until he left after the group recorded "Juke," an instrumental that typically began or ended a set. Cut during a 1952 session for Waters, it was released under Walter's name and became a chart-topping R&B hit.

Little Walter scored fourteen top-10 R&B hits during the 1950's, even more than Chess stars like Waters, Howlin' Wolf, and Sonny Boy Williamson. "He was a good boy," said Waters, "but he had that bad, mean temper, that kind of thing, like, 'You don't mess with me too much.' Then when we got together, I found out I was the only somebody that could do anything with him when he really got out of hand. He began acting like I was his daddy."

Little Walter's hits stopped at the end of the decade, and in subsequent years, the hard-drinking musician with the volatile temper lived from gig to gig. In the early '60s, he shared an apartment with his drummer, Sam Lay, but they had a falling out when Lay quit to play with Howlin' Wolf (Lay would later leave Wolf to join the Butterfield Blues Band). Walter was loath to give other players harmonica tips; when James Cotton, who was playing with Muddy Waters, asked him about a certain technique, Walter obliged by playing with his back turned to Cotton. Butterfield once plied Walter with liquor in hopes of getting an impromptu lesson. "You think Walter was a helpful kind of guy who'd show you stuff?" said Butterfield. "Well he wasn't, he was a nasty son of a bitch who'd tell you to get the fuck away from him."

Charlie Musselwhite, another white harmonica player, saw Walter play a neighborhood bar in Chicago called the Red Onion in 1967. "It was kinda like a party, a get together," said Musselwhite. "Totally informal, like the music was just sort of a thing to bring people together, part of the neighborhood." The Red Onion was far cry from star time. Other nights in Chicago he'd play with Sam Lay's band. "He had to play with me to makes ends meet," said Lay. "So did John Lee Hooker, Jimmy Reed, Eddie Taylor—all of 'em has been in my midst at one time or another. I was paying $17 a night, that was good money, more than I had got from him."

Little Walter died on Valentine's Day in 1968; accounts vary as to the circumstances. "Honeyboy" Edwards said that Walter was routinely taking money from a girlfriend that was sent by an absent father for the care of the couple's children. The irate dad was said to have confronted Walter and knocked him unconscious with a blackjack. The more commonly accepted account is that Walter was hit in the head during a dice game. Junior Wells, another gifted harmonica player, claimed to be a witness.

"Cat threw the dice, but he threw 'em at Walter's butt," said Wells. "The dice came up with the winning combination, but Walter said it wasn't fair—you couldn't roll the dice against no one's ass and call it a winner. When the cat reached for the money, Walter grabbed it first. Then the cat took a hammer and hit Walter upside the head." Walter went home, complained of a headache, and died in his sleep.

Little Walter left a legacy both as an instrumentalist and the personification of a certain lifestyle. "The black players have a pretty limited perspective—it's drinking, and playing, and chasing girls," said Nick Gravenites. "White guys had other choices. . . . People would say, 'Walter's in town!' And they still use that [expression] when someone hits the scene and they're partyin' like mad, chasing after women and drugs and going crazy."

On a February day in 1975, a crowd of two hundred gathered on the village green of Woodstock, New York, to give Muddy Waters, who was at a local studio recording an album, the key to the town. Woodstock, on the edge of the Catskill Mountains, had been a rural magnet for visual artists and writers for much of the twentieth century. But after Albert Grossman and his most prominent client, Bob Dylan, moved to town, its arty population expanded to include folk, rock, and jazz musicians. Dylan left town after the famous Woodstock festival (held sixty-five miles away in Bethel, New York) drew a steady stream of geographically challenged hippies to the event's namesake town. Around this time, Dylan also instigated a long and acrimonious legal battle with Grossman over his management of Dylan's career, particularly as it concerned his song publishing.

Grossman had plenty of other clients living in town, including the Band, Paul Butterfield, and Todd Rundgren. Geoff and Maria Muldaur moved to Woodstock in the late '60s after the breakup of the Kweskin Jug Band. "Cambridge was very social," said Geoff Muldaur. "Then I got to Woodstock and it was a whole other world. People were buying fancy cars if they had a little success." With Grossman continuing to manage their careers, the Muldaurs recorded a pair of blues-inflected records produced by their old Cambridge roommate, Joe Boyd. Boyd had secured his reputation in England overseeing influential folk-oriented records by Fairport Convention, the Incredible String Band, and Nick Drake. After the Muldaurs' marriage broke up, Geoff joined Paul Butterfield's new band, Better Days, and Boyd produced Maria's 1974 solo debut, which included a major hit, "Midnight at the Oasis."

Waters had come to upstate New York to record *The Muddy Waters Woodstock Album*, an amiable, Grammy Award–winning collection orchestrated by Levon Helm, the drummer in the Band. Helm enlisted a studio ensemble that included Garth Hudson and Dr. John on keyboards, and Butterfield on harmonica. Waters was subsequently asked to perform at "The Last Waltz," a lavish concert held in November of 1976 at Bill Graham's Winterland Ballroom that commemorated the effective end of the Band's career; besides playing its own music, the Band also backed such influential peers as Bob Dylan, Van Morrison, and Neil Young. The backstage was filled with musical stars. "Joni Mitchell introduced herself to Muddy," said his guitar player, Bob Margolin, "and he definitely hit on her without knowing she was famous, which made her laugh."

John Simon, who'd produced the Band as well as Janis Joplin's *Cheap Thrills*, was hired to be musical director for the event that was filmed by director Martin Scorsese. "My favorite rehearsal was with Muddy Waters and Paul Butterfield at the Miyako Hotel," said Simon. "Muddy Waters had the dignity of a King, but he also responded to this great, powerful band, and generally radiated tremendous authority. Muddy Waters and The Band. It was like the confluence of two rivers of music."

"I wish somebody had filmed the guitar players in the room watching Muddy," said Dr. John, who played The Last Waltz and saw the rehearsal. "There were so many great guitar players there—Robbie Robertson, Eric Clapton, Bob Dylan, Neil Young, Stephen Stills—and the looks on the faces of these guys was worth the price of admission."

By now, Waters was opening concerts for some of those white stars. "By the mid-1970s," said Dick Waterman, "Bonnie [Raitt] wanted opening acts of people whose music she really loved. She wanted to come to the gig and sit and listen to Fred McDowell or Sippie Wallace. She was initially uncomfortable with having Muddy Waters open for her. She said, 'This should not be.'" Raitt finally agreed to the arrangement when she was assured that Waters was being well paid and gaining valuable exposure to her audience. At every show, Raitt would proudly say what a thrill it was to be on a bill with such a legendary bluesman.

The Muddy Waters Woodstock Album, released in 1975, would be the last new music he would record for Chess Records. Blues-rock guitarist Johnny Winter soon proposed that he produce Waters for his manager's cbs-affiliated record label, Blue Sky. Winter had first met Waters in 1968. "'Man, you got to go places,'" said Waters at the time, "'because ain't many white kids sounding like you at playing music.' He's albino white, he's not jiving white, he all white." After hitting the big time in 1969, Winter had largely gone the way of rock 'n' roll, but that changed after going into the studio with Waters. "Working with Muddy made me realize that blues was what I wanted to do," said Winter. "I might not make as much money as a rock and roll player, but blues made me happier."

Winter's preparation for recording 1977's *Hard Again* included a pre-session huddle with engineer Dave Still. "I played him the good [Muddy] records," said Winter, "and told him why they were good, and played him the bad ones and told him why they were bad." In the studio, Winter knew to trust the musicians. "Johnny didn't take things apart," said guitarist Bob Margolin. "It was just, 'We know how to play this stuff. Let's get the arrangement and cut the tune.'" Waters was pleased with the results. "The music makes my pee pee hard again," said Waters, according to Winter, "so I'll name it *Hard Again*.

Winter bonded with the bluesman, and visited Waters at his Chicago home for a meal of chili while sitting in the kitchen by the stove. "Muddy was a great host, and his cookin' was the best part of it," said Winter. "I had a big bowl and I was sweatin', really big drops of sweat. . . . It was gumbo, but Muddy called it chili. He put okra in it, and other vegetables, too."

Winter added a special ingredient to Muddy's next album, 1978's *I'm Ready*, reuniting Waters with his original guitar partner, Jimmy Rogers. Rogers had given up music in the 1960s to run a Chicago clothing store that was burned to the ground during riots after the assassination of Dr. Martin Luther King. "I set them up to have pretty distorted guitar sounds," said Margolin. "Muddy and Jimmy liked that—it was the way they sounded in the '50s when they played together. Johnny was up in the control room, and said, 'Are you sure you want those amps that dirty?' They said, 'Yeah, we like that.'" Just like a couple of blues-rockers.

The albums Waters made with Winter were praised for a hard, punchy sound that recalled his classic music from the 1950s. They also provided a valuable career boost. "When I started working with Muddy back in 1971," said manager Scott Cameron, "he was not in much demand for anything, and his engagements were very, very few. . . . Without Johnny Winter, I don't think there would have been a *Hard Again*, which was the rebirth of Muddy's career." That revival included opening for Eric Clapton at arenas in Europe and the United States.

"Long before we ever met," said Clapton, "he [Waters] was the most powerful of all the modern blues players I had heard on record, and the sheer strength of his musical character had a profound effect on me as a green young scholar listening my way forward. Later on, right up until the day he died, he was very much a part of my life, touring with me, counseling me, and generally acting as the father figure I never really had."

Everything changed for B.B. King after the mainstream success of 1969's "The Thrill Is Gone"; now, when he played Chicago, instead of a predominantly black venue or a rock ballroom, he was just as likely to be booked into a fancy nightclub. Around the time that Bruce Iglauer launched Alligator Records to record Hound Dog Taylor and the Houserockers, he took Taylor to see King play the London House. They sat at the bar to keep expenses to a minimum.

"About halfway through the show," said Iglauer, "B.B. announced that Hound Dog was there. He said something like, 'We have a very distinguished blues musician in the house.' . . . And Hound Dog of course was glowing and stood up and got a lot of applause, and it was a great moment in his life.

"Right after that, B.B. started a slow blues. And he only sang one verse. He sang, 'I can hear my black name ringing all up and down the line.' Now that verse dates back to the beginnings of the blues. . . . B.B. was reaching out over the head of all those upper-middle-class, rich, white business people and speaking directly to Hound Dog and sayin', 'All these people are here to be entertained, but only you and I understand what's really going on.'"

When King played Chicago's Mister Kelly's, Mike Bloomfield's mother sought his counsel. "She was feeling that he wasn't playing—something to that effect," said King. "She said, 'If you could talk to him, I'm sure that would help him out.'" At the time, Bloomfield was more likely to watch TV in a drugged stupor than to pick up his guitar. "B.B. King wrote me a letter," said Bloomfield, "and he called me on the phone. He said, 'You gotta keep those fingers in shape. . . . You can't let what you've got go to hell like that.' . . . And, my God, the next time I had a chance to see B.B. King, I was embarrassed to face this man who had meant so much to me and who I so much wanted to be like and play like, and he knew I didn't want to play anymore."

At the Fillmore in San Francisco, Bloomfield reluctantly strapped on his guitar to jam with King. "I just had to play the best I could because he was there," said Bloomfield, "this guy that had took the time out, you know, to write me a letter and tell me keep on keeping on."

Howlin' Wolf, though greatly admired within the fraternity of blues musicians, never achieved the mainstream popularity of B.B. King or Muddy Waters. During the 1970s, he played around Chicago and mounted the occasional tour. Touring the South in 1971, Wolf played in Clarksdale, Mississippi, where he met a local who knew his mother, from whom the bluesman had been long estranged. Then, as if in a dream, Gertrude Burnett appeared on the street.

Wolf cried out in joy, gave his mom a big hug, and slipped something into the pocket of her housedress. They talked for a few minutes before Gertrude discovered the contraband. "I don't want your dirty old money," she said, tossing it to the ground. "You play them dirty blues!" She walked away, turned, and repeated, "Dirty!" Hubert Sumlin approached Wolf to offer his comfort, and bent over to pick a $500 bill off the ground. "Wolf cried all the way to Memphis," said Sumlin.

Sumlin was all but Wolf's next of kin. "Hubert was the heart, and that's the way Wolf planned it," said Vaan Shaw, the son of Wolf's saxophone player, Eddie Shaw. "Where Wolf was disciplined, Hubert was a maverick. . . . Where Wolf was structured, Hubert was spontaneous. . . . Wolf did all the planning, and Hubert was the heart and soul."

By the 1970s, Wolf's health was deteriorating; he'd suffered a heart attack, and his failing kidneys requiring dialysis. His wife, Lillian, cared for him at home when he was in Chicago; on the road, the Army veteran was treated at government facilities. Wolf would do his best to save his energy for show time, but where he used to stalk the stage (if not the entire premises) as he sang, he now mostly sat in a chair.

In the early '70s, Wolf spent $100,000 to buy the 1815 Club on Chicago's West Side (when Sumlin declined the offer, he put the club in the name of Eddie Shaw). Wolf would frequently play at the club. "I walked up to Wolf and I said, 'Why are you in this shitty little club?'" said Vaan Shaw. "Wolf looked at me and said, 'Don't worry. When I'm dead, I'll get all the greatness I was supposed to get when I was alive.'" Truth be told, it was in joints like the 1815 Club where Wolf and his relatively few peers found their unique voices. "You got to remember, these guys didn't have blueprints," said Shaw. "And here's a guy using just his ego, creating lyrics in a room full of smoke, alcohol, four-letter words, and intimidating individuals—and yet he still creates. And that's the magic."

And it was magic that one could take to the bank. When Chess Records was being sold to GRT, Arc Publishing's Gene Goodman traveled to Chicago to get Wolf to resign with Arc. To help in the negotiation, Goodman brought a $2,000 check and a bottle of whiskey. Wolf signed an "employee-for-hire" contract that essentially gave Arc ownership of all the songs he'd written and recorded before March 1971. He was unaware that his early songs would soon be up for copyright renewal and worth a pretty penny.

In 1974, Wolf sued Arc for $2.5 million claiming that Goodman had "resorted to guile and cunning and made false statements and representation" in his effort to get Wolf to sign the contract. His lawyers put on the record the kind of underpayment that was involved. Between 1966 and 1974, Wolf received $105,000 from Arc including $45,000 from a settlement with Led Zeppelin over their appropriation of Wolf's "Killing Floor" for the tune they called "The Lemon Song." Wolf's lawsuit rocked the Chicago blues community, and within two years, both Willie Dixon and Muddy Waters entered into similar litigation. Both suits were settled out of the court; when copyright renewals came up, Arc returned the songs to Waters and Dixon. The Wolf suit was also settled before trial, with Arc retaining his copyrights.

When the Rolling Stones played Chicago in 1975, bassist Bill Wyman arranged for a limousine to bring Wolf, his wife, and Buddy Guy to the concert. Mick Jagger gave a shout out from the stage, and when a spotlight found Wolf, he got a standing ovation. "You would've thought Wolf was one of the Rolling Stones," said Lillie Burnett. "When they introduced him to the crowd," said Guy, "I could see the pain in his eyes from how much it hurt to stand. The Wolf was once a powerful man. . . . Now the Wolf was old and feeble."

Wolf died on January 10, 1976; the cause of death was complications from a brain tumor, but it might as well have been a broken heart. In the hospital, Wolf asked his wife to call his mother. "Tell her if I ever needed her, I need her now," said Wolf. But when Gertrude was reached by phone, she refused to stay on the line, let alone travel to Chicago. Wolf asked Lillie, "'Did you get my mother?' 'Yeah.' 'What did she say?' 'She didn't say anything.' 'That's okay, Lillie.'"

Chicago radio station WVON dedicated a day to Wolf's music the Sunday after he passed. Eddie Shaw hosted a jam session in his honor at the 1815 Club. More than ten thousand people showed up to file past Wolf's body at the funeral home. Willie Dixon spoke at the funeral, and the Reverend Henry Hardy concluded his eulogy with shouts of "You ain't dead, Wolf. Howl on! Howl on!" The funeral program listed two sons: Floyd Lee Burnett, born in 1939 before Wolf had left the Delta for Memphis, and Hubert Sumlin, who was conceived playing the blues with the mighty Howlin' Wolf.

FIFTEEN

TEXAS (ROCK STAR) BLUES

Jimmie Vaughan, joined the Chessmen at the age of sixteen. After the band played on a Dallas TV dance show called *Sump'n Else*, the young guitarist spotted a promotional copy of Jimi Hendrix's "Purple Haze" in the studio trash. He took the 1967 release home, where he and his kid brother Stevie Ray were floored by what they heard.

Texas has a rich history of blues music, ranging from Blind Lemon Jefferson, the best-selling country-blues artist of the 1920s, to T-Bone Walker, who made the electric guitar the primary soloing instrument of modern blues. The list of formidable Lone Star bluesmen also includes Lightnin' Hopkins, Freddie King, and Albert Collins. But by the time Jimmie Vaughan was playing fraternity parties and teen clubs, the world had been transformed by the unimaginable success of bands like the Beatles and the Rolling Stones. For a young musician, music wasn't just a cool way to meet girls and make a few bucks; now it might actually be a career.

The Chessmen's competition on the local circuit included the Marksmen, a combo led by guitarist Steve Miller that also included Boz Scaggs, and Billy Gibbons's band, the Moving Sidewalks. Both the Chessmen and the Moving Side-

Stevie Ray Vaughan 1954–1990

walks played on Lone Star concert bills opening for the Jimi Hendrix Experience. Hendrix was impressed by Vaughan's guitar tone, and asked to borrow his Vox wah-wah pedal. When Hendrix broke it during his set, he gave Vaughn forty dollars and one of his own pedals. He sweetened the deal with a spangled jacket adorned with ostrich feathers that Jimmie passed along to his kid brother.

Billy Gibbons was the son of a society bandleader who also wrote arrangements for Hollywood films and conducted the Houston Philharmonic. But his father wasn't the only musical influence in the house; the family maid, Big Stella, and her daughter, Little Stella, exposed Gibbons to black music. "My dad certainly wasn't doin' gut-bucket blues," said Gibbons. "But Little Stella was always buying the records and that's what we were listening to. All the Little Richard stuff, Larry Williams' 'Short Fat Fanny,' Jimmy Reed, T-Bone Walker, B.B. King, the usual lineup of R&B stars." Gibbons got a Gibson Melody Maker guitar and a Fender Champ amplifier for Christmas in 1963, four weeks after President Kennedy was assassinated and just before the Beatles conquered America.

Five years later, when the Moving Sidewalks were on a Dallas concert bill with Hendrix, Gibbons happened to peek in the open door of Jimi's hotel room, where he'd set up a stereo and was playing the Jeff Beck Group's *Truth*. Hendrix looked up to see Gibbons and invited him in for a listen. "We were both fascinated with Jeff Beck's incendiary, wicked six-string thrashing," said Gibbons. "It was the most interesting, relaxed presence of power, observing Jimi doing things to a guitar definitely not designed to be done."

The idea of popular teenage bands opening shows for a superstar like Hendrix suggests just how wide open the music world was in the late '60s. No wonder both Vaughan and Gibson skipped college to continue playing in bands. By contrast, only after Steve Miller attended the University of Wisconsin did he disappoint his parents by moving to Chicago to pursue a full-time career in music. Finding success in blues or rock was far from a sure thing, but within the context of the burgeoning counterculture, it certainly seemed like an attractive alternative to attending an 8 AM class.

The Moving Sidewalks was a psychedelic band—the band's regional hit, "99th Floor," paid tribute to the Texas' premiere acid band, the 13th Floor Elevators—but was also influenced by blues-rock groups like Cream and Fleetwood Mac. One afternoon in 1969, the Moving Sidewalks were rehearsing in a basement club in Houston called the Catacomb. As they roared through their cover of "Crossroads," a local promoter entered the club with Eric Clapton, who was in town on Cream's Farewell tour. When the song was over, Clapton stepped up to the stage to shake the hand of Gibbons, whose next group, ZZ Top, would fully embrace Cream's power-trio format with a rhythm section of bassist Dusty Hill and drummer Frank Beard. Bill Ham, ZZ Top's manager (and virtual fourth member) groomed the group for commercial success. "We played a lot of the out-of-the-way places, playing for the people at people's prices," said Ham. "It's harder that way and takes much longer, but once the band had established itself as a people's band, the people won't leave you."

The "'lil ol' band from Texas" headlined dumps and opened shows for touring bands, including a few gigs in which they backed both Chuck Berry and Bo Diddley. "Neither kept a setlist," said Gibbons. "It was really twisted 'coz they expected us to know every single song in their repertoire. They would just call out a tune. . . . Completely off the cuff. They might play a verse, solo, then we'd have to fall in line and finish it out."

Heavy touring sharpened the band's sound, and it crystallized on ZZ Top's third album, 1973's *Tres Hombres*, which featured an enduring barn burner called "La Grange." The song's irresistible boogie beat rocketed the track into the top 10, and it didn't hurt that the tongue-in-cheek lyrics were an homage to the "Chicken Ranch," a well-known Lone Star brothel. "I went there when I was 13," said Dusty Hill. "A lot of boys in Texas, when it's time to be a guy, went there and had it done. Fathers took their sons there. . . . Oil field workers and senators would both be there."

"La Grange" put ZZ Top on the map and the whorehouse out of business, as the hit single brought so much publicity that the authorities had little choice but to close it down. Blues fans recognized that the propulsive lick of "La Grange" was not unlike that of John Lee Hooker's "Boogie Chillen." Bernard Besman, who owned the copyright to the 1949 Hooker hit, sued ZZ Top in 1992; though the courts ruled that the song had entered the public domain, the suit was settled out of court. By then, ZZ Top had sold more than fifty million albums.

ZZ Top's success came from a combination of raw rhythms and a wry bravado epitomized by titles like "Tush" and "I'm Bad, I'm Nationwide." 1976's "Worldwide Texas Tour" sported a Texas-shaped stage that was home to a buffalo, a longhorn steer, a rattlesnake, and five buzzards. The big payday came in the 1980s, when ZZ Top became video rock stars on MTV with clips that featured sexy babes, cool cars, and Gibbons and

Hill sporting outrageously long beards (Beard, naturally, remained clean-shaven). The theatrics were playfully cheesy, but the band's success was clearly due to Gibbons's virtuosic guitar playing on the band's hard-driving blues-rock songs.

"I picked up the guitar because of Muddy Waters as much as anyone," said Gibbons. "Jimmy Reed, Howlin' Wolf, T-Bone Walker, Albert King, B.B. King, Freddie King—they all had an impact too, but they all followed Muddy Waters." Waters was the opening act on a ZZ Top tour in 1981, and made a great impression on Gibbons. "Three chords," said Gibbons. "To expand on that would be an injustice. . . . Keith Richards made a real apropos statement. He said, 'As long as I can just introduce some new twists to those same three chords, we'll stay in business.' He pointed out that Muddy Waters, Mississippi Fred McDowell, all these cats were doin' it till the day they died, and having a great time."

Steve Miller, like ZZ Top, found a way to alchemize his affection for blues into million-selling rock albums. After tasting the blues life in Chicago, Miller moved to San Francisco and became a fixture on the rock ballroom circuit. "I thought in terms of myself as a band leader," said Miller. Though he didn't play a lot of straightforward blues songs, the genre was a major influence on his most successful mid-1970s work. "I said to myself," said Miller, "'I'll never be Eric Clapton on guitar, I'll never be the writer that Paul McCartney is, I'll never be B.B. King, I'll just be Steve Miller, with a lot of limitations. . . . So I went in the studio and made a very simple album, spent nineteen days doing it—done, mixed, finished, and I had no idea that 'The Joker' was a hit single."

"The Joker" was the first of a string of hits that made Miller a main-stream rock star. Songs like "Rock'n Me," "Fly Like an Eagle," and "Take the Money and Run" were rock songs that were composed and executed using a bluesy aesthetic that exploited simplicity and musicianship in service of a good sharp arrangement. Miller also had a far more commercially oriented worldview than a blues musician. "I finished off the next two albums, *Fly Like an Eagle* and *Book of Dreams*," said Miller, "because I'd learned from *The Joker* that if I was going to go out and tour and do all that stuff again, I really needed to have a couple of albums in the can, because I wasn't going to be able to stop in the middle and start writing again."

The Steve Miller Band's hot streak cooled in the 1980s, but the singer-guitarist would continue to mount successful tours reprising his many hits. In 2011, Miller recorded *Bingo!*, a collection that included some of the same blues songs he performed in mid-'6os Chicago, when Buddy Guy would insist that his group drink a shot of liquor before taking the bandstand. For even the most successful blues-rock musicians, the old tunes never die.

Jimmie Vaughan played an assortment of rock and roll cover tunes with the Chessman, but after seeing Muddy Waters and Freddie King play in Dallas, he quit in 1969 to form a blues band called Texas Storm. "When I started out playing guitar," said Vaughan, "all I wanted to do was play that Jimmy Reed groove—it just feels real good. Then I made it my business to figure out the guitar interplay between Reed and his co-guitarist Eddie Taylor. I tell you what, it sounds real easy when you first hear it, but listen closely and the way they lock and form that deep groove is not easy. It's a whole other thing."

If they were lucky and bold, the young Texas musicians could find a way to learn those grooves by playing with masters of the blues. At a luncheon-ette in Austin, guitarist Marc Benno (best known for cutting a couple of *Asylum Choir* albums with Leon Russell) approached a man he thought was Lightnin' Hopkins but who turned out to be songster Mance Lipscomb. Lipscomb, who'd become popular on the folk-blues circuit, had a lyrical fingerpicking style and an uncommonly deep repertoire of songs. Lipscomb invited Benno to bring his guitar to a jam session at his house the following Saturday night.

"So we drove out into the middle of nowhere," said Benno, "and we saw this old flop-house with Christmas tree lights on it and a whole new world opened up for me. Mance was playing through a jukebox, and he had another guy that had on a Texaco uniform that said 'Willie,' and he was playing a bass with one string on it. The whole thing was just amazing. . . . He told me, 'Yeah, lots of boys been coming around to my house trying to get my style. Cooder Brown been spending a lot of time.' Cooder Brown turned out to be Ry Cooder. And then he said, 'And then there's this other boy, Bobby. He came in and he even took my lyrics, man, he took my lyrics.' And that was Bob Dylan."

To accompany Lipscomb's essentially self-contained style, Benno added complementary lead guitar lines. He used the same strategy when he got a gig leading combos for Lightnin' Hopkins. Playing with Hopkins could be perilous. "He fired the bass player on stage one night," said Benno. "He [Hopkins] said, 'Little man, come here, fire the bass player. I don't like the way he plays.' I said, 'Man, he doesn't want you to play,' and he said, 'You mean this is my last gig?' And I said, 'No, that was your last song.'"

Doyle Bramhall, who drummed with Jimmie Vaughan in Texas Storm and later wrote songs with Stevie Ray Vaughan, also backed Hopkins. "He was a tough bird," said Bramhall. "There weren't any rehearsals or sound checks or anything like that. You just showed up, and you immediately jumped in the deep end. . . . He would stop the whole show with a packed house at the Granada and say, 'Man, this bass player just got to get it together.' . . . He used to say, 'Lightnin' change when Lightnin' change,' as far as his chord playing went."

Hopkins could be just as cranky with a documentary filmmaker as a guy who played bass. In the late 1960s, Les Blank pitched the idea of making a film about Hopkins by showing him a movie that he'd done about trumpeter Dizzy Gillespie. Hopkins didn't say no, and Blank got a friend's father to put up $5,000. Hopkins wanted the full five grand but settled for three payments of $500, and then told Blank to go home after one day of shooting. "He announced to us that he had recorded ten songs that day," said Blank, "and when he did an LP album, ten songs was all he ever did, and he wanted us to pay him the rest of the money we owed him and clear out and not come back." Blank finagled another six weeks to shoot what became *The Blues Accordin' to Lightnin' Hopkins*. "Like Shakespeare, he had an understanding of all people and all their feelings," said Blank of Hopkins, who took him to the cleaners gambling on a card game called Pitty Pat. "Whether he was singing other people's songs, or as it more often happened, making a song up as he played, Lightnin' Hopkins was a man of all colors and classes, and of all times."

Sam Charters recorded Hopkins for Folkways in 1959, as he was completing *The Country Blues*, and came back for more in 1974. Charters had followed his scholarship and field recordings with a job at Vanguard Records recording everybody from Buddy Guy and John Fahey to Country Joe and the Fish. By the end of the '60s, he'd moved to Sweden, spurred, in part, by opposition to the war in Viet Nam. (Charters and his wife, Beat Generation scholar and college professor Ann Charters, typically spent part of their year in Connecticut, where their archives are held at the University of Connecticut.) At the time, Charters was producing records for Sweden's Sonet Label, and asked Hopkins to be Volume 12 of his "Legacy of the Blues" series.

"He [Hopkins] started with the point of view that I was a white motherfucker," said Charters. "He insisted, because of his distrust for whites, that he had to be paid in cash a five-thousand-dollar advance, but I wasn't going to pay him until I did the recording." Charters got his album, but it wasn't well received, and didn't turn a profit. "His singing and guitar work was more sloppy," said Charters. "I knew it was not going to add one iota to what had been done."

Hopkins was both irascible and one-of-a-kind. Robert Palmer wrote in the *New York Times* of a hostile Hopkins demanding his money before playing a 1980 date at Tramps in Manhattan. "Though blues musicians are often called 'folk poets,' most of them are heavily dependent on traditional lines and stanzas," said Palmer. "Mr. Hopkins is a real folk poet, a chronicler of his life and his community who's the closest thing to the tradition-bearing 'griots' of West Africa and Alex Haley's *Roots* that one can find in the United States."

In early 1981, Hopkins was diagnosed with cancer of the esophagus, and succumbed a year later. Everyone knew that an original had passed. "Once I heard Sam playing in the beer joints making up these songs about anything that happened that day and about the folks right there in front of him I just couldn't believe my ears," said Chris Strachwitz, who was inspired to create Arhoolie Records when he saw Hopkins in 1959. "I had never heard anything quite like it in my life and have never heard anyone since then who could do this with the intensity Lightning put into his singing."

In the 1970s, Lightnin' Hopkins shared various concert bills with both Jimmie Vaughan's Texas Storm and Stevie Ray Vaughan's Double Trouble. By the middle of the decade, the Texas blues had a new headquarters, an Austin club called Antone's named after its owner, Clifford Antone. Before he ran the club, the bass-playing Antone had an Austin clothing store; he used the store's back room to host jam sessions with Jimmie Vaughan and his new friend, singer and harmonica player Kim Wilson.

Antone, like Billy Gibbons, was introduced to black music by the hired help. "A maid named Mary Hinton raised me and she was a gospel singer," said Antone, who was of Lebanese descent. "She was as close to me as my mother. She would sing gospel to me as a kid and I would lose it. It was just so good." Antone soon found the blues. "During the hippie days," he said, "I was listening to Fleetwood Mac before it was a rock band, when it was a straight blues band. So this guy in the record store shows me a double record called *Fleetwood Mac in Chicago*." The record hipped Antone to Chicago musicians like Willie Dixon and Otis Spann and gave him a bug for the blues that led to the opening of his club in 1975.

"Clifford Antone brought Chicago blues to Austin," said Buddy Guy. "He brought people like Muddy Waters and Howlin' Wolf, Jimmy Reed,

T-Bone Walker, everybody who the young white generation of the '6os and '7os didn't know anything about." The fact that bands were booked into the club for five-day runs encouraged them to feel at home and to interact with the local musicians, especially the Fabulous Thunderbirds, the new group that Jimmie Vaughan had formed with Kim Wilson. The Thunderbirds frequently accompanied or jammed with the visiting bluesmen.

How did the Thunderbirds become the house band? "Because we wouldn't leave," said Vaughan, "and because our bar tabs were so big that we had to do something to work it off." Antone's offered the black blues musicians good money and r-e-s-p-e-c-t. "They knew we were in it for one reason," said Antone, "that we loved the blues and that we wanted to see them play. So they let their guard down that they kept up all the time. We had just beautiful, family-type relationships with all the blues guys. . . . That's my main reward in my life, that I know that they trusted me, and that I was their friend, and they were mine."

The music was the ice cream on the pie. "You see a guy that's a King," said Antone of Muddy Waters, "an immortal from Mt. Olympus. First time I heard him play slide it almost scared me. It touched something in me I didn't know I had." Waters also appreciated the local talent. "We put Jimmie Vaughan on stage with Muddy, he played slide and Muddy's head snapped. He told me that Kim Wilson was the best harmonica player he'd heard since Little Walter. The blues players had never seen no kids like this."

Offstage was a whole other experience. "Muddy would have a big room," said Antone, "and [piano player] Pinetop [Perkins] would have an electric deep fryer. They'd be drinking champagne and eating fried chicken. I was 25 and in heaven. And the chicken was good." When Muddy Waters was booked to play Antone's on his sixty-third birthday, Clifford paid for Buddy Guy and Junior Wells to fly to Austin to surprise their old boss and mentor. "When it was time to sing 'Happy Birthday," said Guy, "me and Junior came waltzing out on stage with the cake. You could've knocked the Mud over with a feather. He was grinning from ear to ear. He told the audience, 'See these here boys? I known 'em since they were kids. I raised 'em.'"

Antone opened his wallet to musicians, paying for medical care and buying them instruments. He was particularly close to Pinetop Perkins and Howlin' Wolf's guitarist, Hubert Sumlin. "You know what they told me in Chicago?" said Sumlin. "'Wolf dead, you dead.'" Sumlin put down the guitar for months after Wolf's death; just touching the strings made him sad. Then Wolf's old band started performing as the Wolf Gang, and came to Austin to play Antone's.

"The day they arrived," said Antone, "all I wanted to do was meet Hubert. I said, 'Which one of you is Hubert?' He had on these long socks and Bermuda shorts and they all had different colors on them. He raised his hand and said, 'I am.' I said, 'C'mon, man. Let's go.' . . . He got in my car and we left. We went to a barbecue my friend was having. We were best friends from the minute we met." It was as if Sumlin had lost a father and found a son. "Antone took care of him," said Kim Wilson. "Fed him. Made sure he was healthy. . . . They put him on a pedestal and made him feel special. That was really good for Hubert and he found himself." Sumlin would spend months at a time in Austin, living with Antone and his girlfriend, singer Angela Strehli, who comanaged Antone's.

Antone's was just this side of Heaven for Jimmie and Stevie Ray Vaughan. "When I got to be 17, 18, I realized it's really great and fun to play like Buddy Guy and B.B. King, but what are you gonna do if you get lucky and meet them," said Jimmie Vaughan. "I have this dream with all my favorite guitar players—Freddie King, Kenny Burrell, Lonnie Mack—and we're each doing a song and it comes around to me, and what do I play?" He had his chance to find out at Antone's. "The guy doesn't have any gimmicks or anything," said Buddy Guy of Jimmie Vaughan. "He just plays it like it's supposed to be played. I was really surprised the first time I played there, because I didn't realize how strong they knew the blues."

Stevie Ray Vaughan had the biggest thrill of his first nineteen years when Albert King came to play Antone's. "Clifford said to Albert, 'You've got to let this kid play, because he's amazing,'" said Jimmie Vaughn. "At first, he said 'No,' but Clifford kept at him. Now Albert had heard it all, but he got Stevie up there, and Stevie commenced doing Albert King licks. There was silence at first. Everyone stood there with their mouths open. They couldn't believe it. But Albert loved it. He put his arm around him, and from then on it was Albert and Stevie. Everybody went, 'Whew, that was scary.'"

While the younger Vaughn's primary influence was King, he also had a special affinity for Hubert Sumlin. "Stevie gave him a suit and a Rickenbacker guitar," said Antone. "Many nights, at the end of the evening, it would be just Stevie and Hubert sitting on chairs at the edge of the stage with their electric guitars and they would be playing something that wasn't even really a song. No band. They'd just be sitting and playing together." Over the years, Antone was busted twice for "possession with intent to distribute marijuana," but everybody knew that the money went into running his club and keeping its stage open for a couple of bluesman to pick their way deep into the wee wee hours. Musicians have never been strangers to drugs and alcohol; after all, Muddy Waters used to make his own moonshine, and Delta bluesmen always knew the best gigs were playing for bootleggers. Some things never changed.

Stevie Ray Vaughan played bass in his brother's Austin band, Texas Storm, but switched to guitar to play with the Cobras and the later Triple Threat, which also featured singer Lou Ann Barton. When she quit the group in 1978, Vaughan both sang and played lead guitar in a band that was now called Double Trouble after an Otis Rush song. Around this time, the Fabulous Thunderbirds were signed to Takoma Records, John Fahey's label, which was subsequently sold to Chrysalis Records. Though well received by critics and opening shows for the Rolling Stones and Eric Clapton, the Thunderbirds didn't catch commercial fire until 1985, by which time Stevie Ray Vaughan was the biggest new names in blues.

Stevie Ray was a much more flamboyant guitar player than his older brother, whose spare style emulated the melodic approach of a horn player. "As I was hearing the original blues masters from the States," said the younger Vaughan, "I was also hearing the English blues boom at the same time, so not only was I getting the original but I was getting this updated, energized version of the same thing. So I had less reservations, and less reasons to be a so-called 'purist.'" Still, Vaughan's most valuable teacher was his brother. "What Jimmie was bringing home was incredible," said Vaughan. "Here he was, a younger teenager, playing his ass off, and listening to everybody from Buddy [Guy] to B.B. King, the Wolf, Muddy Waters, Django Reinhardt, Kenny Burrell, Wes Montgomery and the Beatles and Hendrix. It was, like, everybody."

The kid brother turned into an inspired cross between Albert King and Jimi Hendrix; Stevie Ray Vaughan hammered out King's clipped blues licks with the kind of volume and rhythmic touch that created a completely different experience. Vaughan covered a pair of Hendrix's greatest hits, "Little Wing" and "Voodoo Chile (Slight Return)," but managed to cut a much more distinctive figure than a slavish imitator like Randy Hansen or even a subtler interpreter like Robin Trower (who'd started his career in Procol Harum). Vaughan seasoned his Hendrix-King fascination with other bluesy influences, and his manner suggested that, as with Jimi, the guitar wasn't an instrument as much as an appendage. Forget about groupies; it was just as easy to picture Jimi and Stevie sleeping with their Stratocasters.

Stevie Ray Vaughan and Double Trouble (drummer Chris Layton and bassist Tommy Shannon, who'd played with Johnny Winter) became regional favorites before recording an album. From the beginning, Vaughan was known to burn the candle at both ends with liquor, speed, and cocaine. He got busted when he and a buddy celebrated opening for Muddy Waters with a backstage snort of coke. Vaughan would sometimes shoot speed and drink a bottle of Chivas Regal before taking the stage. C. B. Stubblefield, who booked the band into his BBQ restaurant, said, "Muddy Waters said, 'Steve could perhaps be the greatest guitar player that ever lived, but he won't live to get forty years old if he doesn't leave that white powder alone. You just don't get over that.' Many times I told him, 'Man, I told you what Muddy Waters said.'"

A buzz developed around the driven guitar player known to wear a big hat and flashy, colorful clothes. When Mick Jagger and Jerry Hall came to Texas to buy a horse, Jagger was slipped a tape of Stevie Ray Vaughan; a week later, the trio played a showcase for Rolling Stones Records at the Manhattan club Danceteria. "It was wild," said Vaughan. "Everyone that you never expected to be there, from Johnny Winter to what's-his-name, the blond-headed guy, Andy Warhol." Though the Stones didn't bite, Atlantic's Jerry Wexler recommended them for a gig at the 1982 Montreaux Jazz Festival, and a live recording of Vaughan's "Texas Flood" won the guitarist his first Grammy Award. His show at Montreaux prompted Jackson Browne to offer him free time in his Los Angeles recording studio and encouraged David Bowie to hire Vaughan to play on his *Let's Dance* album. Vaughn spent about four hours in a New York studio adding his lead guitar to six already recorded instrumental tracks. Vaughan's *Let's Dance* strategy was to play like Albert King.

By then, Vaughan and Double Trouble had traveled to Browne's studio and cut what became its debut album, *Texas Flood*. Talent scout John Hammond had already been pitched by Vaughan's manager, but listened only after his blues singer son sent him a tape of the Texan's incendiary performance at Montreaux. Hammond signed the band after hearing the studio recordings, though he insisted on a remix. Then Bowie asked Vaughan to join his band for his "Serious Moonlight" tour. After a couple of rehearsals, Bowie (and/or Vaughan) pulled the plug. "Bowie stole my licks," said Vaughan after Bowie mimed his guitar fills in the video to "Let's Dance." "Naw," said Jimmie Vaughan. "He didn't steal them. He's just playing them 'cause they're the best thing on the album."

Vaughan recorded an album and video with Albert King and lent the guitarist some money. Later, Vaughan asked to be repaid. "Albert says, 'Money?'" said drummer Layton. "'Come on now, son. You know you owe me, don't you?' And he left without ever paying. The back end of the story is that a good friend who heard what happened said later, 'Well, Stevie, with all the stuff you got from Albert, did you consider that a good deal?' Stevie thought for a second and said, 'Yeah, I did.'"

Texas Flood, which quickly sold more than a half-million copies, made Stevie Ray Vaughan a major star. "He brought back a style that had died," said John Hammond of his biggest discovery since Bruce Springsteen, "and he brought it back at exactly the right time. The young ears hadn't heard anything with this kind of sound." In the early '80s, Vaughan was virtually the only blues-rock guitar hero at a time when all the other ones were either dead or old. Today, it's no stretch to contend that Stevie Ray Vaughan was the last true giant of the blues.

Vaughan introduced a generation of rock fans to the blues and lived a predictably intoxicated lifestyle. Playing in Australia, he ran into Eric Clapton outside a Sydney hotel. "I went out to talk with him," said Vaughan, "hangover and the whole bit, you know? He was sober, of course, and was really calm the whole time while I sat there downing two, three shots of Crown [Royal]. And he just sort of wisely looked at me and said, 'Well sometimes you gotta go through that, don'cha?'" (Clapton kicked his heroin habit in the '70s, but was a heavy drinker until finding sobriety in the '80s.)

Vaughan's party was just hitting high gear. His second album, *Couldn't Stand the Weather*, sold more than a million copies, and the day after his thirtieth birthday in 1984, he played Carnegie Hall with an expanded band that included Dr. John on keyboards, Jimmie Vaughan on second guitar, and a horn section. His parents were in the audience, on their first trip to New York City. In 1985, Vaughan was the first white musician to win two different W. C. Handy National Blues Awards—"Entertainer of the Year" and "Blues Instrumentalist of the Year."

Vaughan looked to his old Texas Storm band mate Doyle Bramhall for original songs; when Double Trouble played Santa Cruz, Bramhall's son, Doyle Bramhall II, came to the concert. Vaughan invited him onstage to jam on the first of a two-night engagement; the next day, Bramhall II returned dressed like a rock star. He would soon become the second guitarist in the Fabulous Thunderbirds, who would score a million-selling success with 1985's *Tuff Enuff*. Both Vaughans were pushing the limit with drugs and alcohol. Stevie Ray would bring the party on stage, where a half-gram of cocaine would be slipped into a glass of Crown Royal. After a 1986 date in

Munich, Germany, the Vaughan entourage bumped into ZZ Top. "I took Stevie backstage," said the band's manager, Bill Ham, "and sat him down and told him it looked to me like he was about to kill himself."

Within a week, Vaughan was in a London hospital suffering from severe internal bleeding. Vaughan's coke-and-booze cocktails had punched holes in his stomach. The rest of the European tour was cancelled, and Vaughan spent a month in a London clinic. Clapton, who'd worked on his own recovery in the same facility, visited his young protégé to offer encouragement and to tell him about nearby parks and attractions. The next day, a forest of flowers arrived courtesy of the guy from Cream who had helped to shape Stevie Ray's music. Vaughan continued his rehabilitation in Atlanta. One night, he attended a solo show by Bonnie Raitt, a friend who'd been an opening act on a Double Trouble tour. Raitt naturally invited Vaughan to come up and play. Vaughan hesitated; he had not performed in months, and could scarcely remember the last time he'd played guitar while sober. Then his fingers hit the strings, and Stevie Ray Vaughan began his second act.

SIXTEEN SWEET HOME CHICAGO

Muddy Waters had by the late 1970s become a lion in winter. After the death of his wife, Geneva, in 1973, Waters reunited with the children he'd had with other women and moved from the South Side of Chicago to a home in suburban Westmont, Illinois, where a vegetable garden was planted in the backyard. The albums Waters had recorded with Johnny Winter had given his career a valuable boost, and he was still a favorite of the rock stars that he'd inspired.

The blues, meanwhile, appealed to an ever more discrete audience. In the early '60s, Waters and his blues-playing peers lost younger listeners to soul and R&B performers. Now, many of those artists found themselves out of step with the overwhelming popularity of disco. Within another decade, rap and hip-hop would become the most popular genre of black American music. The blues was not about to die, but the genre increasingly catered to older fans and followers of rock stars like Eric Clapton and Stevie Ray Vaughan. Some were introduced to the music by the Ray-Ban-wearing caricatures that comedians John Belushi and Dan Aykroyd presented in the

Buddy Guy 1936–

1980 film *The Blues Brothers*. Blues aficionados considered the duo's music superfluous and the movie borderline minstrelsy, but nobody would begrudge Ray Charles, Aretha Franklin, and John Lee Hooker for appearing in the film and cashing a Hollywood paycheck.

In July of 1978, Waters played the Quiet Knight, a folk club on Chicago's North Side and received a surprise visit by members of the Rolling Stones. Keith Richards got down on his knees and kissed Muddy's hand. Waters had grown accustomed to such tributes. Later that summer, while playing the Cellar Door in Washington, D.C., he got a last-minute invitation to play at the White House. "From where I'm from," said Waters, "a black man couldn't even get inside a white man's front room." President Jimmy Carter introduced the band. "Muddy Waters is one of the great performers of all time," said Carter, but the band was not especially moved by their visit to the seat of power. "We didn't get paid nothing," said bassist Calvin Jones. "They didn't even give us good dinners; just some hot dogs."

In the autumn of 1978, Muddy Waters toured Europe opening shows for Eric Clapton. Waters wasn't familiar with Clapton's music, and typically left after his own set. One night, Bob Margolin encouraged him to stick around to see the headliner. "Eric did a killer open-G slide guitar [version of] 'Come See Me Early in the Morning,'" said Margolin, "in which he used a trademark Muddy Waters turnaround lick. Muddy got a big smile and said, 'That's my shit!' From then on, they were very close, and Muddy used to call Eric 'my son,' his highest compliment to a younger musician."

For the Clapton tour, Mike Kappus, Muddy's booking agent, took the opportunity to add a rock-star rider to his client's contract requiring high-end champagne and at least a half dozen fluted glasses. Waters liked his bubbly, and made sure it was available. "If they [the concert promoters] didn't have it," said Kappus, "Muddy had several bottles that he would sell to them to give to him."

When the Clapton/Waters tour stopped in Chicago in 1979, the rock star attended the bluesman's wedding to Marva Jean Brooks. In the late 1950s, Waters had recorded a sexy blues called "She's Nineteen Years Old," which was his new bride's age when they met in Florida. "Muddy was speaking to me in earnest about carrying on the legacy of the blues," said Clapton, "calling me his adopted son, and I assured him that I would do my best to honor this responsibility."

When the Rolling Stones played Chicago in 1981, they jammed with Waters at Buddy Guy's Chicago club, the Checkerboard Lounge. Muddy and Mick shared the lead vocal of "Hoochie Coochie Man," and Muddy and Keith entwined their guitars on "Baby Please Don't Go." The set list also included "Champagne and Reefer," a tune that the Stones would perform with Guy in a 2008 concert film directed by Martin Scorsese, *Shine a Light*. Scorsese is a fan of both Waters and the Rolling Stones, and has used many of their tunes in such films as *Goodfellas* and *Casino*.

A bad auto accident in 1969 had killed Waters's driver and put Muddy in the hospital for two months. Since then, Waters traveled mostly by plane while the band drove. That's why Peter Wolf of the J. Geils Band had occasion to spend time in a Boston airport with Waters. "I would find myself looking at him with some wonderment not just that I was sitting in a lonesome air terminal next to the great Muddy Waters," said Wolf, "but that it was so ordinary somehow. . . . Sometimes I thought about the journey he had traveled, how he had known the young Robert Johnson and Son House, seen Louis Jordan and all the great jump bands, absorbed a tradition that went back more than a century."

One night at Logan Airport, Wolf had a premonition that it might be the last time he saw his famous friend: "'Peter the Wolf,' he said, 'thank you, thank you, thank you, my friend,' said Waters. He repeated it once or twice more, and then, with that regal bearing that never lets you forget you were in the presence of a king, he walked down the jet way to the plane, turning just once before he disappeared from sight."

Muddy Waters died in his sleep from heart failure on April 30, 1983; he'd already endured an operation to remove a tumor from his lung. Muddy's last public performance came when he surprised Eric Clapton at a 1982 Miami concert by walking onto the stage when the guitarist was playing "Blow Wind Blow," a Waters tune from the early '50s. Returning to Chicago, Waters once more took ill—the cancer had returned—and he declined further treatment.

B.B. King and Johnny Winter were among the mourners at Waters's funeral. "I sort of thought like they do in New Orleans," said King, "like you should cry at the incoming and rejoice at the outgoing. I remembered the days that I could talk to him, the days he tried to help me, the music he could play." Winter was inconsolable. "I was trying to talk to B.B. King," said Winter, "and I couldn't even talk to him I was crying so much." Nobody had to be told that the death of Muddy Waters anticipated the end of an era that saw the blues move from the Mississippi Delta to Chicago and the world at large. "When the older guys are gone," said Winter, "it makes it harder on the blues. . . . The new players are not as real, and not as much from the heart."

Waters requested that he be buried with his red Telecaster. But between the bluesman and his guitar, it was a tight fit; when the coffin was finally shut, the neck of the Tele snapped in two. Muddy Waters always did know how to make a guitar cry.

Paul Butterfield was a respected musician and harmonica player even before recording his first record in 1965. In the early '60s, drummer Levon Helm made a point to seek him out in Chicago during his pre-Band travels with Ronnie Hawkins and the Hawks. Helm, who'd grown up in Arkansas listening to such mouth harp masters as Little Walter and Sonny Boy Williamson, liked what he heard. Coincidentally, Helm was brought to see Butterfield (and a later performance by Howlin' Wolf) by guitarist Mike Bloomfield.

Great bands depend on chemistry, and for both Butterfield and Bloomfield, nothing in their entire careers duplicated the incendiary musical rapport they enjoyed on the Butterfield Blues Band's first two albums. "Paul fascinated and intimidated Michael," said Bloomfield's brother Allen. "But [Michael] immediately recognized the virtuosity of [Paul's] playing—he was in a league with the best of the Chicago guys. There was an attitudinal problem between the two—Paul was the hard ball bearing and Mike the soft marshmallow. It took a certain period of time before Paul recognized that underneath that veneer there was sincerity and earnestness. Mike had to be the very best he could be on his ax. . . . That was the common denominator. He saw Mike as a player."

Butterfield was the undisputed boss of the band, but his group never flew higher than when Bloomfield was shooting off fireworks with his lead guitar. Still, Butterfield's leadership role—and Bloomfield's relative reticence—would be reflected in the two men's careers following Bloomfield's departure after the *East-West* album, a collaboration that captured both men at the peak of their improvisational powers. Butterfield soldiered on with the group's original guitarist Elvin Bishop and a new horn section.

In the early 1970s, Butterfield moved to Woodstock, New York, and formed his last great band—Better Days—consciously taking his name off of the brand, broadening the repertoire beyond blues, and sharing vocal duties with Geoff Muldaur and keyboardist Ronnie Barron. "The battle of music was helpful to guys like Butterfield," said Muldaur. "We had some dates with Muddy and he said, 'Are you going to sit in with me, Paul?' 'Not if you don't do "Mannish Boy."' And one night, he never sat in!" How did Waters take to Butterfield's goading? "He loved it," said Muldaur. "And Muddy was right about his whole thing about 'No white boy can sing the blues.' But Paul was upsetting in that way, because he's got to be one of the top five harmonica players ever. And his singing was better than you thought, too. I used to sing next to him, and let me tell you, he was very emotional."

Albert Grossman had negotiated a $250,000 recording contract for Butterfield, but insisted that he not share the advance with the band. "The band was bitching and moaning," said Nick Gravenites. "And Albert just said 'No, forget it. If you're gonna do that I'm not gonna get you the deal.'" Grossman finally prevailed. "Though it was good business," said Gravenites, "I think it helped bring Butterfield down. He went along with it in the end, but I believe he never forgot that." Mike Friedman worked for Grossman, and said, "Albert knew that Butterfield was his ward for the rest of his life. There was never going to be a time when Butter wasn't broke and he wasn't going to have to support him, which happened. This was probably [Grossman's] way to get somebody else's money to do that."

The Better Days group made two records—the 1973 self-titled debut is the better of the pair—after which Butterfield stayed around Woodstock and played the occasional recording sessions, including those for the Muddy Waters album. "Paul had the long relationship with Muddy," said Levon Helm. "That's why Muddy was so comfortable coming up to Woodstock. I'm sure his hot idea when he woke up in the morning wasn't to go find a bunch of white boys to play with! But with Butter, it gave Muddy confidence that there were some players up here. If Paul was playing with them they had to be alright." Butterfield was also invited to play "The Last Waltz."

Like Waters and Wolf and the other Chicago bluesman, Butterfield mostly made his living playing live. Sometimes he'd team up with Rick Danko, the bass-playing singer of the Band, and reprise the songs from their glory days to increasingly smaller audiences. No matter. Musicians live to play, and performing provides an identity through good times and bad. Around this time, Butterfield also recorded an instructional tape about how to play blues harmonica for Woodstock's Homespun Music.

Mike Bloomfield's post-Butterfield career started strong with the short-lived Electric Flag and his collaboration with Al Kooper, *Super Session*. But after cutting a successful live album with Kooper, his recording career vacillated between low-budget albums for small labels (including Fahey's Takoma) and half-hearted shots at the big time. He mostly liked getting high and watching TV. One time, Bloomfield quit dope after Carlos Santana and other Bay Area guitarists staged an intervention. "They said to me, 'Man, you ought to be ashamed of yourself," said Bloomfield, "because you're a laughingstock. We used to learn from you. When Butterfield came to town, we all came to see you. . . . How can you put your name on a marquee and charge money to see this ludicrous exhibition of what Michael Bloomfield used to be?"

But he had trouble staying clean, and then developed a dependency on the prescription drug Placidyl. Bloomfield was a rare musician with a safety net; a trust fund from his grandmother generated about $50,000 a year in interest, and his wealthy father helped to pay the bill for his son' unpaid taxes. "I think it was a sort of defiance," said Allen Bloomfield. "It goes back to this childhood thing of 'somebody's going to bail me out, somebody's going to show me that they love me, somebody's going to be the father and take care of this business.'"

The troubled son and reluctant rock star made three mediocre bids for mainstream success in the 1970s: a brief reunion with the Electric Flag; an undercooked collaboration (*Triumvirate*) with Dr. John and John Hammond Jr.; and a record with a band called KGB that featured Bloomfield, bassist Rick Grech (of Blind Faith), and drummer Carmine Appice (of Vanilla Fudge). Bloomfield subsequently retreated to Mill Valley, where (with the help of his friend Norman Dayron) he made records for small labels, improvised soundtracks for porn movies, and played local gigs with various musical pals. One of his best records, made for *Guitar Player* magazine, was called *If You Love These Blues, Play 'em as You Please* and featured Bloomfield performing in a variety of blues-oriented styles.

Bloomfield's most consistent Bay Area collaborator was Mark Naftalin, with whom he'd played in the Butterfield Blues Band. "During the years when we worked together as Michael Bloomfield and Friends," said Naftalin, "we would go along for a while, and then Mike would pull the plug. I never asked him, but I figured that those times probably coincided with the arrival of a trust fund check."

To help curb his drug abuse, Bloomfield took to drinking a fifth of gin. "All of a sudden, he was a drunk," said Nick Gravenites. "Not just a drinker, but a drunk, to the point where he'd be passed out in the gutter in downtown Mill Valley, and they had to get the Fire Department to take him home." Local officials, having also responded to his drug overdoses, called this "the Bloomfield call."

In November of 1980, Bob Dylan was playing a pair of concerts in San Francisco, and tracked down Bloomfield at his Mill Valley home. Dylan invited him to play at that night's performance, and a hesitant Bloomfield showed up at the Warfield Theater. "So Dylan gave this tremendous intro-duction," said Norman Dayron, "and there was Michael by the side of the stage, holding on to some guitar, wearing his bedroom slippers and a black leather jacket, and he shuffled on to the stage, plugged in, and just brought the house down."

Dylan and Bloomfield performed the hit song they'd recorded in their youth, "Like a Rolling Stone." "Afterwards, Dylan was so happy," said Day-ron. "He said, 'Man, I had no idea how much I'd missed you, how much I've missed hearing you in my music, those notes that ring, that guitar style!' He begged Michael to come back the next night, and I think we all knew it wasn't going to happen, that Michael wasn't capable of repeating that magic, that it would spoil the occasion."

Two months later, on a February morning in 1981, Mike Bloomfield was found slumped over in the front seat of a banged-up Mercury. The car doors were locked, and the key was in the ignition. Bloomfield had died of a drug overdose, and his companions had apparently moved his car, and left him for dead. His mother, father, and brother identified the body. "I'm not born to the blues, it's not in my roots, it's not in my family," said Bloomfield at the 1965 Newport Folk Festival, where he performed with the Butterfield Blues Band and Bob Dylan. "Man, I'm Jewish, you know? I'm not Son House. I haven't been pissed on and stepped on like he has. I haven't gone through that. My father's a multi-millionaire. I've lived a rich, fat, happy life. I can play blues, and I can feel it in a way, but those guys are a different story."

Bloomfield's life suggested that there was more than one route to the blues. Paul Butterfield was also on a downward spiral. He'd undergone multiple operations for an abdominal condition diagnosed as peritonitis. Grossman helped with the medical bills, but Butterfield resisted the doc-tor's order to quit drinking, and he'd also developed a heroin habit. "A lot of people worried about Paul," said Bonnie Raitt. "The '80s were a very rough decade for a lot of us. Our kind of music was almost completely off the air, disco was in and then power pop and New Wave. We felt disenfranchised on a lot of levels. For a lot of people what had been habit became serious vices. A whole line-up of people showed it—drug problems, heart attacks, health problems. And a lot of people fell by the wayside."

Butterfield was living in Los Angeles in January of 1986 when he learned that Albert Grossman had suffered a fatal heart attack while bound for London on the Concorde. Grossman was fifty-nine, and both an emotional and financial anchor to the few clients who remained on his roster after he shifted his energies to his other business interests, which included a recording studio and restaurant complex in Woodstock. Within months of Grossman's death, Richard Manuel of the Band, who'd long struggled with drugs and alcohol, hanged himself hours after a less-than-glamorous gig at the Cheek to Cheek Lounge in Winter Park, Florida. Butterfield died in May of 1987 from peritonitis, a condition exacerbated by his consumption of drugs and alcohol. It was a month after he'd participated in an HBO special called "B.B. King & Friends" during which he collaborated with Albert King and Stevie Ray Vaughan on an Elmore James song that suggested one source of the tears shed over the sad ends of both Butterfield and Bloomfield: "The Sky Is Crying."

In the late 1960s, when Peter Wolf was a deejay at Boston's WBCN, he'd field frequent late-night requests for records by John Lee Hooker from a listener with an Irish accent. The caller was Van Morrison, who was about to record his ruminative song cycle, *Astral Weeks*. At the time, Wolf was also playing music with his pre–J. Geils Band group, the Hallucinations, and was excited when Hooker was booked to play the local Odyssey Coffeeshop.

"There were only about five people in the place when Hooker went on," said Wolf. "He was sensational." To help draw a crowd, Wolf proposed that the Hallucinations back Hooker. Hooker gave the okay, and Wolf and his cohorts alerted their friends and plastered the neighborhood with posters. The next night, the club was filled. "We got real friendly with John" said Wolf. "In the daytime we'd get together and show him around Boston." A few years later, Wolf would sing Hooker's "Serve You Right to Suffer" on the first album by the J. Geils Band.

Hooker worked with a wide variety of blues-rock musicians over his long career, and famously collaborated with Canned Heat in 1971. Over subsequent decades, he would record and perform with Van Morrison, sing the title role on a Pete Townshend concept album (1989's *The Iron Man*), perform a song in *The Blues Brothers* movie, and create a soundtrack for a 1990 Dennis Hopper movie called *The Hot Spot* with an ensemble that included Taj Mahal on guitar, drummer Earl Palmer (who'd played on Little Richard's early hits), and Miles Davis. "The guy liked me a lot," said Hooker of Davis, "and when he got through playing . . . he give me a big hug, and he say, . . . 'You the funkiest man alive. You in that mud right up to your neck.' That means the deep, deep blues, you know, and I think that was a great compliment coming from him."

In the late '80s, Hooker reached a new level of popularity with a series of albums that paired him with a host of blues-rock stars, including Morrison, Carlos Santana, John Hammond Jr., Ry Cooder, Robert Cray, Johnny Winter, and Keith Richards. "You're not going to mistake John Lee Hooker for anybody else," said Richards, "and [his stuff] was just such a fascinating sound, and so different to other stuff I'd heard; in a way more archaic. . . . It was so dark and swampy. I learned those John Lee Hooker chords, which are very strange shapes, and it immediately affected everything I did since."

The Healer, released in 1988, won Hooker his first Grammy Award for a duet remake of his 1951 hit "In the Mood" with Bonnie Raitt. The two had known each other for nearly twenty years but had never shared a song before they met in the studio. "It was really one of the most erotically charged afternoons of my life," said Raitt. "He had his sunglasses on and I was just staring at him, head to head, sitting on chairs. At the end of it I just said, 'I need a towel.' If I was still smoking I would have had a cigarette."

At the time she sang with Hooker, Raitt was without a record contract after making nine albums. "My spirit was broken when Warner Brothers dropped me," she said of a label shakeout that also saw the departure of Van Morrison. Like the blues performers she adored, Raitt had always made the bulk of her income playing live shows, but was now forced to support her band by playing solo concerts with just one other musician. Through it all, Raitt remained a born performer, and a true child of show business.

"One of my most poignant memories," said John Raitt, "was when Bonnie was about 14 and I had to come home to literally change suitcases and take off again. I heard her crying in her bathroom and when I asked what was wrong, she said, 'You're never home! We don't have to have these houses. I miss you!'" Eventually, perhaps inevitably, Bonnie Raitt embraced the same peripatetic lifestyle. One time, their tour buses passed in the middle of the night; when he arrived at his next stop, the dad received a call from his daughter reporting that the concierge at her hotel said that her father had forgotten his sports coat.

The road posed more problems than lost clothing. "I was anesthetized by drugs and alcohol and also the life-style," said Raitt. "At an early age, I became 'Bonnie Raitt' at a time when I was still very unformed. I had to crystallize this personality before I was really ready to do it. . . . I think the responsibility for being rewarded for something I didn't feel I deserved made me hide behind the alcohol. I got sucked into the life-style of a 'rock and roll blues mama.'"

A skiing accident left Raitt with a mangled right thumb during a 1987 acoustic tour of Colorado. Forced off the road, Raitt quit drinking, bought a bicycle to get back in shape, and went into therapy. "I got out of touch with the person who's underneath all those layers," said Raitt. "I built myself a personality. I think it worked in the beginning, but then as I got older, it didn't serve me as well. I think the life-style encouraged the music somewhat. I don't think it always got in the way. It's just that the drugs and alcohol part of it became physically and creatively debilitating and starting running me at the end."

The sober Raitt found a new focus in songwriting and got a new manager after years of overseeing her own career. "Let's face it," said Bonnie Raitt upon the release of 1989's *Nick of Time*. "This is my 10th album, and every time, somebody says, 'This is the one, this is going to do it.' At this point, I expect nothing. But I'm no longer going to undermine my own success. I used to feel a lot of guilt about getting more attention than some of the blues people that I admired. At the same time, I'd also see myself not doing as well as somebody who was doing lesser work." Around this time, Raitt helped to launch the Rhythm and Blues Foundation, an organization that helps musicians in need and fights to collect unpaid record royalties.

Nick of Time sold more than six million copies, and in 1990, won three Grammy Awards, including Album of the Year. That same year, Raitt won a fourth Grammy for her "In the Mood" duet with John Lee Hooker. *Nick of Time* would insure her an enduring career, and while it was considered an adult contemporary album, Raitt would always have a slide on her middle finger, and her heart in the blues.

"Hello everybody. I'm Stevie and I am an alcoholic, and an addict and I too am nervous," said Stevie Ray Vaughan. "I am sober today by the grace of God and that is the only way I know of. Everything I've done got me here." Vaughan was addressing an Alcoholics Anonymous gathering in January of 1990. He'd been sober for three years, and given the depths of his dependency, it was a remarkable feat while working in a music culture quick to accommodate excess. After a little more than a month in rehabilitation, he'd resumed touring in early 1987 and removed the rider in his contract that called for two fifths of Crown Royal and a fifth of Smirnoff to be in his dressing room. Vaughan even quit smoking cigarettes.

The sobriety greatly improved his playing, with his more disciplined attack adding finesse to his always-fiery performances. (The distinction is clear on Vaughan's *Live From Austin, Texas* DVD, which contains televised performances from 1983 and 1989.) In 1988 he made an album with a title that referenced Alcoholics Anonymous—*In Step*—and the powerful playing on tunes like "The House Is Rockin'" and "Crossfire" suggested that hard-driving blues-rock was now his intoxicant of choice.

Vaughan and Double Trouble (the group now included keyboardist Reese Wynans) promoted *In Step* on a co-headlining tour with Jeff Beck dubbed "The Fire and the Fury." Beck spoke highly of his touring partner. "I felt very amateurish alongside him," said Beck of Jimi Hendrix, "because he lived and breathed it. [Vaughan is] very similar to Jimi in that way." Eric Clapton, who like Beck was challenged by Hendrix's supernatural talent, also saw the similarity. "We played together only a couple of times," said Clapton of Vaughan, "but it was enough to be able to link him with Jimi Hendrix in terms of commitment. They both played out of their skin . . . as if there was no tomorrow, and the level of devotion they both showed to their art was identical."

Vaughan's increasingly mature musicality truly came to the fore on his next recording, a collaboration with his brother Jimmie, who'd left the Fabulous Thunderbirds and also gotten sober. *Family Style*, which was credited to the Vaughan Brothers, picked up a musical story that had begun decades before in their boyhood home. But while the record would win the Contemporary Blues Grammy (plus the Rock Instrumental Grammy for "D/FW"), the collection had more to do with stripped-down R&B than blustery blues. Produced by Nile Rodgers, guitarist in the disco-flavored group Chic, *Family Style* saw the younger Vaughan playing with the musical economy that was more typical of his older brother. Only on "Brothers" do the siblings showcase their different approaches to the blues guitar. With the two Vaughan's sharing vocal and guitar duties, *Family Style* was a record that must have made their mom proud.

Before the release of *Family Style*, Stevie Ray Vaughan and Double Trouble went on tour with Eric Clapton. Jimmie Vaughan was also on the bill that played Alpine Valley in East Troy, Wisconsin, on August 27, 1990. Robert Cray filled out the program. Virginia-born Cray is a soul-inflected singer and guitarist who epitomized a younger generation of blues players who learned as much from Clapton as B.B. King, let alone Muddy Waters. "I can't sing the songs with the same kind of emotion, or the same kind of stories as those guys that lived in the South and picked cotton," said Cray, who got his first guitar after he heard the Beatles.

The day of the show, Clapton invited Buddy Guy to brunch at the Four

Seasons in Chicago, where he confessed to his drugged-out state when he tried to produce Guy and Junior Wells on their *Layla*-era Atlantic album. The two guitarists then took a helicopter to Wisconsin. By the time Stevie Ray Vaughan took the stage with Double Trouble, he knew that Guy was in the audience. "He brings me back home," said Vaughan of Guy. "It's easy to get off into just going through the motions. I try not to do that, but I catch myself. But to come out and see somebody like Buddy or Otis Rush, it's like they shake you, and that's when I find the kind of emotion I really want."

At Alpine Valley, Vaughan played a song that had inspired Guy, Guitar Slim's "The Things That I Used To Do," and "Let Me Love You Baby," a tune that Guy had written with Willie Dixon that was a favorite of British blues-rock bands. "I heard a Buddy Guy song," said Cray. "It started up, and I ran up to the stage because I thought Buddy had joined Stevie on stage. But it was Stevie singing a Buddy Guy song. And I walked up to see a big old smile on Buddy's face."

"Never heard Stevie wail so hard," said Guy of the performance. "I got goose bumps. I felt proud. Just like Muddy had felt he had raised me, I felt like Stevie was my boy." After Clapton's headlining set, he invited the other guitarists onstage for a jam session. "I took a look at everybody grabbing Stratocasters off the racks," said Cray, "so I went and grabbed a steel-bodied Telecaster." Spread across the stage was Clapton, Guy, two Vaughans, and Cray. Clapton chose the encore: Robert Johnson's "Sweet Home Chicago."

"Whenever I'm around," said Guy, who's lived in Chicago for more than fifty years, "Eric always calls that tune. We wore it out, and the fans went home smiling. Backstage, with everybody glowing, Eric talked about how we'd be together again at his [typically annual] concerts at the Royal Albert Hall in London. He was going to bring us all in."

Stevie Ray Vaughan grabbed a seat on the first of four helicopters flying back to Chicago, leaving his brother to catch one of the others. Clapton and Guy took the next copter, and said their goodbyes at Midway Airport. Around dawn, Clapton and Jimmie Vaughan awoke to the news that one of the helicopters had slammed into the side of a mountain less than a mile after takeoff. They took a long, silent limousine ride to Wisconsin to identify the bodies of Stevie Ray Vaughan and three members of Clapton's crew. In the morning sun, their sad eyes took in the debris spread across a hillside. Vaughan spotted a familiar broad-brimmed hat. An official approached him holding out his younger brother's Coptic cross. The big brother slipped it around his neck.

Four days later, family and close friends attended Stevie Ray Vaughan's funeral in Dallas, with another three thousand outside the chapel. Mourning alongside Jimmie Vaughan and his mother, Martha, were Eric Clapton, an inconsolable Buddy Guy, and ZZ Top. Stevie Wonder sang the Lord's Prayer while Dr. John played piano. Nile Rodgers spoke and played "Tick Tock," a sweet soul song from the soon-to-be-released album by the Vaughan Brothers. Then Bonnie Raitt, Jackson Browne, and Steve Wonder sang "Amazing Grace." Behind the bar at Antone's, the Austin club where Stevie Ray Vaughan had played with the giants of the blues, his portrait was hung alongside one of Muddy Waters.

SEVENTEEN
FURTHER ON UP THE ROAD

In 1992, thirty years after releasing his first album, Bob Dylan used his acoustic guitar and harmonica to record *Good as I Been to You* in the garage of his home in Malibu, California. It consisted of thirteen solo performances of songs, that he might have sung in 1962 when he opened for John Lee Hooker at the Gaslight Café in Greenwich Village. He played "Frankie and Albert" in the style of Mississippi John Hurt, Blind Boy Fuller's "Stop It Up and Go," a blues classic first recorded by the Missisippi Sheiks, "Sittin' On Top of the World," and "Tomorrow Night," a song that was a hit for Lonnie Johnson in 1947. The album initially shocked Dylan fans, who were once aghast when he swapped his Martin guitar for a Fender Stratocaster.

Ry Cooder 1947–

On *World Gone Wrong*, released a year later, Dylan reprised the format, and sang "Ragged and Dirty," a song by Son House's old partner, Willie Brown. Dylan also wrote liner notes titled "About the Songs (what they're about)." "'Broke Down Engine' is a Blind Willie McTell masterpiece," said Dylan. "It's about revival, getting a new lease on life, not just posing there—paint-chipped & flaked, mattress bare, single bulb swinging above the bed." (Dylan had already paid homage to the bluesman with a haunting original called "Blind Willie McTell.") The title song, "World Gone Wrong," was by the Mississippi Sheiks.

"Strange things alright," said Dylan of the tune. "Strange things like courage becoming befuddled & nonfundamental. Evil charlatans masquerading in pullover vests & tuxedos talking gobbledygook, monstrous pompous superficial pageantry parading down lonely streets on limited access highways."

Some thought that these quickie, low-tech albums might have been a clever ploy to complete his contract with Columbia Records. But then Dylan re-signed with the label, and in 1997, released *Time Out of Mind*, the first of a series of outstanding late-career recordings that were suffused with the blues (the others were 2001's *Love and Theft*, 2006's *Modern Times,* and 2012's *Tempest*). In this context, Dylan's early-'90s rapprochement with his folk-blues roots rekindled the inspiration he found when, in 1961, John Hammond sent his newest signing home with an advance copy of *Robert Johnson: King of the Delta Blues Singers*. That record had a profound influence on Dylan during the early years of his long career, and thirty-five years later, he seemed revitalized having revisited the repertoire that had moved him in his youth.

Dylan was hardly alone. Blues are in the bloodstream of generations of musicians. Tom Waits was a bohemian singer-songwriter who emerged in the early 1970s with tunes that were soon covered by the Eagles and Bruce Springsteen. Blues were always a part of his musical palette, but beginning with 1983's *Swordfishtrombones*, when Waits's music took a more experimental turn, blues was in the stylistic forefront, with his Beefheart-meets-Wolf vocals suggestive of a kind of post-modern Delta blues. It was only fitting that in 2001, John Hammond Jr. recorded *Wicked Grin*, a bluesy collection of Waits songs that was produced by their composer.

Musicians schooled in jazz have recorded some of the very best recent blues. Think of Cassandra Wilson singing songs by Robert Johnson and Son House; or Olu Dara, the father of the rapper Nas, who played trumpet with avant-garde bands before making albums that blended blues, folk, and jazz. Similarly, guitarist James "Blood" Ulmer played free jazz with Ornette Coleman before he turned to playing the blues. Popular electric guitarists like Kenny Wayne Shepherd, Joe Bonamassa, and Gary Clark Jr. play a blues-rock style reminiscent of Stevie Ray Vaughan. Acoustic players like Keb' Mo', Corey Harris, Alvin Youngblood Hart, and Kelly Joe Phelps mix various elements of soul, folk, and pop into their blues. Chris Smither continues to combine bluesy musicianship with a singer-songwriter sensibility, while Rory Block revisits classics of the Delta blues. Record labels like Alligator and Blind Pig market contemporary variants on the electric blues of the 1960s. Music fans book passage on sailing ships for "Blues Cruises" that feature oceans of booze and performances by everybody from Taj Mahal to the latest blues-rock bands. But for all of these examples, the blues, like rock 'n' roll, has become a distinctly (pardon the pun) minority taste.

The mass audience mostly hears blues on television commercials, and lately, performances by both Muddy Waters and Howlin' Wolf have been used in TV ads for Viagra. "I've heard more slide guitar on television than I have in mainstream radio over the last thirty years," said Bonnie Raitt, a master of the bottleneck style. "Anytime you want to connote danger or sex, or you have a truck driving over a dirt road, it's there to signify that whole sense of foreboding. It's the same reason they use blues images in ads for cigarettes and alcohol: it's the devil side. So they play those slinky grooves to get people to give in to their deep dark passions."

Sometimes, the blues stands out by being the antithesis of the often synthetic, high-gloss music that dominates the top of the pops. "ZZ Top's show at the Beacon was all base line," said Ben Ratliff in the *New York Times* in 2010. "Not bass lines—there were those, too, and very steady—but an unbroken rumble to authority, an adherence to rules and a celebration of them . . . this was, more or less, a perfect concert." That same year, *Times* critic Jon Pareles reviewed Eric Clapton's Crossroads Guitar Festival: "While the concerts are benefits for Crossroads Center, Antiqua, a nonprofit addiction-treatment clinic that Mr. Clapton founded in the Caribbean, they are also rallies for what sometimes seems to be an endangered species: the guitar hero, the kind of player who can seize and hold an audience with chorus after chorus of an instrumental solo."

Talk about old school! Clapton, of course, is uniquely successful among blues-rock stars, and has drawn from the blues songbook throughout a hugely successful career that's seen him play a wide variety of rock and pop. His 1992 collection, *Unplugged*, was the soundtrack of his performance on the acoustic-oriented MTV show of the same name. The disc included "Tears in Heaven," a touching ballad dedicated to his son Connor, who'd died at the age of four after falling from an upper-story window of a Manhattan apartment. *Unplugged* was otherwise pretty much a blues album, with Clapton performing tunes by Robert Johnson ("Walkin' Blues" and "Malted Milk"), Big Bill Broonzy ("Hey Hey"), Jesse Fuller ("San Francisco Bay Blues"), and a song popularized by Muddy Waters that Clapton had once performed with Cream ("Rollin' and Tumblin'").

On Clapton's 1994 album, *From the Cradle*, he turned to electric blues and covered songs by Willie Dixon, Eddie Boyd, Tampa Red, Freddie King, and

Muddy Waters. The tone was almost academic, as if Clapton was fulfilling his pledge to Muddy to keep the blues alive; while performing the album on tour, pictures of the artists who'd originated the songs Clapton played were displayed on video screens. Clapton's fealty to the blues continued with 2000's *Riding with the King*, a collaboration with B.B. King, and his tribute to Robert Johnson, *Me and Mr. Johnson*. The accompanying DVD found Clapton performing at the Dallas address of Johnson's second and last recording sessions.

Clapton's devotion to the blues canon turned out to be a surprisingly robust commercial success—*Unplugged* sold over ten million copies, *From the Cradle* moved three million units, with two million buying *Riding with the King* (the Johnson disc moved a half million). Such sales say at least as much about Clapton the rock star as they do about the mass market for the blues. After all, he was also able to tap into his more rock-friendly past. In 2005, Clapton reunited with Cream for a series of concerts in London and New York that generated CD and DVD releases. More live discs resulted from his 2008 tour with Steve Winwood, his partner in the short-lived Blind Faith.

Clapton strengthened his own concerts by trading solos with a pair of gifted young guitarists, Doyle Bramhall II and Derek Trucks. Both players are from musical families. Bramhall II is the son of Doyle Bramhall, who drummed and sang with Jimmie Vaughan's Texas Storm, and later wrote songs recorded by Stevie Ray Vaughan. Bramhall II played with the Fabulous Thunderbirds before joining forces with Clapton. Derek Trucks is the nephew of drummer Butch Trucks, a founding member of the Allman Brothers Band, and perhaps the most gifted slide guitarist since Duane Allman. Trucks joined the Allman Brothers in 1999, and also plays in the Tedeschi-Trucks Band with his wife, blues guitarist and singer Susan Tedeschi.

But no second-generation story beats the family of Jim Dickinson, a primary player on the Memphis blues scene during the 1960s who played with the Rolling Stones and Ry Cooder before producing records by rock acts like Big Star and the Replacements. Dickinson had a couple sons who grew up playing music, with Cody sitting behind the drums, and Luther playing guitar. "They tried to get me to teach 'em," said Jim Dickinson, "especially Luther, but I told 'em that you've gotta learn the way I did. . . . You have to teach yourself to rock."

The Dickinson boys grew up in northern Mississippi during the 1990's vogue for the "hill country blues" marketed by Fat Possum Records. Previously unrecorded artists like Junior Kimbrough, R. L. Burnside, and

T-Model Ford played a raw, ramshackle style of blues that typically employed a single chord. The minimalist aesthetic appealed to latter-day punk rock fans, prompting the Jon Spencer Blues Explosion to record a successful album with Burnside called *A Ass Pocket of Whiskey*. Writer and musician Robert Palmer, who died of liver disease in 1997 at the age of fifty-two, produced Fat Possum records by both Burnside and Junior Kimbrough. The label's most famous act turned out to be the Black Keys, a blues-rock duo from Akron, Ohio, that hit the big time with its 2010 Nonesuch album, *Brothers*.

At the age of fifteen, Luther Dickinson began hanging around with Othar Turner, a fife player who was a contemporary link to a Mississippi tradition of fife and drum bands. "I used to sit on Otha's porch and play [guitar] until Otha would jump up and start hopping around," said Dickinson. "When he threw his hat down and started singing field hollers, I knew I'd come up with something good."

"What Otha taught Luther," said Jim Dickinson, "wasn't how to play but how to feel. A monkey can learn the notes, and many monkeys do. But to learn what a black man feels when he plays his own music—that's the trick. It's the same trick as Elvis. . . . I know some people think it's exploitive, but I think it's a miracle." Luther Dickinson learned his lessons well. He and his brother Cody formed the North Mississippi Allstars, and cultivated a rocky version of the hill county blues. Their father died in August of 2009, secure that his sons were carrying on the family business.

"Dad always said that the essence of rock 'n' roll was young white boys crossing the tracks to hang out in the juke joints and soak up the blues," said Luther Dickinson. "It's all about racial collision. It's Chuck Berry trying to play Bob Wills and getting it not quite right. It's the Beatles and the Rolling Stones trying to play Chuck Berry and getting it not quite right. It's me trying to play like Otha [Turner] and R. L. [Burnside] but letting Duane Allman get in there, too." This potluck stew of black and white music pretty much defines what Jim Dickinson called "world boogie."

In the late 1960s, around the time that Ry Cooder recorded with the Rolling Stones, he was offered his own deal with the devil. "This is the way it was presented to me," said Cooder of his conversations with record executives. "'Play the blues loud and be a star.' I figured that you'd have just one run and that you could cut your options off. A lot of people made that deal and never got out." The guitarist chuckled at his words. "Have hits, get rich," said Cooder. "What a chump's play."

Instead of turning up the volume, Cooder has spent his life refining his ability on the guitar. "I'm not some kind of Egyptologist, a hopeless antiquarian," said Cooder. "I've just been looking for what I can use, absorb into my own playing." Cooder aimed for what he has called "chicken skin," the state of exhilaration incited by great music. In that pursuit, only one thing comes between Cooder and the steel-wound strings of his electric guitar—a glass slide. "I've found that sherry bottles are the best," said Cooder, "because they have a long neck that bells out and are made of the thickest glass. So what I do is take a dozen bottles down to the auto glass place, give them some money, and they cut it up right. I tell them they can keep what's inside the bottles."

For much of the 1970s and '80s, Cooder made critically acclaimed solo albums and created soundtracks for films. The instrumental template for Wim Wenders's *Paris, Texas* was Blind Willie Johnson's "Dark Was the Night, Cold Was the Ground." Cooder did lots of films with Walter Hill, including *Crossroads*, a kind of *Karate Kid Gets the Blues* in which Ralph Macchio played a young guitarist studying music at the Julliard School who goes to Mississippi to help an aging bluesman win his soul back from the devil. No surprise that the music was better than the movie.

Cooder learned to play Mexican Tejano music sitting alongside accordionist Flaco Jimenez, and studied Hawaiian slack-key guitar playing with singer and guitarist Gabby Pahinui. (The term "slack-key" refers to the numerous open tunings used in a finger-style guitar technique that was developed to accommodate the rhythms and harmonies of Hawaiian music.) Cooder said Pahinui and Bahamian guitarist Joseph Spence were "My musical beacons. . . . They had what I call high-zen understanding. . . . As they got older, they got better." Cooder hit a mother lode of mature musical wisdom when he recorded with a group of traditional Cuban musicians for an album called *Buena Vista Social Club* in 1997. The album revived Cuban styles popular in the 1940s and '50s, and featured players like singer Compay Segundo and pianist Ruben Gonzalez who hadn't had high-profile work since Cuba's 1959 revolution. The worldwide popularity of the *Buena Vista Social Club*, which generated a concert film by Wim Wenders, various off-shoot recordings, and a sold-out show at Carnegie Hall, represents a rediscovery that was just as unlikely as Depression-era bluesmen like Son House and Mississippi John Hurt performing at the Newport Folk Festival in the 1960s.

Cooder had a more blues-oriented partnership when he cut 1994's *Talking Timbuktu* with Malian guitarist Ali Farka Toure, who has been called "the Malian John Lee Hooker." "The journalists always want to know about the blues," said Toure. "I say the word blues means nothing to me. I do not know the blues. I know the African tradition." Toure agreed that he heard a kindred spirit in Hooker. "This music is 100 percent African," said Toure. "Some of the tunes he plays are in the Tamashek style, some in the Boze style, some in the Songhai style. I respect him and appreciate his genius as a translator of African music in the United States, but my music is the roots and the trunk and he is the branches and the leaves."

Hooker wouldn't have known the Songhai style from a Shanghai noodle. And Cooder, who played with Hooker on many occasions, would likely agree that Hooker's elemental guitar style is more of a root than a branch. But that's the way musical styles evolve. Hooker's music might carry traces of black America's African origins, but the sound of "Boogie Chillen" was cultivated in both the soil of Mississippi and the concrete of Detroit. Hooker, a master of the endless beat, died in June of 2001, two months shy of his eighty-fourth birthday.

Ry Cooder has lately focused on solo albums (*My Name is Buddy*, *Chavez Ravine*) that reflect the politically leftist leanings of the folk music he heard in his youth. Cooder released *Election Special* in August of 2012, a work that left little doubt that he would not be voting for Mitt Romney. Indeed, Cooder had already expressed his choice for president on his previous record, 2011's *Pull up Some Dust and Sit Down*. On "John Lee Hooker for President," Cooder accompanied his masterful interpretation of Hooker's hypnotic guitar style with a properly guttural vocal drawl. "Every man and woman," he said, referencing a famous Hooker song, "gets one scotch, one bourbon, one beer, three times a day, if they stay cool." As for who would be in Hooker's administration? "Jimmy Reed, vice president," said Cooder. "Little Johnny Taylor, secretary of state."

The man who first taught Ry Cooder about the slide, John Fahey, died in February 2001 after undergoing a sextuple coronary bypass operation at the age of sixty-one. It had been a long, often hard road since Fahey had rediscovered Skip James and founded Takoma Records. The label, set up to promote Fahey's music, had found its greatest success with guitarist Leo Kottke. Another Takoma artist, pianist George Winston, would later became a superstar of contemporary instrumental music. Fahey sold Takoma to Chrysalis Records in 1979.

By then, Fahey was drinking heavily, and after the dissolution of his first marriage, he relocated to Salem, Oregon. In the mid-'80s, he fell victim to Epstein-Barr syndrome, a viral infection that exacerbated his diabetes and other health problems. Two more failed marriages and a sputtering career left him in virtual poverty in the early 1990s. Living in cheap motels, he supported himself by pawning his guitars, and reminiscent of his teenage days collecting 78s with Dick Spottswood in Washington, D.C., selling rare records that he'd discovered in thrift stores.

Fahey rebounded in the mid-'90s after the release of a career retrospective, *Return of the Repressed: The Anthology*, underscored his influence on such alternative musicians as the members of Sonic Youth and Jim O'Rourke, who produced his thorny 1997 album, *Womblife*. At the same time, an inheritance from his late father gave Fahey the means to start Reverent Records, which released an acclaimed seven-disc retrospective (*Screamin' and Hollerin' the Blues: The Worlds of Charley Patton*) focused on the bluesman who'd been the subject of Fahey's master's thesis. In a final, oddly fitting twist, Fahey won his only Grammy Award for the liner notes to Reverant's *Anthology of American Folk Music, Vol. 4*, which forty-five years after the release of 1952's *Anthology*, recreated what was to be the fourth volume of Harry Smith's enduring, epic collection of great American music.

A different kind of music collector, Alan Lomax, died in 2002. Lomax had spent much of the last twenty years of his life working on a project he called the Global Jukebox. The idea was to digitize Lomax's vast holdings of recordings, photos, and films and create an interactive multimedia archive accessible via the World Wide Web. Such a resource, which began to be realized in 2012, is a 180-degree reversal of the folklore premise with which Lomax started his career, wherein exposure to outside influences were presumed to compromise an artist like Lead Belly. Now, with everything at everybody's fingertips, such purity had to be considered a thing of the past.

"I don't recommend heroin for anybody," said Keith Richards, "but I don't regret it for myself. I could have become just another horrible, bigoted megastar. In a weird way, it put my head in the clouds, but kept my feet on the ground. Maybe I'm really not too happy with the rarefied atmosphere of stardom. With junk, I was just another guy on the street trying to get a fix."

The Stones celebrated their golden anniversary in 2012, but back in 1986, when I spoke to all of its members, the band had been in peril of coming unglued. The occasion was the release of the group's latest album, *Dirty*

Work, and the rift centered upon the fact that Mick Jagger had decided to forgo a Rolling Stones tour to make a solo album. It also turned out that for the first time in his life, Charlie Watts was abusing drugs, a period that he later attributed to a "mid-life crisis." Spending an afternoon as a fly-on-the-wall while the group made a video for the album's first single, "Harlem Shuffle," it appeared that the band was all but broken. The tensions were nothing new; in the 1970s, when Richards was largely lost to heroin, Jagger took control of (and essentially saved) the Stones. Years later, he and Richards were still struggling to reestablish an amicable balance of power.

The Stones had always boiled down to Jagger and Richards, and the circumstances of our chats suggested why Keith has typically won the public relations war. Mick telephoned from Antigua, a scenario that gave the savvy, press-wise entertainer prone to obfuscation a clear, gotta-run advantage. I met Keith in the Manhattan office of his manager, where we shared a bottle of Maker's Mark bourbon, the kind of gesture nearly certain to make a rock critic an ally.

"People are sometimes drawn to play with fire," said Richards when asked about members of the group's inner circle who burned out early. "But if you want to play with fire, you've got to be prepared to burn." Richards took a cigarette from his lips and placed its fiery tip to the end of his left index finger. "I can do that because I've got 20 years of calluses from playing the guitar. It's easy for me to play Keith Richards"—the cigarette again touched the finger—"because I've had lots of practice."

Saxophone player Bobby Keys, who has toured with the Rolling Stone since he added his horn to "Brown Sugar," and who shared a birth date and drug habit with Richards, learned this the hard way. "That's the thing about the rock 'n' roll lifestyle," said Keys. "When I was hangin' out with Keith and Mick, hell, I just lived the life that they did. Fuck it. But I'd forget, of course, that I was on salary and those guys weren't. It just didn't seem relevant to me at the time. I thought, 'Well, if they can have it, I can have it too.' That was an error of calculation."

During the late 1980s, Jagger and Richards went their separate ways, but nobody mistook their solo work for that of the Rolling Stones, especially the accountants. Richards also served as the musical director for an all-star concert honoring the ever irascible Chuck Berry, captured in the 1987 documentary *Hail! Hail! Rock 'n' Roll*. Relations between the principals mellowed after the Stones were inducted into the Rock and Roll Hall of Fame, setting the stage for the "Steel Wheels" tour that established a routine by which the band would periodically release a largely ignored new album and then mount a hugely lucrative tour that featured their greatest hits. Like the bluesmen they had once sought to emulate, the Stones now made their money on the road.

In sense and sensibility, Jagger had always been more attuned to the musical flavor-of-the-month than the resolutely rootsy Richards. In 1982, Keith went to see Tina Turner at a New York club, and invited her and David Bowie back to his suite at the Plaza Hotel. "He had this great big tape machine set up there," said Turner, "and you could see that he used it constantly. We had some champagne, and Keith cranked up his machine and started playing all this old music, and it suddenly dawned on me: This is what these guys did. They would go back to this old music that they loved—blues and R&B—and they would change it around and make something of their own out of it."

Turner was by then divorced from Ike Turner, and on the cusp of a remarkable career revival with the release of 1984's *Private Dancer*. Her 1986 autobiography, *I, Tina*, detailed the physical abuse she'd endured from her cocaine crazy husband before she fled the relationship in 1976. Ike Turner, who served an eighteen-month prison term after a 1989 drug bust, was unrepentant. "Tina exaggerated about me beating her," said Turner. "Have you seen how big she is? . . . Ain't it part the woman's fault if she stays around and lets me hit her?" Ike Turner passed away in December 2007; the coroner said he died of cocaine toxicity complicated by other medical issues.

During the Rolling Stones "A Bigger Bang" tour, Martin Scorsese filmed an October 2006 show at New York's Beacon Theater that was released two years later as *Shine a Light*. (In 2003, Scorsese produced a comprehensive, seven-part documentary broadcast on PBS called *The Blues*.) Backstage at the Beacon, Ahmet Ertegun, eighty-three, stumbled in the VIP lounge and struck his head on the concrete floor. In the hospital, he slipped into a coma, and died a week later. Ertegun was buried not in the land of blues and jazz, but in his native Turkey. Like Mick and Keith, Ahmet was a foreigner beguiled by the music of America.

The Stones marked their fiftieth year with concerts in London and New York; what else can a poor boy do? The Rolling Stones are lifers, like guitarist Hubert Sumlin, who got Richards, Eric Clapton, and James Cotton to play on his 2008 album, *About Them Shoes*. Sumlin had already enjoyed the help of a host of musicians who'd played benefits to help pay his medical bills after a 2002 operation in which a cancerous lung was removed. Sumlin died in December of 2011; Jagger and Richards paid for his internment and funeral service. Sumlin had once more tumbled through a transom to land alongside his old boss and another hero of the Rolling Stones, Howlin' Wolf.

By 1970, many people had heard the songs of Robert Johnson, but nobody had seen his face. A handful of the curious had been searching for biographical details ever since Alan Lomax made his 1942 trip through the Delta and heard about Johnson from Muddy Waters and Son House. Still, Sam Charters had only a sketchy portrait in 1959's *The Country Blues*. Soon, though, researchers would be on Johnson's trail like a pack of hungry hellhounds.

Gayle Dean Wardlow was a teenager in 1954 when he began knocking on doors in Mississippi looking to buy old records by Roy Acuff, an influential country singer and promoter. Wardlow quickly discovered that one rare jazz or blues disc could be traded for a whole lot of Acuff. So he explored the black side of town and found that a house with a well-tended lawn and a flowerpot on the porch was a good prospect because it suggested a female resident of long standing. Men, he found, were more apt to move and dump their records. Wardlow cultivated an interest in the men behind the music. He solicited the state of Mississippi for the death certificates of Charley Patton, Willie Brown, Tommy Johnson, and Robert Johnson. He got three out of four, and obtained Johnson's death letter when he directed a specific request to LeFlore County. Wardlow published the fruits of his research in obscure publications devoted to the blues and record collecting.

Mack McCormick, a Texas researcher who'd helped to discover Mance Lipscomb and revive the career of Lightnin' Hopkins, had long been collecting information on Johnson. In 1970, he interviewed two people who told similar stories about having witnessed Johnson's poisoning, and pointed to the same killer. The LeFlore county sheriff, however, showed little inclination to pursue the very cold case. McCormick continued his research and planned to write a book called *Biography of a Phantom*. When he found two of Johnson's half-sisters, he came away with something special—the first known pictures of the phantom bluesman.

But before McCormick could publish his book, another researcher staked a competing claim. Steve LaVere, a record collector who'd worked around the blues and record business, found one of Johnson's half-sisters, Carrie Thompson, who'd uncovered two more photos of Johnson in the year since her meeting with McCormick. LaVere left with copies of the photos and a much more valuable document: a signed contract that gave him the rights to commercially exploit the photos and recordings of Robert Johnson with a fifty-fifty split of any royalties with Thompson.

LaVere was presumably aware that Johnson's songs had never been copyrighted; after all, on the LP reissues of his work, the fine print said the songs were in the public domain. LaVere approached Columbia Records around 1975 about producing a complete collection of Johnson's recordings and let them know about his deal with a Johnson heir. John Hammond, perhaps because he'd known LaVere's father, the late jazz vocalist and pianist Charles LaVere, agreed to grant LaVere ownership of copyrights that, in truth, nobody seemed to own. Frank Driggs, who produced the original Johnson reissues, was already at work on a comprehensive package when LaVere made his pitch. "LaVere," said Driggs, "got a deal such as nobody I've ever heard of getting in the history of the business."

One explanation for the pact could be that a record company preferred paying publishing royalties to somebody (anybody!) to avoid potential litigation from an unknown third party. In this case, McCormick informed Columbia that he had his own deal with Johnson's half-sisters, a threat which served to delay the release of the boxed set until 1990. By then, LaVere had established a reputation as a fearsome litigator against anybody who encroached on his claim to the Johnson estate, including the celebrated cartoonist R. Crumb, who'd produced T-shirts sporting his portrait of Johnson. McCormick, possibly fearing such a lawsuit, retreated and never finished *Biography of a Phantom*. The issuing of the 1990 collection established that the copyright to Johnson's songs belonged to LaVere's company, "Delta Haze Corporation." He subsequently sued the Rolling Stones (via Allen Klein) over the band's recording of two Johnson tunes.

LaVere was meanwhile busy being sued by Carrie Thompson's heirs over his management of the estate. But the legal imbroglio took an unexpected turn when it turned out that the phantom had fathered a son. McCormick had interviewed Claude Johnson in the early 1970s, and was told that the grandparents who brought him up had never hid the fact that he was the son of the bluesman. Johnson eventually retained a lawyer in 1988 and began a ten-year legal battle that included two visits apiece to the Mississippi and the U.S. Supreme Court. "He's just a little old country boy from Crystal Springs, Mississippi," said Gayle Dean Wardlow of Claude Johnson, who made his living hauling gravel. "It's almost like one of those Shakespearean things. He got pulled into it, totally."

The Robert Johnson paternity case turned on the testimony of Johnson's seventy-nine-year-old mother, Virgie Mae Smith, and a best friend from her youth, Eula Mae Williams. They spoke of dark clubs where the bluesman could still the room with his voice and guitar, and related how Johnson had met the seventeen-year-old Smith on her way to school. Williams testified to attending a "house party" with her fiancé and Smith, and how during the evening, Johnson accompanied them on a romantic walk in the pine forest. The couples paused to make love in a standing position that permitted eye contact. This last detail seemed to flummox the judge overseeing the bench trial. He questioned the witness:

Q: Well, let me share something with you, because I'm really curious about this. Maybe I have a more limited experience. But you're saying to me that you were watching them make love?

A: M-hm.

Q: While you were making love?

A: M-hm.

Q: You don't think that's at all odd?

A: Say what?

Q: Have you ever done that before or since?

A: Yes.

Q: Watch other people make love?

A: Yes, I have done it before. Yes, I've done it after I married. Yes.

Q: You watched other people make love?

A: Yes, sir. Yes, sir.

Q: Other than . . . other than Mr. Johnson and Virgie Cain.

A: Right.

Q: Really?

A: You haven't?

Q: No. Really haven't.

A: I'm sorry for you.

Claude Johnson won his case and became a millionaire after he produced a birth certificate that listed his father as "RL Johnson, laborer." He testified that he'd seen his father twice. The second time was in 1937, when he was living with his grandparents, and Johnson approached the house with a guitar slung over his shoulder.

"We were living in my granddaddy's and grandmama's house," said Johnson. "They were religious people, and they thought that the blues was the devil's music. People back then believed that. They told my daddy they didn't want no part of him. They said he was working for the devil, and they wouldn't even let me go out and touch him. I stood in the door, and he stood on the ground, and that is as close as I ever got to him."

Stefan Grossman sat in the control room of Murray Hill Studios, a production facility near the entrance to the Queen's Midtown Tunnel in Manhattan. He's looking through a window onto the sound stage where Ernie Hawkins was making an instructional guitar video about how to play the country blues of Lightnin' Hopkins. The format is that Hawkins first plays the song, and then slowly demonstrates its individual components. But when the cameras rolled, he blew the first take of "Santa Fe Blues." "This guitar sucks," said Hawkins with a smile; the instrument he played was not just any old Martin, but a Stefan Grossman Signature Model.

Half a century ago, Grossman and Hawkins studied with the Reverend Gary Davis. Happy Traum took lessons with Brownie McGhee. Traum and Grossman authored books teaching the music of a broad swath of country blues fingerpickers. These weren't collections of sheet music, or words and chords; these pages contained a graphic style of "tablature" that used the six strings of the guitar to illustrate the location and sequence of "notes" in a finger-style guitar piece. It was a visualization that became a staple in guitar magazines, but what's significant about Traum and Grossman, is that they weren't documenting the work of some rock guitar hero, but classics of country blues.

Traum and Grossman both started companies to market guitar lessons. Traum's Homespun Music offers lessons on a wide variety of genres and instruments, while those offered by Stefan Grossman's Guitar Workshop are focused exclusively on the guitar, and include lessons on virtually every style of blues. In a sense, these tutorials, taught by many of the musicians who've appeared in this text, have recreated the sort of oral folk tradition by which Muddy Waters learned from watching Son House. Today, however, it's less likely to be a young black man looking to play country blues than a middle-aged white professional revisiting a youthful passion for the guitar now that his own children have left the nest. Some of these well-heeled players signed up for Grossman's "Workshop Safari," which offered "a great opportunity to improve your guitar skills and go on an African Safari." Others attend a summertime music camp for a week of guitar immersion. Ernie Hawkins was teaching at a "Guitar Intensive" program on a college campus in Bar Harbor, Maine, when I took his class in "Texas Blues." Guitar camp is typically a live-in-a-dorm room get-away during which a variety of instructors lead hands-on-guitar lessons with students also looking forward to the after-hour concerts and jam sessions. "When I've taught at these camps," said Traum, "I'm mostly working with doctors, lawyers, and business guys who've got much nicer guitars than mine." Sitting in a sunny classroom with a view of the ocean is not where one might expect to learn how to make your thumb thump on the bass strings with a steady rolling pulse. Lightnin' Hopkins refined this style on dusty roads and in ghetto bars. These days, his music is likely to be studied by a white guy with a $5,000 guitar. It's an odd and revealing twist in the history of the blues.

"In the '60s," said Hawkins, "we were in thrall of the romance and myth of the black man. Before my senior year in high school, I hitchhiked down to Statesboro, Georgia, looking for Blind Willie McTell (who wrote "Statesboro Blues"). I had a great time and was living out the myth of the wandering musician. Turned out I couldn't find anybody who even knew who he was. And I was so broke that I ended up playing guitar for tips at a drive-through hamburger joint. Later, I found out that McTell had died in 1959, and that he'd also played at a drive-through."

After high school, Hawkins spent a year studying with Gary Davis. "He was a mythic figure," said Hawkins, "like Homer. He was the blind blues singer. But when he talked about his life, or when I'd read his welfare records, I realized, phew, man, this is poverty. This is struggle, this is painful, this is sores on his legs. This is no heat, no money, no food. And in the midst of it all, Gary Davis, genius musician, singing for the glory of God."

Hawkins went to college and got a degree in philosophy and then a PhD in phenomological psychology. He went from graduate school to playing electric guitar in Pittsburgh blues bands, but Davis lingered in his fingers, and his soul. "For years I tried to puzzle out what he'd taught me," said Hawkins. "By the '90s, I realized that learning Gary Davis was a lifelong project, because the more I learned, the more I recognized how much depth was there. I realized that if I wanted to be more than a dilettante, I'd really have to keep devoting myself to digging deeper into what I'd learned, and what he could still teach me."

After inhaling Davis's cigar smoke during his teenage lessons, Woody Mann went to Julliard and then studied with jazz pianist Lennie Tristano. He produced taped lessons and numerous books devoted to the works of Robert Johnson, Blind Blake, and Lonnie Johnson. He's taught guitar workshops from Tokyo to Tuscany, and performed jazz and sophisticated acoustic music, but lately he's been working on a documentary about his first musical mentor. Mann, Hawkins, Grossman, and Roy Book Binder have all been featured participants in "Gary Davis Weekend," an annual event at the Cadillac of guitar camps, Jorma Kaukonen's Fur Peace Ranch, which was established in 1989, and is located in southeastern Ohio.

Kaukonen and bassist Jack Casady left the Jefferson Airplane in the early 1970s to focus on their coffeehouse blues band, Hot Tuna. "The Airplane thing was a blessing," said Kaukonen, "because it allowed me to be a better-than-decently paid folk musician." 1970s *Hot Tuna* popularized such Davis tunes as "Hesitation Blues" and "Death Don't Have No Mercy." Kaukonen employed three fingers when he picked (Davis used two), which gave his interpretations a folksier spin. "Anywhere you go in the world," said Hawkins, "somebody's going to be able to play [Davis's] 'I Am the Light of This World' just like Jorma."

To this day, there's a small but strong community of acoustic musicians who were touched by the blues revival of the 1960s. On the road, they have boxes of CDs in the trunk of the car to sell at gigs on a national network of clubs that often exist on the edge of solvency. Paul Geremia, a gifted country blues guitarist, recently played the Rosendale Café in New York's Hudson Valley and crashed at my house. Over morning coffee, he ruminated over his nearly fifty years playing country blues, telling me how he once blew harmonica with Peter Wolf's first group, the Hallucinations, and that Patrick Sky had produced his first album in 1968. He laughed at the memory of the time he invited Howlin' Wolf and his band to a party at his pad and had only a pint of whiskey and a handful of beers for refreshments.

"The first place I played was a little coffeehouse in Providence," said Geremia, "and one night this guy Dick Waterman showed up." Geremia took Waterman up on his offer of a place to stay in Cambridge. Four decades later, he found himself in the guest room of Waterman's home in Oxford, Mississippi. "Sometimes it seems like nothing has changed," said Geremia. "Here I am sleeping in Dick Waterman's spare room."

Musicians born into the blues revival of the 1960s were blessed to live through a golden era. "I haven't even added up yet what happened at Newport," said Geoff Muldaur, "because it was so important and so incredible. That is why I believe in the zeitgeist. You can't plan on who's going to be on the planet, who might create something significant. The people who came out of the American blues and jazz scene are beyond comprehension. It's just astounding to me that I could actually go to see a show by Louis Armstrong or Duke Ellington, and hang out with somebody like Mississippi John Hurt. You cannot come even close to matching them today. It's just not on the planet. When B.B. King dies, every major inventor of the [blues] form will have passed. So from that point on, it really becomes like a classical music form."

In the 1960s, when Muldaur played with the Kweskin Jug Band, the group performed on *The Steve Allen Show*. After the music, the host talked to the band. "He turns to me," said Muldaur, "and said, 'What are you going to do with the rest of your life?' I froze. . . . 'I don't know. Find peace?' The embarrassment. I choked national. Well here it is, years later, and I'm starting to like my answer. I'm traveling around the world playing for people, mostly in humble settings, very few big deals."

By 2012, John Hammond had four hundred songs at the tips of his fingers, and had played Robert Johnson songs more than twice as long as the devil let that bluesman live. Consider the motor memory in his fingers. "The blues was what made me feel good about my life and about who I was," said Hammond. "And it gave me my life." It's those individual lives, from the rock star in the private jet to the guitar player with 250,000 miles on a beat-up car that has carried the blues into the twenty-first century. And then there are the guys that don't go from town to town, but from the couch to the porch; the musician who just might live next door. The blues is in our musical DNA; that's what keeps it alive. Styles come and go, but nothing can replace the emotional alchemy of a voice alongside fingers pressed against steel strings.

Dave "Honeyboy" Edwards played for coins on the streets of Memphis in the 1930's, where the best tips came when the farmers from Mississippi and Alabama would bring their livestock to the city's killing floors and blow their payday on liquor and whores. When the night got quiet, Edwards would pack away his guitar and go to see a piano player like Roosevelt Sykes or Memphis Slim. "We'd come in late at night, come off the streets around midnight and them dives stayed open till three in the morning," said Edwards. "Women would be sitting all on top of the damn piano, drinking white whiskey. We'd just get drunk then, try to get us a woman to carry home with us. It was plenty of fun. Musicians have plenty of fun. My God, the world don't owe me nothing." Robert Johnson, and all the other bluesmen who've passed through the crossroads, would surely agree.

LAST CALL

Thanks most to the gifted musicians who populate these pages. They rock my world. I'm grateful to the Woodstock Library and the Mid-Hudson Library System for providing a steady stream of pertinent books. Thanks also to the New York Public Library for the Performing Arts and the Schomburg Center for Research in Black Culture. Please use and support your local library, one of our most valuable public resources.

Appreciation for the biographers of the principal players in *Crossroads*: Daniel Beaumont; Stephen Calt; Martin Celmins; Alice Echols; Deborah Frost; Tony Glover, Scott Dirks, and Ward Gaines; Robert Gordon; Alan Govenar; Peter Guralnick; Charles Shaar Murray; Joe Nick Patoski and Bill Crawford; Philip R. Ratcliffe; Bob Riesman; Will Romano; James Segrest and Mark Hoffman; Mary Lou Sullivan; John Szwed; Elijah Wald; Ed Ward; David Ritz; and Jan Mark Wolkin and Bill Keenom. The interviews conducted or edited by Jas Obrecht were most useful, as were W. John Tomas's insights into the legal legacy of Robert Johnson.

John Lee Hooker 1917–2001

Two books were particularly helpful: *Baby, Let Me Follow You Down*, by Eric Von Schmidt and Jim Rooney; and Christopher Hjort's *Strange Brew*. Two others deserve special mention. Robert Palmer's *Deep Blues* is a perceptive and beautifully written history of the blues. And read David "Honeyboy" Edwards's memoir, *The World Don't Owe Me Nothing*, to get the feel of walking in a bluesman's shoes.

While working on the book, it was an informative pleasure to speak with Stefan Grossman, Geoff Muldaur, Ernie Hawkins, Patrick Sky, Dick Waterman, Woody Mann, John Sebastian, Dick Spottswood, Happy Traum, Jorma Kaukonen, David Bromberg, Roy Book Binder, Paul Geremia, Steve James, George Worthmore, David Bennet Cohen, and Pete Kuykendall,

Thanks to my agent (and longtime friend) Paul Bresnick, my editor (and blues-band drummer) Stephen P. Hull, and to Gary J. Hamel for the conscientious copyediting. I'm grateful for the valuable feedback and encouragement of my writer's group: Laura Claridge, Richard Hoffman, and Holly George-Warren. Holly also let me use her interviews with Marc Benno and Clifford Antone. Paul Jellinek and I loved the Beatles and B.B. King as teenagers; I'm thankful that he's still my friend, and for the astute comments he gave me on my manuscript.

For the past fifteen years I've had the pleasure to play in a Hudson Valley blues-rock band, the Comfy Chair. For a rock critic who'd spent decades chasing after the stars, it's been an eye-opening experience to make music with players who've worked with them, including some of the musicians in this book. So thanks to the Comfy Chair: Josh Roy Brown, Steve Mueller, Larry Packer, Eric Parker, Baker Rorick, and the late, great Steve Burgh. Come on over for a supper-jam; the rice and chicken gizzards are on the stovetop. Baker and I also perform as the Sunburst Brothers, and are grateful to our Cousins, Chuck Cornelis and Jake Guralnick. All you guys have made me both a better musician and a more-informed writer.

Finally, my heart belongs to my lovely and talented wife, Margie Greve, who not only provided loving support throughout the project, but also produced the portraits that make it sing. This one's for you.

NOTES

PREFACE

vii "Ladies and gentlemen": *Live at the Regal*, ABC Records, 1965.

viii "They were not ghosts": Von Schmidt and Rooney, *Baby, Let Me Follow You Down*, 189.

ix "If you come": Doyle, *Rolling Stone*, 3/15/12.

PRELUDE

xii "When he finished": Guralnick, *Searching for Robert Johnson*, 17.

xiii "In the early thirties": Ibid., 37.

xiii "I got my style": Romano, *Jimmy Reed*, 18.

xiv "When you playing": Graves, *Crossroads*, 42.

xv "the greatest Negro blues": Thomas, "The Devil and Mr. Johnson," 7.

xv "Johnson makes Lead Belly": Ibid., 7.

ONE. RARE RECORDS AND WORKING MUSICIANS

2 "I guess he": Author interview, Dick Spottswood, 9/28/11

3 "If he was in a good mood": Smith, *Just Kids*, 114.

3 "there were big piles of 78s": Ed Sanders, Liner notes to *Harry Smith's Anthology of American Folk Music, Volume 4* (Reverent Records, 2000), 8.

4 "I was looking for exotic records": Marcus, *The Old Weird America*," 10.

4 "In 1952 fiddler Eck Dunford": Marcus, *The Old Weird America*," 94.

4 "The set became our Bible": Van Ronk with Wald, *The Mayor of MacDougal Street*, 46.

4 "I'd match": Liner notes to *Anthology of American Folk Music*, Smithsonian Folkways Recordings, 1997, 8.

5 "It was in Friar's Point": Palmer, *Deep Blues*, 111.

6 "Man, you don't know": Gordon, Can't Be Satisfied, xv.

6 "I used to say to Son House": Beaumont, *Preachin' the Blues*, 92.

6 "Anytime that you end a piece": Ibid. 64.

6 "with [House] the sorrow of the blues": Szwed, *Alan Lomax*, 181.

6 "He [Lomax] came down and recorded": Waterman, *Between Midnight and Day*, 42.

7 "We was playing": Govenar, *Lightnin' Hopkins: His Life and Blues*, 67.

9 "I came to Chicago": Rooney, *Bossmen: Bill Monroe & Muddy Waters*, 109.

9   "All of a sudden": Filene, *Romancing the Folk*, 88.

9   "We come in": Gordon, *Can't Be Satisfied*, 75.

9   "When I run up on Little Walter": Cohen, *Machers and Rockers*, 111.

9   "Muddy would cook some rice": Gordon, *Can't Be Satisfied*; 87.

10 "Muddy was playing when I was plowing": Ibid., 94.

10 "Christmas of 1937": Edwards, *The World Don't Owe Me Nothing*, 114.

10 "He'd [Bukka] been a boxer": King and Ritz, *Blues All Around Me*, 113.

10 "That night I couldn't sleep": Ibid., 113.

10 "He played piano and made us sound": Ibid., 140.

11 "The top job for anybody": Collis, *Ike Turner: King of Rhythm*, 43.

11 "Muddy, Jimmy Rogers, and Little Walter": Palmer, *Deep Blues*, 231.

12 "When I heard Howlin' Wolf": Segrest and Hoffman, *Moanin' at Midnight*; 87.

12 "He would sit there with these feet": Ibid., 89.

12 "Leonard Chess kept worryin' me": Ibid., 102.

TWO. CHICAGO BLUES AND THE BIRTH OF FOLK-BLUES

13 "They'd be shaking": *Guitar Player* Editors, *The Guitar Player Book: Artists, History, Technique, and Gear*, 51.

13 "The beat is almost": Gordon, *Can't Be Satisfied*, 210.

14 "Why should I fight to save": Cohen, *Machers and Rockers*, 141.

14 "He took me in": Segrest and Hoffman, *Moanin' at Midnight*, 108.

15 "It got to the place": Milward, "Willie Dixon: The Man Who Built the Blues."

15 "That's nice": Gordon, *Can't Be Satisfied*, 135.

15 "Muddy had a plantation": Ibid., 181.

16 "Wolf had to match whatever": Segrest and Hoffman, *Moanin' at Midnight*, 179.

16 "Well, these Coke cases started to come": Obrecht, *Rollin' and Tumblin'*, 213.

16 "When he got there": Ibid., 213.

16 "I was as green": Guy & Wilcock, *Damn Right I Got the Blues*, 32.

16 "I'm in there trying": Ibid., 33.

17 "It was like": Ibid., 40.

17 "I'm a blues player": King and Ritz, *Blues All Around Me*, 162.

17 "Mother-fucking blues-singing": Ibid., 189.

17 "They would take": King and Waterman, *The B.B. King Treasures*, 60.

17 "They never had a lawyer": Dixon, *I Am the Blues*, 192.

17 "That generation": Cohen, *Machers and Rockers*, 151.

18 "Some of the statements": Berry, *The Autobiography*, 104.

18 "full well that I'd sign": Ibid., 104.

19 "The roots of rock 'n' roll": King and Ritz, *Blues All Around Me*, 184.

19 "When I was": Lawrence, *Jimi Hendrix*, 110.

19 "Sometime around 1954": Van Ronk and Walk, *The Mayor of MacDougal Street*, 24.

20 "When I got off": Ibid., 58.

20 "The musicians": Author interview with Happy Traum, 9/20/11.

20 "His name was Ian Buchanan": Ibid.

20   "Some of the first": Author interview with Jorma Kaukonen, 1/15/10.

21   "Brownie had two": Author interview with Traum, 9/20/11.

21   "I was at the Washington": Author interview with David Cohen, 10/2/11.

21   "Then one day": Von Schmidt and Rooney, *Baby, Let Me Follow You Down*, 68.

21   "It was like finding": Ibid., 71.

21   "I'd go hunting records": Author interview with Spottswood, 9/28/11.

22   "A couple hours later": Ibid.

22   "I still have a letter": Interview of John Fahey from website of Stefan Grossman's Guitar Workshop.

23   "A car pulled up": Govenar, *Lightnin' Hopkins: His Life and Blues*, 74.

23   "I did it all with": Ibid., 74.

23   "He is one of the last": Charters, *The Country Blues*, 266.

THREE. BOHEMIAN BLUES AND THE FOLK REVIVAL

24   "Sure, come up and": Author interview with Stefan Grossman, 12/17/08.

24   "bombed out as Dresden" and "in a three-room" and "a musical genius": Ibid.

25   "Play what you know": Author interview with Woody Mann, 12/10/08.

25   "On Friday night": Milward, "The Sons of Gary Davis," 119.

26   "His sermons were remarkable": Ibid., 120.

26   "When he taught me": Author interview with David Bromberg, 1/10/09.

26   "My blues-guitar-artist-to-be": Kalb, "My Scene: Greenwich Village, Early 1960s," *Fretboard Journal*, Fall, 2009

27   "By New Haven": Van Ronk and Wald, *The Mayor of MacDougal Street*, 136.

27   "Peter, Paul & Mary wanted": Milward, "The Sons of Gary Davis," 121

28   "During the session": Sanders, *Fug You*, 142.

28   "One thing I regret": Ibid., 82.

28   "I spent a lot": Von Schmidt and Rooney, *Baby, Let Me Follow You Down*, 126.

28   "He'd sit around": Murray, *Boogie Man*, 232.

29   "Without him there would be no": Ibid., 275.

29   "In about 1964 and '65": Dylan, *Chronicles: Part One*, 287.

29   "I was just trembling": Obrecht, *Blues Guitar*, 65.

30   "He was playing": Shapiro and Glebbeek, *Jimi Hendrix Electric Gypsy*, 103.

30   "Later, somebody": Von Schmidt and Rooney, *Baby, Let Me Follow You Down*, 75.

32   "a silver-voiced heavenly choir": Lomax, *The Land Where the Blues Began*, 353.

32   "The party was in 1959": Author interview with Geoff Muldaur, 2/5/10.

33   "That was it for being": Ibid.

33   "My dad liked him more": Govenar, *Lightnin' Hopkins*, 111.

33   "I was beginning": Boyd, *White Bicycles*, 20.

34   "One way I learned": Von Schmidt and Rooney, *Baby, Let Me Follow You Down*, 167.

34   "The record took": Ibid., 224.

35   "John Sebastian": Ibid., 178.

35 "He just said, 'It was'": Ibid., 178.

35 "I was sharing": Ibid., 191.

35 "When I moved in with Al": Ibid., 191.

35 "While Bukka was staying": Ibid., 191.

35 "Manny was a great guy": Author interview with Muldaur 2/5/10.

36 "We were a family": Ibid.

36 "I realized that I": Ibid.

36 "When I went into labor": Segrest and Hoffman, *Moanin' at Midnight*, 232.

FOUR. BRITISH BLUES

37 "*The Best of Muddy Waters* album": Jagger, Richards, Watts, and Lane, *According to the Rolling Stones*; p. 42

37 "Did we hit it off?": Richards and Fox, *Life*, 79.

38 "Brian and I": Jagger, Richards, Watts, and Lane, *According to the Rolling Stones*, 39.

38 "The main man for me": Clapton, *The Autobiography*, 29.

38 "At three or four or five": Richards, *Life*, 56.

38 "I started to meet people": Clapton, *The Autobiography*, 35.

39 "I would take the bits": Ibid., 40.

40 "You had a sense": Dixon, *I Am the Blues*, 129.

40 "I felt through": Schwartz, *How Britain Got the Blues*, 74.

40 "In my early teens": McStravick and Ross, *Blues-Rock Explosion*, xxii.

40 "what kind of car": Schwartz, *How Britain Got the Blues*, 236.

40 "Muddy made a typical": Ibid., 148.

41 "So far as the groups": Ibid., 152.

41 "Can you imagine": Dixon: *I Am the Blues*, 131.

41 "I'll never forget": Ibid., 135.

41 "I'd make tapes": Ibid., 135.

41 "Brian and I": Jagger, Richards, Watts, and Lane, *According to the Rolling Stones*, p. 41.

42 "There was no space": Ibid., 44.

42 "They were playing": Bockris, *Keith Richards: The Biography*, 58.

42 "Andrew was a publicist": Jagger, Richards, Watts, and Lane, *According to the Rolling Stones*, 56.

42 "I couldn't wait": Clapton, *The Autobiography,* 47.

43 "Those English kids": Ibid., 48.

43 "You get Hooker": Schwartz, *How Britain Got the Blues*, 154.

43 "Mr. Burnett": Segrest and Hoffman, *Moanin' at Midnight*, 215.

43 "We're all anticipating": Ibid., 219.

44 "What I would do": Clapton, *The Autobiography*, 73.

44 "We had an": Hjort, *Strange Brew*, 29.

44 "He had exquisite": Wilcox and Guy, *Damn Right I've Got the Blues*, 65.

44 "His look, everything": Ibid., 66.

45 "I was very nervous": Hjort, *Strange Brew*, 46.

45 "I remember": Ibid., 46.

45 "I thought maybe": Brunning, *Blues: The British Connection*, 92.

46 "At first the music": Clapton, *The Autobiography*, 40.

46   "Eric absolutely insisted": Hjort, *Strange Brew*, 48.

46   "I went to talk to Eric": Ibid., 48.

46   "When I asked him": Celmins, *Peter Green: The Biography*, 37.

47   "I was absolutely": Clapton, *The Autobiography*, 64.

47   "Down in the basement": Dixon, *I Am the Blues*, 163.

48   "When we got to": Wilcox and Guy, *Damn Right I've Got the Blues*, 64.

48   "We did 'Train Kept A-Rolling'": Ibid., 64.

48   "It was a milestone event": Wyman, *Stone Alone*, 227.

48   "Sonny Boy Williamson": Wilcox and Guy, *Damn Right I've Got the Blues*, 58.

48   "Berry himself": Wyman, *Stone Alone*, 228.

49   "It seemed to us": Jagger, Richards, Watts, and Lane, *According to the Rolling Stones*, 92.

49   "All the amps": Schwartz, *How Britain Got the Blues*, 244.

FIVE. OUT OF THE PAST

51   "John Hurt": Von Schmidt and Rooney, *Baby, Let Me Follow You Down*, 189.

52   "It's too bad": Ratcliffe, *Mississippi John Hurt*, 123.

53   "Seventeen states": Author interview with Spottswood 9/28/11.

53   "If he ain't died": Ratcliffe, *Mississippi John Hurt*, 128.

53   "I thought the man": Ibid., 127.

53   "John, we have been": Ibid., 128.

53   "If you listen to John": Author interview with Dick Waterman, 10/2/11.

53   "When you think of Mississippi": Author interview Grossman, 12/10/08.

54   "When we heard the tape": Author interview with Spottswood, 9/28/11.

54   "John was the only Negro": Ibid.

54   "He realized": Ratcliffe, *Mississippi John Hurt*, 133.

54   "We recorded": Author interview with Pete Kuykendall, 10/1/11.

54   "My thought at the time": Author interview with Spottswood, 9/28/11.

55   "In Chicago, Illinois": *Newport Folk Festival: Best of the Blues, 1959–68*, Vanguard Records.

55   "We could not keep up": Author interview with Muldaur, 2/5/10.

55   "John Hurt": Van Ronk with Wald, *The Mayor of MacDougal Street*, 184.

55   "I went to Newport": Von Schmidt and Rooney, *Baby, Let Me Follow You Down*, 217.

56   "John Hurt was": Author interview with Spottswood, 2/28/11.

56   "Some of the rediscovered bluesmen": Author interview with Muldaur, 2/5/10.

56   "I don't play 'em, I stomp 'em": Beaumont: *Preachin' the Blues*, 87.

57   "Bill and John, they just outtalked me": Calt, *I'd Rather Be the Devil*, 248.

57   "Skip sat down": Von Schmidt and Rooney, *Baby, Let Me Follow You Down*, 197.

58   "You don't get it, do you": Waterman, *Between Midnight and Day*, 67.

59   "When we found Son": Beaumont, *Preachin' the Blues*, 20.

59   "Al Wilson taught": Ibid., 22.

59   "What really happened": Beaumont, *Preachin' the Blues*, 23.

60   "How are you, Son?": Waterman, *Between Midnight and Day*, 37.

60 "Son only had about a third": Beaumont, *Preachin' the Blues*, 21.

60 "Son House would get himself": Author interview with Ernie Hawkins, 2/18/11.

61 "These worlds were coming together": Author interview with Muldaur, 2/5/10.

61 "John Lee Hooker": Bego, *Bonnie Raitt*, 22.

SIX. UNIVERSITY OF CHICAGO BLUES

62 "Muddy thought they were": Gordon, *Can't Be Satisfied*, 165.

62 "hurt the blues": Palmer, *Deep Blues*, 255.

63 "Blues represented, at that time": Adelt, *Blues Music in the Sixties*, 15.

63 "Being a blues singer": King and Ritz, *Blues All Around Me*, 216.

63 "The University was sort of a pocket": Ward, *Mike Bloomfield*, 23

63 "I got a job as a driver": Wolkin and Keenom, *Michael Bloomfield*, 55.

64 "Muddy Waters, he was like a god": Ibid., 25.

64 "We got to be friends": Ibid., 27.

64 "So Michael and I get up there": Segrest and Hoffman, *Moanin' at Midnight*, 223.

64 "Being with Big Joe": Bloomfield and Summerville, *Me and Big Joe*.

65 "To hear him talk about Robert Johnson": Ibid.

65 "Well, Michael, we really had" Ibid.

65 "I went to the South Side": Sullivan, *Raisin' Cain*, 59.

66 "I'd get up and do a couple of Lightnin'": Ward, *Mike Bloomfield*, 24

66 "I went down": Wilcox and Guy, *Damn Right I've Got the Blues*, 76.

67 "I joined up": Dalton, "Steve Miller: Still Flying on His Own Terms."

67 "I had a talk": Wilcox and Guy, *Damn Right I've Got the Blues*, 62.

67 "Wolf had a regular": Segrest and Hoffman, *Moanin' at Midnight*, 224.

67 "I got him into a studio": Ward, *Mike Bloomfield*, 36.

68 "We was looking": Segrest and Hoffman, *Moanin' at Midnight*, 233.

68 "I told Paul": Boyd, *White Bicycles*, 61.

69 "I was in Dylan's": Ward, *Mike Bloomfield*, 52.

69 "I don't want any of the B.B. King": Ibid., 51.

69 "Suddenly Dylan exploded": Kooper and Edmonds, *Backstage Passes*, 54.

69 "I think they picked us to close": Ibid., 92.

69 "He was a scary guy": Ibid., 121.

70 "Hendrix knew who I was": Shapiro and Glebbeek, *Jimi Hendrix*, 104.

70 "At workshops": Von Schmidt and Rooney, *Baby, Let Me Follow You Down*, 253.

70 "Alan Lomax got up on stage": Ibid., 253.

71 "We were boogying and totally": Ibid., 253.

71 "Lomax walked down": Ibid., 258.

71 "They [Lomax and Grossman] were right in front": Ward, *Mike Bloomfield*, 44.

71 "rooting for Albert": Author interview with Muldaur, 2/5/10.

72 "There was a clear generational and cultural gap": Hedin, *Studio A: The Bob Dylan Reader*, 42.

72 "You said that you weren't": Silber, "An Open Letter to Bob Dylan."

72 "To me, the Butterfield": Author interview with Muldaur, 2/5/10.

74 "I'd like to tell you a little story now": B.B. King, *Live at the Regal*, ABC Records, 1965.

75 "I had never seen": B.B. King interview on the "Academy of Achievement" website.

75 "We got to the": Ibid.

75 "Ladies and gentlemen": Ibid.

75 "It was a very emotional night": King and Waterman, *The B.B. King Treasures*, 86.

75 "When he hit the note": Ibid., 89.

75 "It was a breakthrough for me": Ibid., 89.

75 "Mike Bloomfield was a special": King and Ritz, *Blues All Around Me*, 230.

76 "That [album] left": Wolkin and Keenom, *Michael Bloomfield*, 112.

76 "I remember one time": Ward, *Mike Bloomfield*, 56.

76 "'East-West' was a radical departure": Ibid., 56.

76 "None of the shows Bill Graham": Ibid., 56.

77 "They were the first": Wolkin and Keenom, *Michael Bloomfield*, 129.

77 "I came to the Airplane": Author interview with Kaukonen, 1/15/10.

77 "Nobody held the guitar": Wolkin and Keenom: *Michael Bloomfield*, 122.

77 "He and just a couple of other": Ibid., 122.

77 "People were running around": Segrest & Hoffman, *Moanin' at Midnight*, 256.

78 "The first night I got to San Francisco": "The Gibson Interview: Steve Miller (Part 2)," www.gibson.com.

78 "I thought most": Ibid.

79 "Probably the biggest gig": Wolkin and Keenom, *Michael Bloomfield*, 146.

79 "I got into playing it": Gleason, *The Jefferson Airplane and the San Francisco Sound*, 110.

80 "She had to change": Sculatti and Seay, *San Francisco Nights: The Psychedelic Music Trip*, 83.

80 "I had two": Nicholas S. Shillace, *John Fahey and American Primitivism*, 66.

80 "He [Alan] was fiendishly intelligent": Ibid., 67.

82 "Albert was born in Indianola": King and Ritz, *Blues All Around Me*, 251.

82 "He was a big strong dude": Ibid., 251.

83 "Wasn't for these English acts": Guy, *When I Left Home*, 205.

83 "I didn't feel that Leonard Chess": Collis, *The Story of Chess Records*, 190.

83 "Charters wasn't all that different": Guy, *When I Left Home*, 195.

83 "Buddy realized": Author interview with Waterman, 10/2/11.

84 "Buddy Guy was one": Wilcox and Guy, *Damn Right I've Got the Blues*, 83.

84 "Jimi [Hendrix] was very into Buddy": Ibid., 85.

EIGHT. OUT OF THE PAST AND INTO THE PRESENT

85 "Them boys were good": Waterman, *Between Midnight and Day*, 18.

86 "What I heard": Author interview with John Sebastian, 4/18/98.

86 "There's a tradition": Ibid.

86 "I remember working": Ibid.

86 "I remember one time": Van Ronk and Wald, *The Mayor of MacDougal Street*, 188.

86 "One time I remember": Author interview with Patrick Sky, 2/12/11.

87 "The thing that made": Ibid.

87 "Some of these olds guys": Ibid.

87 "They had John sitting": Ibid.

87 "There were some religious things": Ibid.

88 "He would always draw": Ratcliffe, *Mississippi John Hurt*, 172.

88 "John Hurt had": Author interview with Sebastian, 4/18/98.

88 "He wasn't a professional": Ratcliffe, *Mississippi John Hurt*, 173.

88 "I remember asking him": Author interview with Spottswood, 9/28/11.

88 "I'm voting for Skip": Ibid.

89 "I found out that he was only": Author interview with Sky, 2/12/11.

89 "John never had": Van Ronk and Wald, *The Mayor of MacDougal Street*, 188.

89 "I'm not prepared": Author interview with Spottswood, 9/28/11.

89 "I had a small part": Author interview with Waterman, 10/2/11.

90 "Hoskins I found": Ratcliffe, *Mississippi John Hurt*, 188.

90 "Uncle John and Skip": Ibid., 188.

90 "By all rights, John went": Obrecht, "Mississippi John Hurt."

91 "Cut to 1965": Block, *When A Woman Gets the Blues*, 138.

91 "Here's to Robert Johnson": Waterman, *Between Midnight and Day*, 37.

91 "I'm glad to be back": Lester, "I Can Make My Own Songs."

92 "House's recording session": Cohn, Liner notes to *Son House: Father of the Delta Blues: The Complete 1966 Sessions*, Columbia, 1992, 10.

92 "He could not be left": Author interview with Waterman, 10/2/11.

92 "He liked the occasional": Milward, "The Sons of Gary Davis."

93 "We had to kick him out": Author interview with Muldaur, 2/5/10.

93 "His head was thrown back": Beaumont, *Preachin' the Blues*, 151.

93 "I bought Skip James": Dean, "Skip James' Hard Time Killing Floor Blues.".

93 "Skip James was dying": Author interview with Spottswood, 9/28/11.

94 "Sometimes they look at me": Calt, *I'd Rather Be the Devil*, 275.

94 "Why don't you take a bath": Ibid., 269.

94 "You know you ought": Ibid., 269.

94 "Heap of time": Ibid., 281.

95 "They all developed something": Ibid., 300.

95 "Don't you be mocking": Gordon, *Can't Be Satisfied*, 190.

96 "This man got the blues": *Devil Got My Woman: Blues at Newport 1966*.

96 "We ain't talking about": Ibid.

96 "The Lomax film": Muldaur, 2/5/10.

97 "If it please the Lord": Calt, *I'd Rather Be the Devil*, 345.

97 "When I met him": Author interview with Mann, 10/20/11.

98 "I'm half inclined": Von Schmidt and Rooney, *Baby, Let Me Follow You Down*, 198.

NINE. THE CREAM OF (MOSTLY) BRITISH BLUES

100 "[We] are tired": Hjort, *Strange Brew*, 66.

100 "I think the John": Ibid., 58.

100   "They got all these white": Palmer, *Deep Blues*, 260.

101   "The blues is": Wilcox and Guy, *Damn Right I've Got the Blues*, 65.

101   "This is where we started": Clapton, *The Autobiography*, 91.

101   "It was the most amazing": Hjort, *Strange Brew*, 130.

102   "Two pressings questions": Ibid., 144.

102   "On the first night": Clapton, *The Autobiography*, 86.

103   "We spent a lot": Celmins, *Peter Green*, 36.

103   "I remember one time": Ibid., 23.

103   "He went immediately": Ibid., 49.

103   "He knew and certainly"; Ibid., 40.

104   "I was in a shocked": Ibid., 41.

104   "He [Mayall] said that if you really": Ibid., 69.

104   "The guy who": Hjort, *Strange Brew*, 173

104   "From then on": Celmins, *Peter Green*, 45.

105   "Peter's a great": Mike Vernon, Liner notes to *Eddie Boyd: The Complete Blue Horizon Sessions*, 16.

106   "We got quite": Fleetwood and Davis, *Fleetwood*, 59.

106   "I will never forget": Clapton, *The Autobiography*, 87.

107   "The song Jimi wanted": Ibid., 80.

108   "In his playing": Henderson, *'Scuse Me While I Kiss the Sky*, 217.

108   "There was a tremendous": Murray, *Crosstown Traffic*, 91.

108   "You know English": Wenner, Eric Clapton Interview in *Rolling Stone*.

109   "I felt threatened": Murray, *Crosstown Traffic*, 46.

110   "We are the first group": Hjort, *Strange Brew*, 153.

110   "The way I've always": Martin Scorsese, *The Blues*, 237.

111   "I met B.B. King": Ibid., 159.

111   "Clapton is a master": Wenner, Eric Clapton Interview in *Rolling Stone*.

111   "When they get over": Ibid.

112   "These guys were": Hjort, *Strange Brew*, 202.

112   "The Cream has": Shelton, "Britain's Cream Skims into City with Blues, Blare and Jazzy Pop."

112   "Before Woodstock": Echols, *Scars of Sweet Paradise*, 264.

TEN. BABY BOOM BLUES

113   "[Butterfield] told": Von Schmidt and Rooney, *Baby, Let Me Follow You Down*, 270.

113   "Between shows": Ibid., 272.

113   "I could never": Scorsese, *The Blues*, 191.

114   "Bloomfield was": *Gordon, Can't Be Satisfied*, 349.

115   "Eric Clapton walked": Segrest and Hoffman, *Moanin' at Midnight*, 270.

115   "Wolf looked": Ibid., 270.

115   "It was a chauffeur": Romano, *Incurable Blues*, 98.

115   "I was a little": *Performing Songwriter*, Jan/Feb 2000.

115   "The Rolling Stones": Phinney, *Souled American*, 188

116   "That's great": Milward, "What More Can This Woman Do?"

116   "I carried": Henke, "Bravo Bonnie," *Rolling Stone*, 5/3/90.

116   "One of the reasons": *Frets*, April 1988.

116 "You have this": *Performing Songwriter*, Jan/Feb 2000.

116 "I was hangin' out": Hubbard, "Veteran Rocker Bonnie Raitt Gets Back on Track in the Nick of Time."

116 "The door flew": Waterman, *Between Midnight and Day*, 86.

117 "When I was coming": Steel, "Ry Cooder."

117 "I'd sit there": Obrecht, "Ry Cooder,"

118 "I found out": Metting, *The Unbroken Circle*, 97.

118 "one of those interplanetary": Ibid.

118 "Once I figured": Murray, *Boogie Man*, 341.

118 "To me [Waters is]": Obrecht, "Go Where It's Dangerous and Say Yes," *Guitar Player*, November 1982.

118 "doorman": Metting, *The Unbroken Circle*, 9.

118 "Listen to all": James, "Blues across the Borders."

119 "My job": Santoro, "Ry Cooder: Blues and Roots," *Downbeat*, August 1986.

119 "I called the club": Ibid.

120 "When I got": Murray, *Boogie Man*, 385.

120 "We built a plywood": Liner notes, *Hooker 'n' Heat*, EMI Records.

121 "In the summer": Gordon, *It Came From Memphis*, 78.

121 "We would go out": Ibid., 121.

121 "It's something none": Ibid., 121

121 "We got out a tape": Tobler and Grundy, *Guitar Greats*, 115.

121 "He [Estes] lived": Brown, Interview with Ry Cooder.

122 "On one side": Steel, "Ry Cooder."

122 "They played these": Gordon, *It Came From Memphis*, 124.

122 "I had been playing": Ibid., 138.

122 "For me": *Perfect Sound Forever*, "The Insect Trust: Bill Barth,".

123 "You listen to Skip": Gordon, *It Came From Memphis*, 153.

123 "The guarantee": Milward, "The Sons of Rev. Gary Davis," 122.

123 "I might not talk": Ibid., 123.

124 "I was looking": Ibid., 123.

124 "We'd go lick by lick": Ibid., 123.

124 "It was like": Ibid., 124.

124 "I asked Reverend Davis": Ibid., 124.

125 "He had a book": Ibid., 123.

125 "Dylan was there": Woliver, *Hoot!*, 45.

125 "We had a couple": Milward, "The Sons of Rev. Gary Davis," 121.

125 "Oh Lord": Boyd, *White Bicycles*, 42.

125 "He gave me": Milward, "The Sons of Rev. Gary Davis," 121.

126 "He weighed": Ibid., 121.

ELEVEN. ROCKIN' THE BLUES

127 "With us, Allen": Keith Richards, *Life*, 179.

128 "We had a company": Ibid., 287.

128 "He started out": Doggett, You Never Give Me Your Money, 67.

128 "People would say": Bockris, *Keith Richards: The Biography*, 132.

129 "I could get": Jagger, Richards, Watts, and Lane, *According to the Rolling Stones*, 114.

129 "We would all sit back": Ibid., 116.

129 "The snare drum": Ibid., 116.

129 "Those chords": Keith Richards, *Life*, 257.

129 "Ry Cooder": Ibid., 242.

129 "Five strings cleared": Ibid., 244.

130 "I had met Ian": Hjort, *Strange Brew*, 132.

130 "was hired for 150": Wyman, *Stone Alone*, 525.

130 "I call that tour": Jagger, Richards, Watts, and Lane, *According to the Rolling Stones*, 142.

131 "He came": Case, *Jimmy Page: Magic Musician Man*, 40.

131 "I watched him": Ibid., 38

131 "I immediately thought": Davis, *Hammer of the Gods*, 51.

132 "I told him": Case, *Jimmy Page: Magic Musician Man*, 41.

132 "The way I see": Davis, *Hammer of the Gods*, 60.

132 "The popular formula": Mendelsohn, Review of *Led Zeppelin I*.

133 "There's this forlorn": Tobler and Grundy, *The Guitar Greats*, 72.

133 "He said, 'Listen'": Wall, *When Giants Walked the Earth: A Biography of Led Zeppelin*, 57.

133 "Before the friendship": Tobler and Grundy, *The Guitar Greats*, 72.

134 "Maybe they": Milward, "The Man Who Built the Blues."

134 "We did a gig": Shadwick, *Led Zeppelin*, 84.

134 "When these first rock": Dixon and Snowden, *I Am the Blues*, 167.

134 "Prior to my working": Ibid., 223.

135 "Every one of us": Palmer, Liner notes, *Led Zeppelin* boxed set, Atlantic Records, 1990.

135 "Only when I began": Ibid.

135 "Does anybody really": Jones, "Apple Cores #2," *Downbeat*, 1965.

136 "One day I went": Herr, *Dispatches*, 181.

138 "There were no": Moskowitz, *The Words and Music of Jimi Hendrix*, 43.

138 "They may have": Kramer, "Classic Tracks."

139 "He was the first": Murray, *Crosstown Traffic*, 151.

139 "We've never played": Jagger, Richards, Watts, and Lane, *According to the Rolling Stone*, 125.

140 "Mick and Keith": Bockris, *Keith Richards: The Biography*, 155.

140 "In 1969": Jagger, Richards, Watts, and Lane, *According to the Rolling Stones*, 143.

140 "We had to learn": Ibid., 143.

140 "When we played": King and Waterman, *The B.B. King Treasures*, 101.

140 "The open tuning": Richards, *Life*, 273.

140 "They [the Stones] were in": Hutton, "Interview with Jim Dickinson."

141 "You wanted to": Jagger, Richards, Watts, and Lane, *According to the Rolling Stones*, 147.

141 "If you listen": Richards, *Life*, 278.

141 "When we went": Jagger, Richards, Watts, and Lane, *According to the Rolling Stones*, 146.

142 "Woodstock was a bunch": Echols, *Scars of Sweet Paradise*, 264.

142 "We could feel": Hjort, *Strange Brew*, 274.

142   "Keep it cool": Bockris, *Keith Richards: The Biography*, 169.

142   "I just stood": *Strange Brew*, 281.

TWELVE. STONED BLUES

143   "They used to": Tobler and Grundy, *The Guitar Greats*, 145.

143   "Michael was very": Ibid., 145.

143   "You could see": Goodman, *The Mansion on the Hill*, 94.

144   "I ain't no": Wolkin and Keenom, *Mike Bloomfield: If You Love These Blues*, 158.

144   "Michael's problem": Ibid., 151.

144   "I just didn't think": Ibid., 151.

144   "There was a real": Ibid., 162.

145   "I think Michael"; Ibid., 162.

145   "He felt like": Ward, *Michael Bloomfield*, 79.

145   "Every time somebody": Tobler and Grundy, *The Guitar Greats*, 146.

145   "He came from": Wolkin and Keenom, *Mike Bloomfield: If You Love These Blues*, 168.

145   "Chemical soul": Echols, *Scars of Sweet Paradise*, 234.

146   "Every time": Echols, *Scars of Sweet Paradise*, 174.

146   "I've seen terrible": Friedman, *Buried Alive*, 91.

146   "Here's this dude": Echols, *Scars of Sweet Paradise*,. 205

146   "She was planning": "Alone with the Blues," *Time*, 8/27/73.

147   "What they [Big Brother] should": Echols, *Scars of Sweet Paradise*, 206.

147   "Big Brother is just": Wenner, "Mike Bloomfield."

147   "Janis wanted to": Echols, *Scars of Sweet Paradise*, 231.

147   "The hottest item": Sepulvado and Burks, "The Texas Scene."

148   "He said, 'Let's go": Sullivan, *Raisin' Cain*, 91.

148   "Muddy's records probably": Ibid., 25.

148   "I said, 'Please": Ibid., 46.

148   "Willie Dixon spent": Ibid., 98.

148   "I remember the Atlantic": Ibid., 111.

149   "I had taken acid": Ibid., 120.

149   "I used to go see": Tobler and Grundy, *The Guitar Greats*, 147.

149   "He [Peter] first did everything": Celmins, *Peter Green*, 70.

150   "At first our heroes": Fleetwood and Davis, *My Life and Adventures in Fleetwood Mac*, 68.

150   "Man, you'd be": Celmins, *Peter Green*, 89.

150   "Around then": Celmins, *Peter Green*, 89.

150   "Here was a young": Ibid., 78.

150   "At one point Peter": Ibid., 97.

151   "Towards the end": Lesh, *Searching for the Sound*, 198.

151   "I remember how upset": Fleetwood and Davis, *My Life and Adventures in Fleetwood Mac*, 79.

151   "We could still be a band": Ibid., 79.

151   "Because of all the adoration": Celmins, *Peter Green*, 101.

151   "We were offered a glass": Ibid., 111.

151   "I opened the door": Ibid., 111.

152   "Peter Green and me"; Ibid., 85.

152   "Peter Green was never": Fleetwood and Davis, *My Life and Adventures in Fleetwood Mac*, 80.

152   "The truth": Brackett, *Fleetwood Mac*, 37.

152   "In the studio": Ibid., 42.

THIRTEEN. EXILES ON STAR STREET

154   "The black man's": Joplin, *Love, Janis*; 110.

154   "Willie Mae was": Woliver, *Hoot!*, 102.

154   "The last thing": Ibid., 102.

154   "We got there": Echols, *Scars of Sweet Paradise*, 253.

154   "The intense": Smith, *Just Kids*, 158.

155   "She was waiting": Sanders, *Fug You*, 383.

155   "Those of us": Willis, Liner notes, *Janis*, Columbia/Legacy, 1993.

156   "[Hendrix] was tryin'": Murray, *Crosstown Traffic*, 91.

156   "He was so happy": Cross, *Room Full of Mirrors*, 121.

157   "Jimi Hendrix": Davis and Troupe, *Miles*, 293.

157   "Jimi was": King and Ritz, *Blues All Around Me*, 241.

158   "The one Clapton": Hjort, *Strange Brew*, 252.

159   "'Mandies' were quite strong": Clapton, *The Autobiography*, 123.

159   "I heard Ry": McStravick and Ross, *Blues-Rock Explosion*, 2.

160   "Man, that record": Allman and Light, *My Cross to Bear*, 90.

161   "We didn't have": Santoro, Liner notes, *The Layla Sessions*.

161   "He [Ertegun] told me": Clapton, *The Autobiography*, 128.

162   "I was three": Wilcox and Guy, *Damn Right I've Got the Blues*, 93.

162   "I was incredibly": Ibid., 93.

162   "I know I am": Hjort, *Strange Brew*, 321.

162   "We're all hooked": Ibid., 321.

162   "By the end": Santoro, Liner notes, *The Layla Sessions*.

162   "Every time I'm": Poe, *Skydog*, 219.

163   "I didn't know": Fleetwood and Davis, *My Life and Adventures in Fleetwood Mac*, 85.

163   "He [Peter] was in a corner": Celmins, *Peter Green*, 125.

163   "the most disturbing": Ibid., 125.

164   "He and Danny": Fleetwood and Davis, *My Life and Adventures in Fleetwood Mac*, 92.

164   "All the while": Ibid., 96.

164   "The fact that Pete": Ibid., 98.

164   "They took me": *Celmins*, Peter Green, 142.

165   "Peter desperately": Ibid., 146.

165   "I can't do this": Ibid., 157.

166   "Up until then Mick": Bockris, *Keith Richards*, 203.

166   "He was my mate": Meyer, *Twenty Thousand Roads*, 439.

167   "It doesn't matter": Bockris, *Keith Richards*, 231.

167   "*Exile on Main*": Jagger, Richards, Watts, and Lane, *According to the Rolling Stones*, 157.

167   "The reason I made": Bockris, *Keith Richards*, 206.

167   "In guys particularly": Ibid., 206

168   "This party is": Greenfield, *S.T.P.*, 327.

168   "the wildest craziest": Ibid., 326.

168   "It's so wonderful": Ibid., 329.

168   "It [was] a party": Ibid., 330.

168   "Right now is when"; Ibid., 330.

FOURTEEN. FATHERS, MOTHERS & SONS

169   "I saw Little": Glover, Dirks, and Gaines, *Blues with a Feeling*, 237.

169   "He was great"; Ibid., 238.

170   "We had heard": Edwards, *The World Don't Owe Me Nothing*, 154.

170   "Next thing I": Ibid., 154.

170   "He was a good": Palmer, *Deep Blues*, 208.

170   "You think Walter": Glover, Dirks, and Gaines, *Blues with a Feeling*, 219.

170   "It was kinda like": Ibid., 255.

171   "He had to play": Ibid., 282.

171   "Cat threw": Buddy Guy, *When I Left Home*, 198.

171   "The black": Glover, Dirks, and Gaines, *Blues with a Feeling*, 282.

172   "Cambridge was": Author interview with Geoff, Muldaur, 2/5/10.

172   "Joni Mitchell introduced": Gordon, *Can't Be Satisfied*, 365.

172   "My favorite": Helm and Davis, *This Wheel's On Fire*, 261.

172   "I wish somebody": Gordon, *Can't Be Satisfied*, 365.

172   "By the mid-'70s": Ibid., 368.

173   "'Man, you got to": Ibid., 367.

173   "Working with Muddy": Ibid., 364.

173   "I played him": Sullivan, *Raisin' Cain*, 208.

173   "Johnny didn't take": Ibid., 209

173   "The music makes": Mattox, "A Fire Still Burns in Winter."

173   "Muddy was a great": Sullivan, *Raisin' Cain*, 215.

173   "I set them up": Ibid., 221.

174   "When I started": Ibid., 230.

174   "Long before": Clapton: The Autobiography, 326.

174   "About halfway": King and Waterman, *The B.B. King Treasures*, 124.

174   "She was feeling": Wolkin and Keenom, *Michael Bloomfield*, 176.

175   "B.B. King wrote": Ibid., 177.

175   "I just had": Ward, *Michael Bloomfield*, 92.

175   "I don't want": Segrest and Hoffman, *Moanin' at Midnight*, 280.

175   "Wolf cried": Ibid., 280

175   "Hubert was the heart": Ibid., 306.

176   "I walked up": Ibid., 316.

176   "You got to remember": Ibid., 310.

176   "You would've thought": Ibid., 311.

176   "When they introduced": Guy and Ritz, *When I Left Home*, 229.

177   "Tell her if I": Segrest and Hoffman, *Moanin' at Midnight*, 317.

177   "Did you get my mother?": Ibid., 317.

177   "You ain't dead, Wolf": Ibid., 320.

179 "My dad certainly": Frost, *ZZ Top: Bad and Nationwide*, 14.

179 "We were both": Gibbons with Vickers, *Rock + Roll Gearhead*, 20.

180 "We played": Frost, *ZZ Top: Bad and Nationwide*, 66.

180 "Neither kept": Gibbons with Vickers, *Rock + Roll Gearhead*, 32.

180 "I went there": *Spin* magazine. See Songfacts.com, www.songfacts.com.

181 "I picked up": Gibbons, "Muddy Waters."

181 "Three chords": Booth, *Rhythm Oil*, 179.

181 "I thought in terms of": Tobler and Grundy, *The Guitar Greats*, 135.

181 "I said to myself": Ibid., 139.

181 "I finished off": Ibid., 140.

182 "When I started": Fox, "Jimmie Vaughan."

182 "So we drove": Benno interviewed by Holly George-Warren.

182 "He fired the bass player": Ibid.

183 "He was a tough": Govenar, *Lightnin' Hopkins*, 214.

183 "He announced to us": Ibid., 176.

183 "Like Shakespeare": Ibid., 235.

183 "He [Hopkins] started with": Ibid., 203.

184 "His singing": Ibid., 203.

184 "Though blues": Palmer, "Still Singing the Blues."

184 "Once I heard": Govenar, *Lightnin' Hopkins*, 230.

184 "A maid named Mary": Interview of Clifford Antone by Holly George-Warren.

184 "During the hippie days": Ibid.

184 "Clifford Antone": Wilcox and Guy, *Damn Right I've Got the Blues*, 11.

185 "Because we wouldn't": From Karlok (dir.), *Antone's: Home of the Blues*.

185 "They knew we": Ibid.

185 "You see a guy": Gordon, *Can't Be Satisfied*, 249.

185 "We put Jimmie": From Karlok (dir.), *Antone's: Home of the Blues*.

185 "Muddy would have": Gordon, *Can't Be Satisfied*, 250.

185 "When it was time": Guy and Ritz, *When I Left Home*, 235.

185 "You know what": Romano, *Incurable Blues*, 112.

186 "The day they arrived": Ibid., 117.

186 "Antone took care": Ibid., 128.

186 "When I got to be 17, 18": Kot, "Jimmie Vaughan a Terrific Team Player."

186 "The guy doesn't": Wilcox and Guy, *Damn Right I Got the Blues*, 9.

186 "Clifford said": Kot, "Jimmie Vaughan a Terrific Team Player."

186 "Stevie gave": Romano, *Incurable Blues*, 135.

186 "Many nights": Ibid., 136.

187 "As I was hearing": Stevie Ray Vaughan guitar lesson, YouTube.

187 "What Jimmie": Wilcox and Guy, *Damn Right I've Got the Blues*, 113.

188 "Muddy Waters said": Potaski and Crawford, *Stevie Ray Vaughan*, 116.

188 "It was wild": Ibid., 147.

188 "Bowie stole my licks": Ibid., 153.

188 "Naw": Ibid.

189 "Albert says": Phinney, *Souled American*, 298.

189   "He brought": Potaski and Crawford, *Stevie Ray Vaughan*, 158.

189   "I went out to talk": Ibid.

190   "I took Stevie backstage": Ibid.

SIXTEEN. SWEET HOME CHICAGO

192   "From where I'm": Gordon, *Can't Be Satisfied*, 258.

192   "Muddy Waters": Ibid., 258.

192   "We didn't get paid": Ibid., 258.

192   "Eric did a killer": Ibid., 259.

192   "If they [the concert promoters] didn't": Ibid., 261.

192   "Muddy was speaking": Clapton, *The Autobiography*, 326.

193   "I would find": Scorsese, *The Blues*, 193.

193   "'Peter the Wolf'": Ibid., 173.

193   "I sort of thought": Gordon, *Can't Be Satisfied,* 272.

193   "I was trying": Sullivan, *Raisin' Cain*, 242.

193   "When the older": Ibid., 243.

194   "Paul fascinated": Ellis, "Paul Butterfield: The Glory Years."

194   "The battle": Author interview with Muldaur, 2/5/10.

195   "He loved it": Ibid.

195   "The band was bitching": Goodman, *Mansion on the Hill*, 106.

195   "Though it was good": Ibid.

195   "Albert knew": Ibid.

195   "Paul had the long": Ellis, "Paul Butterfield: The Final Note."

195   "They said to me": Ward, *Mike Bloomfield*, 91.

196   "I think it was": Wolkin and Keenom, *Michael Bloomfield*, 190.

196   "During the years": Ibid., 206.

196   "All of a sudden": Ward, *Mike Bloomfield*, 107.

197   "So Dylan gave": Ibid., 107.

197   "Afterwards, Dylan": Ibid., 107.

197   "I'm not born": From Lerner (dir.), *Festival*.

197   "A lot of people": Ellis, "Paul Butterfield: The Final Note."

198   "There were only": Von Schmidt and Rooney, *Baby, Let Me Follow You Down*, 268.

198   "We got real friendly": Ibid.

198   "The guy liked me": Murray, *Boogie Man*, 442.

199   "You're not going": Ibid., 458.

199   "It was really": Ibid., 442.

199   "My spirit": Milward, "What More Can This Woman Do?"

199   "One of my most poignant": Ibid.

199   "I was anesthetized": Boyd and George-Warren, *Musicians in Tune*, 202.

200   "I got out of touch": Ibid., 203.

200   "Let's face it": Milward, "What More Can This Woman Do?"

200   "Hello everybody": Address to Aquarius Chapter of Alcoholics Anonymous, 1/3/90, www.srvrocks.com.

201   "I felt very amateurish": Patoski and Crawford: *Stevie Ray Vaughan*, 241.

201   "We played together": Clapton, *The Autobiography*, 325.

201   "I can't sing": Rosenberg, *Transforming Tradition*, 253.

202   "He brings me": Wilcox and Guy, *Damn Right I've Got the Blues*, 125.

202   "I heard a Buddy": Ibid., 127.

202   "Never heard Stevie": Guy, *When I Left Home*, 250.

202   "I took a look": Wilcox and Guy, *Damn Right I Got the Blues*, 127.

202   "Whenever I'm around": Guy, *When I Left Home*, 251.

SEVENTEEN. FURTHER ON UP THE ROAD

204   "'Broke Down Engine' is": Dylan, Liner notes, *World Gone Wrong*, Columbia Records, 1993.

205   "Strange things alright": Ibid.

206   "I've heard more": Phinney, *Souled American*, 300.

206   "ZZ Top's show": Ratliff, "Sure, Those Beards Remain, But Their Music Has Legs, Too."

206   "While the concerts": Pareles, "Eric Clapton's Crossroads Guitar Festival."

207   "They tried to get": Hutton, "Jim Dickinson."

208   "I used to sit": Hines, "Luther Dickinson."

208   "What Otha taught Luther": Ibid.

208   "Dad always said": Ibid.

208   "This is the way": Milward, "Ry Cooder Lets It Slide."

209   "I'm not some": Scherman, "Ry Cooder's Crossroads Blues."

209   "I've found that sherry bottles": Milward, "Ry Cooder Lets It Slide, by John."

209   "My musical beacons": Ibid.

210   "The journalists": Metting, *The Unbroken Circle*, 257.

210   "This music is": Trillo, *World Music: The Rough Guide*, 198.

211   "I don't recommend": Milward, "Only Rock 'n' Roll? It Was Far More."

212   "People are sometimes": Ibid.

212   "That's the thing": Keys and Ditenhafer, *Every Night's a Saturday Night*, 121.

213   "He had this great": Bockris, *Keith Richards*, 335.

213   "Tina exaggerated": Collis, *Ike Turner*, 126.

215   "Lavere got a deal": DiGiacomo, "Searching for Robert Johnson," *Vanity Fair*, November 2008.

215   "He's just a little": Barry, "Bluesman's Son Gets His Due."

216   "Q: Well, let me share": Ibid.

216   "We were living": Thomas, "The Devil and Mr. Johnson."

218   "In the '60s": Author interview, 11/4/11.

218   "He was a mythic": Ibid.

218   "For years": Ibid.

219   "The Airplane thing": Author interview, 1/15/10.

219   "Anywhere you go": Author interview, 1/14/11.

219   "The first place": Author interview, 7/20/11.

219   "Sometimes it seems": Ibid.

219   "I haven't even added": Author interview, 2/5/10.

220   "He turns to me": Muldaur biography, Hightone Records, 2008.

220   "The blues was what": Douglas, Interview with John Hammond.

220   "We'd come in late": Edwards, *The World Don't Owe Me Nothing*, 65.

BIBLIOGRAPHY

Adelt, Ulrich. *Blues Music in the Sixties: A Story in Black and White*. New Brunswick, NJ: Rutgers University Press, 2010.

Allman, Gregg, and Alan Light. *My Cross to Bear*. New York: Harper Collins, 2012.

Barry, Ellen. "Bluesman's Son Gets His Due." *Los Angeles Times*, June 2, 2004.

Beaumont, Daniel. *Preachin' the Blues: The Life and Times of Son House*. New York: Oxford University Press, 2011.

Bego, Mark. *Bonnie Raitt: Just in the Nick of Time*. New York: Birch Lane, 1995.

Berry, Chuck. *The Autobiography*. New York: Harmony Books, 1987.

Block, Rory. *When a Woman Gets the Blues*. Aurora Productions, 2011.

Bloomfield, Michael, with S. Summerville. *Me and Big Joe*. San Francisco: Re/Search Publications, 1980.

Bockris, Victor. *Keith Richards: The Biography*. New York: Poseidon Press, 1992.

Booth, Stanley. *The True Adventures of the Rolling Stones*. Chicago: A Capella Books, 2000.
———. *Rhythm Oil: A Journey through the Music of the American South*. New York: Da Capo Press, 2000.

Boyd, Jenny, with Holly George-Warren. *Musicians in Tune: Seventy-Five Contemporary Musicians Discuss the Creative Process*. New York: Fireside, 1992.

Boyd, Joe. *White Bicycles: Making Music in the 1960s*. London: Serpent's Tail, 2006.

Brackett, Donald. *Fleetwood Mac: 40 Years of Creative Chaos*. Westport, CT: Greenwood, 2007.

Broonzy, Big Bill, as told to Yannick Bruynoghe. *Big Bill Blues*. New York: Oak Publications, 1964.

Brown, Mick. Interview with Ry Cooder. *Sunday (London) Times Magazine*, November 1980. Available at www.ryland-cooder.com/198011st.html.

Brunning, Bob. *Blues: The British Connection*. London: Blandford Press, 1986.

Calt, Stephen. *I'd Rather Be the Devil: Skip James and the Blues*. New York: Da Capo Press, 1994.

Carson, Annette. *Jeff Beck: Crazy Fingers*. San Francisco: Backbeat Books, 2001.

Case, George. *Jimmy Page: Magic Musician Man*. Milwaukee, WI: Hal Leonard, 2007.

Celmins, Martin. *Peter Green: Founder of Fleetwood Mac, the Biography*. London: Castle Communications, 1995.

Charters, Samuel. *The Country Blues*. London: Michael Joseph Ltd., 1960.

Clapton, Eric. *The Autobiography*. New York: Broadway Books, 2007.

Clayson, Alan. *The Rolling Stones: Beggar's Banquet*. New York: Billboard Boos, 2008.

Cohn, Lawrence, ed. *Nothing but the Blues*. New York: Abbeville Press, 1993.

Cohodas, Nadine. *Spinning Blues into Gold: The Chess Brothers and the Legendary Chess Records*. New York: St. Martin's Press, 2000.

Cohen, Rich. *Machers and Rockers: Chess Records and the Business of Rock & Roll.* New York: W.W. Norton, 2004.

Collis, John. *The Story of Chess Records.* London: Bloomsbury Publishing, 1998.

——. *Ike Turner: King of Rhythm.* London: Do-Not Press Limited, 2003.

Cross, Charles R. *Room Full of Mirrors: A Biography of Jimi Hendrix.* New York: Hyperion, 2006.

Dalton, Craig. "Steve Miller: Still Flying on His Own Terms." *Mix*, October 1, 2006.

Davis, Francis. *The History of the Blues.* New York: Hyperion, 1995.

Davis, Miles, and Quincy Troupe. *Miles: The Autobiography.* New York: Simon & Schuster, 1989.

Davis, Stephen. *Hammer of the Gods.* New York: Harper Entertainment, 2008.

Dean, Eddie. "Skip James' Hard Time Killing Floor Blues." *Washington City Paper*, November 25, 1994.

De La Parra, Fito, with T. W. McGarry and Marlane McGarry. *Living the Blues: Canned Heat's Story of Music, Drugs, Death, Sex and Survival.* Record Grafix, 1999.

Devil Got My Woman: Blues at Newport 1966. Vestapol DVD 13049.

DiGiacomo, Frank. "Searching for Robert Johnson." *Vanity Fair*, November 2008.

Dixon, Willie, with Don Snowden. *I Am the Blues.* New York: Da Capo Press, 1990.

Doggett, Pete. *You Never Give Me Your Money: The Beatles After the Breakup.* New York: Harper Collins, 2009

Douglas, Bob. Interview with John Hammond. *Fretboard Journal*, Winter 2011–2012.

Dylan, Bob. *Chronicles: Volume One.* New York: Simon & Schuster, 2004.

——. Liner notes. *World Gone Wrong.* Columbia Records, 1993.

Echols, Alice. *Scars of Sweet Paradise: The Life and Times of Janis Joplin.* New York: Henry Holt, 1999.

Edwards, David "Honeyboy," as told to Janis Martinson and Michael Robert Frank. *The World Don't Owe Me Nothing.* Chicago: Chicago Review Press, 1997.

Ellis, Tom III. "Paul Butterfield: The Glory Years." *Blues Access*, Spring 1996.

——. "Paul Butterfield: The Final Note." *Blues Access*, Fall 1997.

Evans, David. *Big Road Blues.* New York: Da Capo Press, 1987.

Ferris, William. *Give My Poor Heart Ease: Voices of the Mississippi Blues.* Chapel Hill: University of North Carolina Press, 2009.

Filene, Benjamin. *Romancing the Folk.* Chapel Hill: University of North Carolina Press, 2000.

Fleetwood, Mick, and Stephen Davis. *My Life and Adventures in Fleetwood Mac.* New York: William Morrow, 1980.

Fox, Darrin. "Jimmie Vaughan." *Guitar Player.* www.guitarplayer.com/article/jimmie -vaughan/1456.

Frost, Deborah. *ZZ Top: Bad and Nationwide.* New York: Collier Books, 1985.

Gibbons, Billy. "Muddy Waters." In "100 Greatest Artists." *Rolling Stone*, December, 2009.

Gibbons, Billy F, with Tom Vickers. *Rock + Roll Gearhead.* St. Paul, MN: MBI Publishing, 2005.

Giola, Ted. *Delta Blues: The Life and Times of the Mississippi Masters Who Revolutionized American Music.* New York: W.W. Norton & Company, 2008.

Gleason, Ralph J. *The Jefferson Airplane and the San Francisco Sound.* New York: Ballantine Books, 1969.

Glover, Tony, Scott Dirks, and Ward Gaines. *Blues with a Feeling: The Little Walter Story.* New York: Routledge, 2002.

Goodman, Fred. *The Mansion on the Hill.* New York: Times Books, 1997.

Gordon, Robert. *Can't Be Satisfied: The Life and Times of Muddy Waters.* Boston: Little, Brown, 2002.

———. *It Came From Memphis.* Boston: Faber and Faber, 1995.

Govenar, Alan. *Lightnin' Hopkins: His Life and Blues.* (Chicago: Chicago Review Press, 2010.

Graves, Tom. *Crossroads: The Life and Afterlife of Blues Legend Robert Johnson.* Spokane, WA: Demers Books, 2008.

Greenfield, Robert. *S.T.P.: A Journey through America with the Rolling Stones.* New York: E.P. Dutton, 1974.

Groom, Bob. *The Blues Revival.* London: Studio Vista, 1971.

Guitar Player Editors, *The Guitar Player Book: Artists, History, Technique, and Gear.* New York: Random House, 1979.

Guralnick, Peter. *Feel Like Going Home.* New York: Vintage Books, 1981.

———. *Lost Highway.* New York: Vintage Books, 1982.

———. *Searching for Robert Johnson.* New York: Dutton, 1989.

Guy, Buddy, and David Ritz. *When I Left Home: My Story.* New York: Da Capo Press, 2012.

Hajdu, David. *Positively Fourth Street.* New York: Farrar, Straus and Giroux, 2001.

Hamilton, Marybeth. *In Search of the Blues.* New York: Basic Books, 2008.

Hammond, John, with Irving Townsend. *John Hammond on Record.* New York: Summit Books, 1977.

Hedin, Benjamin, ed. *Studio A: The Bob Dylan Reader.* New York: W.W. Norton, 2005

Helm, Levon, with Stephen Davis. *This Wheel's On Fire: Levon Helm and the Story of the Band.* New York: William Morrow and Company, 1993.

Henderson, David. *'Scuse Me While I Kiss the Sky: The Life of Jimi Hendrix.* New York: Bantam Books, 1981.

Henke, James. "Bravo Bonnie." *Rolling Stone,* May 3, 1990.

Hines, Geoffrey. "Luther Dickinson": *Fretboard Journal,* Fall 2010.

Hjort, Christopher. *Strange Brew: Eric Clapton & the British Blues Boom 1965–1970.* London: Outline Press, 2007.

Hubbard, Kim. "Veteran Rocker Bonnie Raitt Gets Back on Track in the Nick of Time." *People,* April 24, 1989.

Hutton, Joss. Interview with Jim Dickinson, *Perfect Sound Forever,* January 2002 www.furious.com/perfect/jimdickinson.html.

James, Steve, "Blues across the Borders." *Acoustic Guitar,* March/April 1993.

Jagger, Mick, Keith Richards, Charlie Watts, and Ronnie Lane. *According to the Rolling Stones.* San Francisco: Chronicle Books, 2003.

Jones, LeRoi. *Blues People.* New York: William Morrow & Co., 1963.

———. "Apple Cores #2." *Downbeat,* 1965.

Joplin, Laura. *Love, Janis.* New York: Villard Books, 1992.

Kalb, Danny. "My Scene: Greenwich Village, Early 1960s." *Fretboard Journal,* Fall, 2009.

Karlok, Dan (director). *Antone's: Home of the Blues.* Film. Silver Star Entertainment, 2004.

Keil, Charles. *Urban Blues.* Chicago: University of Chicago Press, 1966.

Keys, Bobby, and Bill Ditenhafer. *Every Night's a Saturday Night: The Rock 'n' Roll Life of a Legendary Sax Man.* Berkeley: Counterpoint, 2012.

King, B.B., with David Ritz. *Blues All Around Me.* New York: Avon Books, 1996.

King, B.B., with Dick Waterman. *The B.B. King Treasures: Photos, Mementos and Music from the B.B. King Collection.* New York: Bullfinch, 2005.

Kooper, Al, with Ben Edmonds. *Backstage Passes: Rock 'n' Roll Life in the Sixties.* (New York: Stein and Day, 1977.

Kot, Greg. "Jimmie Vaughan a Terrific Team Player." *Chicago Tribune,* August 14, 2011.

Kramer, Eddie. "Classic Tracks: Jimi Hendrix Experience All Along the Watchtower." *Sound on Sound,* November, 2005.

LaVere, Stephen. Liner notes, *Robert Johnson: The Complete Recordings.* Columbia Records.

Lawrence, Sharon. *Jimi Hendrix: The Man, the Magic, the Music.* New York: Harper Entertainment, 2005.

Lerner, Murray (director). *Festival.* Film. Patchke Productions, 1967.

Lesh, Phil. *Searching for the Sound: My Life with the Grateful Dead.* San Francisco: Back Bay Books, 2006.

Lester, Julius, "I Can Make My Own Songs." Son House interview. *Sing Out!* July, 1965.

Lipscomb, Mance. *I Say Me For a Parable: The Oral Autobiography of Mance Lipscomb, Texas Bluesman, as Told to and Compiled by Glen Alyn.* New York: W.W. Norton, 1993.

Lomax, Alan. *The Land Where the Blues Began.* New York: Dell, 1993.

Marcus, Greil. *Mystery Train.* New York: E.P. Dutton, 1975.

———. *Invisible Republic: Bob Dylan's Basement Tapes.* New York: H Hold & Co., 1997.

Mattox, T. E. "A Fire Still Burns in Winter." *Traveling Boy.* travelingbluesboy.com.

McStravick, Travick, and John Summer Ross, ed. *Blues-Rock Explosion.* London: Old Goat Publishing, 2001.

Mendelsohn, John. Review of *Led Zeppelin I. Rolling Stone,* March 15, 1969.

Meyer, David. *Twenty Thousand Roads: The Ballad of Gram Parsons and His Cosmic American Music.* New York: Villard, 2008.

Metting, Fred. *The Unbroken Circle: Tradition and Innovation in the Music of Ry Cooder and Taj Mahal.* Lanham, MD: Scarecrow Press, 2001.

Miller, Jim, ed. *The Rolling Stone Illustrated History of Rock & Roll.* New York: Random House, 1980.

Milward, John. "Only Rock 'n' Roll? It Was Far More." *USA Today,* April 16, 1986.

———. "Ry Cooder Lets It Slide." *Newsday,* October 6, 1987.

———. "Willie Dixon: The Man Who Built the Blues." *Philadelphia Inquirer,* December 1, 1988.

———. "What More Can This Woman Do?" *Philadelphia Inquirer,* June 11, 1989.

———. "The Sons of Gary Davis." *No Depression,* Fall 2009.

Molenda, Mike, ed. *The Guitar Player Book.* New York: Random House, 1979.

Moskowitz, David. *The Words and Music of Jimi Hendrix,* Santa Barbara, CA: Praeger, 2010.

Mullen, Patrick B. *The Man Who Adores the Negro: Race and American Folklore.* Urbana: University of Illinois Press, 2008.

Murray, Charles Shaar. *Boogie Man: The Adventure of John Lee Hooker in the American Twentieth Century.* New York: St. Martin's Press, 2000.

———. *Crosstown Traffic: Jimi Hendrix and Post-war Pop.* London: Faber and Faber, 1989.

Norman, Philip. *Sympathy for the Devil: The Rolling Stones Story.* New York: Simon & Schuster, 1984.

Obrecht, Jas. "Go Where It's Dangerous and Say Yes." *Guitar Player,* November 1982.

———. *Rollin' and Tumblin': The Postwar Blues Guitarists.* San Francisco: Miller Freeman, 2000.

———. "Ry Cooder—Talking Country Blues and Gospel." Jas Obrecht Music Archive, May 24, 2010. http://jasobrecht.com/ry-cooder-talking-country-blues-and-gospel/.

———. "Mississippi John Hurt." Jas Obrecht Music Archive, October 10, 2010. http://jasobrecht.com/mississippi-john-hurt-life-music/.

Obrecht, Jas (ed.). *Blues Guitar: The Men Who Made the Music.* San Francisco: Miller Freeman Books, 1993.

Oliver, Paul. *Conversations with the Blues.* Cambridge: Cambridge University Press, 1997.

Palmer, Robert. *Deep Blues.* New York: Viking Press, 1981

———. Liner notes, *Led Zeppelin* boxed set. Atlantic Records, 1990.

———. *Blues & Chaos: The Music Writing of Robert Palmer.* Edited by Anthony DeCurtis. New York: Scribner, 2009.

———. *The Rolling Stones.* New York: Doubleday & Co., 1983.

———. "Still Singing the Blues." *New York Times*, October 31, 1980.

Pareles, Jon. "Eric Claptons Crossroads Guitar Festival." *New York Times*; June 29, 2010.

Patoski, Joe Nick, and Bill Crawford. *Stevie Ray Vaughan: Caught in the Crossfire*: Little, Brown, 1993.

Pearson, Barry Lee, and Bill McCulloch. *Robert Johnson: Lost and Found.* Urbana: University of Illinois Press, 2003.

Perfect Sound Forever. "The Insect Trust: Bill Barth." *Perfect Sound Forever* online magazine. www.furious.com/perfect/billbarth.html.

Phinney, Kevin. *Souled America: How Black Music Transformed White Culture.* New York: Billboard Books, 2005.

Poe, Randy. *Skydog: The Duane Allman Story.* San Francisco: Backbeat Books, 2006.

Ratcliffe, Philip R. *Mississippi John Hurt: His Life, His Times, His Blues.* Jackson: University Press of Mississippi, 2011.

Ratliff, Ben. "Sure, Those Beards Remain, But Their Music Has Legs, Too." *New York Times*, September 13, 2010.

Richards, Keith, with James Fox. *Life.* New York: Little Brown, 2010.

Riesman, Bob. *I Feel So Good: The Life and Times of Big Bill Broonzy.* Chicago: University of Chicago Press, 2011.

Rolling Stone. "Bravo Bonnie." *Rolling Stone*, May 3, 1990.

Romano, Will. *Incurable Blues: The Troubles and Triumphs of Blues Legend Hubert Sumlin.* San Francisco: Backbeat Books, 2005.

———. *Big Boss Man: The Life and Music of Bluesman Jimmy Reed.* San Francisco: Backbeat Books, 2006.

Rooney, James. *Bossman: Bill Monroe and Muddy Waters.* New York: Da Capo Press; 1991.

Rosenberg, Neil V., ed. *Transforming Tradition: Folk Music Revivals Examined.* Urbana: University of Illinois Press.

Sanders, Ed. *Fug You: An Informal History of the Peace Eye Bookstore, the Fuck You Press, and Counterculture in the Lower East Side.* Cambridge: Da Capo Press, 2011.

Santelli, Robert. *The Big Book of Blues.* New York: Penguin, 1993.

Santoro, Gene. "Ry Cooder: Blues and Roots." *Downbeat*, August 1986.

———. Liner notes. *The Layla Sessions 20th Anniversary Edition*, Polydor, 1990.

Scaduto, Tony. *Mick Jagger: Everybody's Lucifer.* New York: Berkley Medallion, 1975.

Scherman, T. "Ry Cooder's Crossroads Blues." *Rolling Stone*, October 19, 1985.

Schwartz, Roberta Freund. *How Britain Got the Blues: The Transmission and Reception of American Blues Style in the United Kingdom.* Aldershot: Ashgate, 2007.

Scorsese, Martin. *Martin Scorsese Presents The Blues*. Edited by Peter Guralnick, Robert Santelli, Holly George-Warren, and Christopher John Farley. New York: Amistad, 2004.

Sculatti, Gene, and Davin Seay. *San Francisco Nights: The Psychedelic Music Trip*. New York: St. Martin's Press, 1985.

Segrest, James, and Mark Hoffman. *Moanin' at Midnight: The Life and Time of Howlin' Wolf*. New York: Pantheon, 2004.

Sepulvado, Larry, and John Burks, "The Texas Scene." *Rolling Stone*, December 7, 1968.

Shadwick, Keith. *Led Zeppelin: The Story of a Band and Their Music*, Milwaukee, WI: Backbeat Books, 2005.

Shapiro, Harry, and Caesar Glebbeek. *Jimi Hendrix: Electric Gypsy*. New York: St. Martin's Press, 1990.

Shaw, Arnold. *Honkers and Shouters: The Golden Years of Rhythm & Blues*. New York: Macmillan, 1978.

Shelton, Robert. "Britain's Cream Skims into City with Blues, Blare and Jazzy Pop." *New York Times*, March 30, 1968.

Shillace, Nicholas S. *John Fahey and American Primitivism: The Process of American Identity in the Twentieth Century*. Master's thesis, Wayne State University.

Silber, Irwin. "An Open Letter to Bob Dylan." *Sing Out!* November, 1964.

Smith, Patti. *Just Kids*. New York: Ecco, 2010.

Steel, Gary. "Ry Cooder." *Witchdoctor*, July 26, 2010. www.witchdoctor.co.nz.

Sullivan, Mary Lou. *Raisin' Cain: The Wild and Raucous Story of Johnny Winter*. Milwaukee, WI: Backbeat Books, 2010.

Szwed, John. *Alan Lomax: The Man Who Recorded the World*. New York: Viking, 2010.

Thomas, W. John. "The Devil and Mr. Johnson." *Texas Review of Entertainment & Sports Law*, Fall 2009.

Time. "Alone with the Blues." *Time*, August 27, 1973.

Tipaldi, Art. *Children of the Blues: 49 Musicians Shaping a New Blues Tradition*. San Francisco: Backbeat Books, 2002.

Tobler, John, and Stuart Grundy. *The Guitar Greats*. New York: St. Martin's Press, 1984.

Tosches, Nick. *Unsung Heroes of Rock 'n' Roll*. New York: Harmony Books, 1991.

Trillo, Richard. *World Music: The Rough Guide*. London, 1994.

Van Ronk, Dave, with Elijah Wald. *The Mayor of MacDougal Street: A Memoir*. New York: Da Capo Press, 2005.

Von Schmidt, Eric, and Jim Rooney. *Baby, Let Me Follow You Down*. Amherst: University of Massachusetts Press, 1979.

Wald, Elijah. *Escaping the Delta: Robert Johnson and the Invention of the Blues*. New York: Amistad, 2004.

Wall, Mick. *When Giants Walked the Earth: A Biography of Led Zeppelin*, London: Orion, 2008.

Ward, Ed. *Michael Bloomfield: The Rise and Fall of an American Guitar Hero*. New York: Cherry Lane Books, 1983.

Wardlow, Gayle Dean. *Chasin' That Devil Music: Searching for the Blues*. San Francisco: Miller Freeman, 1998.

Waterman, Dick. *Between Midnight and Day: The Last Unpublished Blues Archive*. New York: Thunder's Mouth Press, 2003.

Wenner, Jann. "Mike Bloomfield." *Rolling Stone*, April 27, 1968.

——. Eric Clapton interview. *Rolling Stone*, May 11, 1968.

Wexler, Jerry, and David Ritz. *Rhythm and the Blues*. New York: Knopf, 1993.

Wilcox, Donald E., with Buddy Guy. *Damn Right I've Got the Blues*. San Francisco: Woodford Press, 1993.

Willis, Ellen. Liner notes, *Janis*. Columbia/Legacy, 1993.

Woliver, Robbie. *Hoot! A 25-Year History of the Greenwich Village Music Scene*. New York: St. Martin's Press, 1986.

Wolkin, Jan Mark, and Bill Keenom. *Michael Bloomfield: If You Love These Blues*. San Francisco: Miller Freeman Books, 2000.

Wyman, Bill, and Ray Coleman. *Stone Alone: The Story of a Rock 'n' Roll Band*. New York: Viking, 1990.

INDEX

Page numbers in *italics* indicate illustrations.